AFROFUTURISM RISING

NEW SUNS

RACE, GENDER, AND SEXUALITY IN THE SPECULATIVE

Susana M. Morris and Kinitra D. Brooks, Series Editors

AFROFUTURISM RISING

The Literary Prehistory of a Movement

Isiah Lavender III

THE OHIO STATE UNIVERSITY PRESS
COLUMBUS

Copyright © 2019 by The Ohio State University.
All rights reserved.

Library of Congress Cataloging-in-Publication Data is available online at catalog.loc.gov.

Cover design by Stacey Robinson & John Jennings
Text design by Juliet Williams
Type set in Adobe Palatino

ALWAYS HEATHER ALWAYS

CONTENTS

Acknowledgments — ix

Introduction On Defining Afrofuturism — 1

PART I 1619–1903: THE AFROFUTURIST VISTA AND THE POSSIBILITY OF FREEDOM

Chapter 1   Hope and Freedom Technologies — 25

Chapter 2   Black Uprisings and the Fight for the Future — 48

Chapter 3   Of Alien Abductions, Pocket Universes, Trickster Technologies, and Slave Narratives — 77

PART II AFROFUTURISM AND CLASSIC TWENTIETH-CENTURY AFRICAN AMERICAN NOVELS

Chapter 4   Black Bodies in Space: Zora Neale Hurston's *Their Eyes Were Watching God* — 107

Chapter 5   "Metallically Black": Bigger Thomas and the Black Apocalyptic Vision of Richard Wright's *Native Son* — 127

Chapter 6   Racial Warfare, Radical Afrofuturism, and John A. Williams's *Captain Blackman* — 153

Conclusion Into the Black-o-Sphere — 186

Works Cited — 197

Index — 217

ACKNOWLEDGMENTS

ABOVE ALL ELSE, I thank God for inspiring me to embrace writing and thinking about stuff in general and science fiction specifically and placing people in my path to activate my ambition from teachers to colleagues, family to friends, and my Miniature Schnauzer Rocco, as well as the owl who stopped by on occasion in the deep night to keep me company, as crazy as that sounds. I never dreamed of doing a second monograph, yet here I am seven years later. Thank you, God!

This monograph consciously began at the 2012 NEH Summer Institute on Contemporary African American Literature held at Penn State University, where I would share ideas ultimately resulting in the fourth chapter of this book. The book chapter has been slightly modified from its originally published version, "An Afrofuturist Reading of Zora Neale Hurston's *Their Eyes Were Watching God,*" which first appeared in *LIT: Literature-Interpretation-Theory,* vol. 27, no. 3, 2016, pp. 213–33. Therefore, I simply must thank Lovalerie King, Maryemma Graham, Trudier Harris, Dana Williams, Thabiti Lewis, Lanisa Kitchiner, Ayesha Hardison, Susan Weeber, Shelli Homer, Brandon Manning, Kameelah Martin, Shaila Mehra, Earl Brooks, Quentin Miller, Nicole Sparling, Beauty Bragg, Therí Pickens, Aisha Damali, David Green, Nancy Kang, and Alicia Inshiradu. But I'd like to especially thank Cherise Pollard, Marlene Allen, and Claudia Dreiling for reading early versions of the chapter after the institute was completed. "Of Alien Abductions, Pocket Universes, and Slave Narratives" first appeared in *Speculating Futures: Black Imagination & the Arts*, a special double issue of *Obsidian: Literature & Arts in the African Diaspora*, vol. 42, no. 1/2, 2016, pp. 191–203, and I have Sheree Renée Thomas to thank for that initial publication. A vastly expanded and revised version now exists as chapter 3. Likewise, I am grateful to Ritchie Calvin of Stony Brook University for inviting me to give my first keynote address drawn from this chapter in February of 2017, which also reminds me to thank Sherryl Vint of the University of California, Riverside; Patrick Sharp of California State University, Los Angeles; and Adilifu Nama of Loyola Mary Mount University for earlier speaking gigs.

Of course, scholarship does not exist in a vacuum, and readers might notice small similarities in terms of theorizing between this book and two other essays of mine that have recently been published. Thus I feel a small recognition is due. The essays themselves are nothing like the book chapters, but the theorizing itself clearly relates to this book. Therefore, I'd like to thank Amandine Faucheux for cowriting "Tricknology: Theorizing the Trickster in Afrofuturism" for the special *Afrofuturism* issue of *MOSF Journal of Science Fiction*, vol. 2, no. 2, 2018, pp. 31–46. Further, I would like to communicate my gratitude to the editing team of Gerry Canavan and Eric Link for publishing "Contemporary Science Fiction and Afrofuturism" in *The Cambridge History of Science Fiction* (2019).

Perhaps my greatest debt of gratitude belongs to Sharon Weltman of LSU, who has read and critiqued every chapter of this manuscript more than once. Likewise, this book would have been impossible to finish without the benefit of my two writing groups at LSU, and I have great affection for Sunny Yang, Chris Barrett, Pallavi Rastogi, and Michael Bibler. I am also indebted to associate dean, and former English chair, Elsie Mitchie for helping me with one last revision of a crucial chapter.

I would be remiss if I failed to mention the stimulating conversations regarding this book I've had with many other of my LSU colleagues—Carl Freedman, Mari Kornhauser, Bill Demastes, and Joseph Kronick, among others. LSU has supported me well with a number of grants over the past several summers to get this book written, and for that I am also grateful. Likewise, I need to thank my former UCA colleague Lori Leavell for continuing to exchange essay drafts with me.

I also owe my thanks to Lisa Yaszek of Georgia Tech, who has offered me a ton of advice on this manuscript over the past five or so years. I greatly value her friendship and mentoring.

In terms of the science fiction world and its scholarly community, I am thankful to Mark Bould, Robin Reid, Doug Davis, Sean Guynes-Vishniac, Brooks Landon, Farah Mendohlson, Edward James, André Carrington, Reynaldo Anderson, John Jennings, Bodhisattva Chattopadhyay, Stacey Robinson, Kinitra Brooks, Bill Campbell, Minister Faust, Nalo Hopkinson, Nisi Shawl, Grace Dillon, Graham Murphy, Stina Attebery, the late great Mike Levy, Neil Easterbrook, Rob Latham, John Rieder, Steven Shaviro, De Witt Kilgore, Joan Gordon, Veronica Hollinger, Jeffrey Weinstock, and Joy Sanchez-Taylor as well as my favorite scholarly organizations, International Association of the Fantastic in the Arts and the Science Fiction Research Association. I also want to give a shout out to Ana Maria Jimenez-Moreno, Tara Cyphers, and Kristina Wheeler for shepherding this book along, as well as the blind reviewers who helped make it a better book.

Most of all, I must acclaim the most important people in my life—Heather, Kingsley, Frazier, Melissa, and John: Heather for being the heart of my family, my ride-or-die chic *Fury Road*–style, bold, beautiful, God-fearing; Kingsley and Frazier for being the best sons a man could ask for; Melissa for being the anchor to my childhood; and John for being the big brother I always wanted. Finally, I'd like to thank my lovely goddaughter Zoë Jenkins for helping me cut a footnote or two in getting the manuscript in its final form.

INTRODUCTION

ON DEFINING AFROFUTURISM

LIKE SCIENCE FICTION (SF) itself, afrofuturism proves notoriously difficult to define. Some people see it as an aesthetic genre unto itself: SF written by black people for black people. Others see it as a way of reading that calls attention to the complex relations between science, technology, and race that always undergirded but are not always made evident in SF. Still others understand afrofuturism as a cultural phenomenon emerging from the relationship between African Americans and Western technology, and they appreciate SF's themes of abduction, displacement, and alienation as fitting symbols for black experience. Yet others see it as a mode of aesthetic production that merges myth and history to imagine new black cultures and futures. These competing and very different connotations suggest that we also comprehend afrofuturism as a moment and as a movement. It fascinates so many people because it explores historical, geographic, and technoscientific forces transforming the world today. Already an important buzzword in literary circles, afrofuturism is likely to only increase in importance as major afrofuturist films such as *Hidden Figures* (2016), *Get Out* (2017), and *Black Panther* (2018), and the upcoming small-screen adaptations of Octavia Butler, N. K. Jemisin, and Nnedi Okorafor, continue to capture the public imagination.[1] While the significance of these new visual avenues for afrofu-

---

1. See Yohana Desta's "Octavia Butler Is Finally Heading to TV, Thanks to Ava DuVernay" (2017); Nellie Andreeva and Denise Petski's "N. K. Jemisin's 'The Fifth Sea-

turism cannot be underestimated, the printed word remains fundamental to understanding the full dimensions of afrofuturism.

In *Afrofuturism Rising* I explore afrofuturism as a narrative practice that enables users to communicate the interconnection between science, technology, and race across centuries, continents, and cultures. Afrofuturism is a historical phenomenon that emerges in parallel with its sister genre, science fiction, at the dawn of modernity, specifically in the period of American chattel slavery, in response to the singular risks and possibilities afforded by industrial capitalism. Throughout this book, I extend existing scholarly conversations about afrofuturism to canonical literary texts by African American writers (most from before the twentieth century) that up to now have not traditionally been thought of as SF. The book accomplishes this task through a transhistorical method that rereads these texts as if they were genre SF, highlighting the way that black experience in America and around the world has *always* been an experience of spatial and temporal dislocation and disorientation, not unlike the events experienced by the protagonists of genre SF. Confronting this real history in science-fictional terms makes it easier for us to grapple emotionally and intellectually with an amnesiac past that most people want left alone—a defamiliarized history, concerned with familiar facts that are made to feel new to our own racialized experiences through the strangeness generated by speculative contexts. Afrofuturism, like SF, is always in dialogue with the present in which it is written. However, unlike SF, afrofuturism looks to the past to move forward the aspirations of an entire race in all of its cultural complexities. The stakes of merging history, black literature, afrofuturism, and SF require dealing with forms of psychological dislocation/disorientation/trauma/white supremacy from the safe distance offered by science-fictional speculation.

Afrofuturism is a set of race-inflected reading protocols designed to investigate the optimisms and anxieties framing the future imaginings of black people. Mark Dery's coining of the term *Afrofuturism*[2] in 1993 provided a reference point to explore issues of race, science, and technology in the art, music, and literature of contemporary black America in relation to

---

son' Book To Be Developed as TV Series at TNT" (2017); and Charles Pulliam-Moore's "HBO and George R. R. Martin Set To Produce Nnedi Okorafor's *Who Fears Death* TV Series" (2017).

2. Dery explains that *Afrofuturism* means "speculative fiction that treats African American themes and addresses African American concerns in the context of twentieth-century technoculture—and, more generally, African American signification that appropriates images of technology and a prosthetically enhanced future" ("Black to the Future" 736). Different forms of afrofuturism—Afro-futurism and Afrofuturism—exist in earlier scholarship because the term itself had not yet been codified.

technoculture and science fiction.³ This definition led the first generation of afrofuturist scholars to treat afrofuturism as a black Atlantic art form that appeared in the wake of World War II and that is, as such, uniquely suited to thinking about issues of social justice in a global and technology-intensive world. Alondra Nelson describes afrofuturism as black voices with "other stories to tell about culture, technology and things to come" ("Introduction" 9). Kodwo Eshun discusses some of these black voices, arguing that "Frantz Fanon revolted in the name of the future against a power structure that relied on control and representation of the historical archive" ("Further" 289).

Yet scholars in the past decade have become gradually more attentive to extending afrofuturism into a deeper past. For instance, Paul Youngquist convincingly argues that much of Amiri Baraka's work belongs to science fiction.⁴ Lisa Yaszek provides a compelling afrofuturist reading of Ralph Ellison's *Invisible Man* (1952), while Mark Bould explores even earlier afrofuturist novels such as Delany's *Blake, or the Huts of America* (1859–62); Griggs's *Imperium in Imperio* (1899); and Hopkins's *Of One Blood: Or, the Hidden Self* (1903), among other novels.⁵ *Afrofuturism Rising* complements these works by drawing conclusions about the relevance of afrofuturism in interpreting black literature written mostly before the 1970s.

To that end, I largely focus on antebellum works, late nineteenth-century fiction, and mainstream twentieth-century black writers in this book. What sanctions my consideration of antebellum texts is less a historical drive to recover evidence of this narrative practice as a way of reading and more a hermeneutic that lets me examine works across centuries on a continuum. The very foundations of afrofuturism—as a literary genre, a cultural aesthetic, and a philosophy—predate the 1993 neologism and extend back centuries to the writings of enslaved blacks in the New World. At the heart of African American literature, slavery's disorienting experience creates the science fictionality of afrofuturism that contests both history and futurity.

But why use afrofuturism to study canonical African American literature? The literary past can help us both to question and to envision what

---

3. Regardless of the obvious analytical significance of Dery's term, Samuel R. Delany, Greg Tate, and Tricia Rose merit further acclaim for taking part in the initial conversations with Dery. From the outset, these scholars have created afrofuturism with their profound understandings of black cultures in relationship to SF. Dery asks the questions guiding these keen black minds and frames them with his brief introduction. Unquestionably, afrofuturism's critical vitality corresponds to these black scholars.

4. See Youngquist's "The Space Machine: Baraka and Science Fiction" (2003).

5. See Yaszek's "An Afrofuturist Reading of Ralph Ellison's *Invisible Man*" (2005) and Bould's "Revolutionary African-American Sf before Black Power Sf" (2010).

will happen next in African American culture and why. Indeed, this book at once outlines a new methodological theory to apply to the classics of the black literary canon and offers a critical reassessment by coupling race criticism with SF. The result will help us to perceive what kinds of reciprocal relationships exist between race and racism, people and technology, culture and time, and how these relationships will produce the black futures we foresee in the present.

As I argue throughout the book, hope structures black life from antebellum America to the present. This powerful feeling orients the future. While the "future" itself is historically and culturally contingent on the past, I conceive of it as an imaginative apparatus of subject-making. Our discernment of afrofuturism as a complex historical phenomenon that expands across time, cultures, and artistic outlets begins by exploring how the central concerns of afrofuturism first emerged in early American scientific and political debates and continues with its reverberations in canonical twentieth-century texts. Crucial to understanding this future imagining—generating alternative futures, recasting the past—is how afrofuturism challenges readers to look past slavery's many tragedies through the science-fictional language employed by twentieth-century black writers. We have to look beyond the past and hope for a different future.

While the first generation of afrofuturist literary scholarship has tended to focus on the proleptic, recovering a tradition of African American science fiction misplaced in time, I propose to open up the ambiguity in Eshun's description of afrofuturism—those works whose prolepsis is interwoven with their retrospection through countermemory "by reorienting the intercultural vectors of Black Atlantic temporality" ("Further" 289). Eshun later remarks, "Afrofuturism, then, is concerned with the possibilities for intervention within the dimension of the predictive, the projected, the proleptic, the envisioned, the virtual, the anticipatory and the future conditional" (293). This move involves transforming afrofuturism from an archive of texts, artifacts, and practices to a reading protocol that can be applied to a much wider range of cultural production—in a manner akin to Ernst Bloch's transformation of "utopia" from a generic category into the principle of hope of which the German Marxist philosopher writes at length in his three-volume *The Principle of Hope* (1955). In fact, Bloch's ideas have been taken up by many scholars in utopian studies and SF studies alike, with Fredric Jameson, Tom Moylan, and Darko Suvin prominent among them.[6]

---

6. See Jameson's *Archaeologies of the Future: The Desire Called Utopia and Other Science Fictions* (2005); Moylan's *Demand the Impossible: Science Fiction and the Utopian Imagination* (1986) as well as *Scraps of the Untainted Sky: Science Fiction, Utopia, Dystopia* (2000);

Bloch perceives that people have dreamed of a better life in all cultures throughout history, resulting in his creation of various strands of utopia as he provides a systematic classification of hope from fairy tales and daydreams to philosophical and religious articulations of utopia. If we follow Bloch's example, the hope for something better, something other, propels the continual drive toward utopia. Bloch's utopian thinking conveys "the search for absolute perfection, and in the future only two possibilities can be sustained: absolute perfection or absolute destruction" (Widdicombe 76). But this dialectic does not represent afrofuturism accurately with its grounding in material reality, its built-in coping mechanism for a terrible racial history. Perhaps Wilson J. Moses's concept of afrotopia, blending "Afrocentric tradition[s]" with "utopian ideas of progress" to produce a wonderful future for black people, might be closer to Bloch's meaning here (44). Likewise, Afro-pessimism's[7] theorizing of a black social death, its deliberate antagonism of the "alien" encounter between blackness and humanity, something incompatible, in the attempt to confirm and confer a fundamental human existence for blacks, seems to fit with the dialectic vacillation Bloch sees in his two absolutes.

Afrofuturism must be considered utopian to some degree because it seeks to perform world-building on a scale that imagines black being in new ways, in new worlds where race and racism sometimes exist and sometimes do not. It also seeks to imagine new ways of being black in the physical world where race and racism persist and have form as a dreadfully marginalizing system of thought control in regard to both individuals and societies.

Critical Terminologies

Afrofuturism Rising demonstrates the value of afrofuturism as a reading practice by tracing three guiding concepts: the black "networked consciousness,"[8]

---

and Suvin's *Defined by a Hollow: Essays on Utopia, Science Fiction and Political Epistemology* (2010).

7. Cameroonian philosopher Achille Mbembe addresses the negative narrative regarding Africa in his book *On the Postcolony* (2000), where he states, "The African human experience constantly appears in the discourse of our times as an experience that can only be understood through *negative interpretation.* Africa is never seen as possessing things and attributes properly part of 'human nature'" (emphasis in the original 1). Such a powerful thought expresses Afro-pessimism.

8. Alondra Nelson credits Anna Everett for theorizing the idea of "the networked consciousness of the African diaspora of necessity prefiguring the network consciousness often hailed as one of the benefits of the Internet" (10).

the hope impulse, and the transhistorical feedback loop. A visual description that illustrates all three interconnected concepts at once better explains them. Black bodies function as *living* circuits per se when race is understood "as a labor-based" technology dependent on dehumanization (Lavender, *Race* 54). More viscerally, a slave starts picking, weeding, or hoeing on one row, goes to the end, and comes back to nearly the same place, trapped in her corporal existence, before starting on the next row on a hot and humid day in Louisiana. In one inspired moment, she begins humming, then singing, shaping words into a work song or a spiritual created from carefully censored Bible verses the master allowed his chattel to hear. Singing transports her tired mind away from the physical drudgery and pain of repetitive motion. Then others take up her song. This torturous, circular journey continues for hours, days, months, and years as the slaves perform their backbreaking tasks under continual threat of violence. But a current materializes between them, almost like electricity, only in thought form.

Agency develops as the slaves gain access to their metaphorical circuitry through communication. They develop mental pathways that allow them to bond with one another in their shared experience in all its misery. Through this sharing, and specifically sharing in the form of aesthetic endeavor, these interactive connections become the basis of a black networked consciousness, a sustainable communal web capable of love, though not protection from slavery's daily traumas while also allowing for betrayals, rivalries, and miscommunications. Only the enslaved blacks discover that such a shared consciousness has always been there ready to be tapped since its origin "in the darkened abyss below the decks of European ships during the infamous middle passage of the transatlantic slave trade" (Everett 125). Survival requires this "webbed network['s]" development as enslaved blacks instigate "a perpetual fight for human status, a yearning for human rights, a struggle for inclusion within the human species" that projects far into the future, hundreds of years (Eshun, *More Brilliant* 00[-006]). A good literary example of such a networked consciousness functioning occurs with the black citizens of Eatonville in Zora Neale Hurston's monumental *Their Eyes Were Watching God* (1937), the subject of chapter 4.

Of course, theorizing on a networked black consciousness already exists. On the one hand, Eshun uses his "webbed network" to discuss a wide range of black music, what he terms *sonic fiction*, such as electronic dance music, jazz fusion, as well as Detroit techno, among several others, and futurist visions in this music at the intersection of black music and SF. On the other hand, Everett discusses an "African diasporic consciousness" in light of blacks using cyberspace to involve themselves with digital culture

(125). While Eshun and Everett have already conceived of aspects relating to this networked black consciousness, and while I am also building on this existing body of knowledge that rightly owes a debt to Paul Gilroy's *The Black Atlantic: Modernity and Double Consciousness* (1993), where he frames his reading of black diasporic experiences in transatlantic terms through DuBois's theory of double consciousness, I combine their concepts into a black networked consciousness from which to analyze literature through an afrofuturistic lens.

A black networked consciousness (sometimes inverted as networked black consciousness or other derivatives as a matter of variety) differs from the notion of community in black studies. Borrowing from traditions of technocultural and science fiction studies in addition to black society, a black networked consciousness suggests that through afrofuturism, communal memories and traditions, which link the past, present, and future, make possible the hope that black people wish to experience from a painful past in building black futures. This is not a desire to escape the pain but to confront and get free of it. What gets done with this changed perceptual filter becomes important. Such desire "charges" the emotional register necessary to force social change by technocultural/technospiritual means. A community, which by definition shares common social interests, does not do that by itself. Each member of the black networked consciousness represents a figurative circuit that powers the network by transmitting hope across the transhistoric feedback loop, chaining together the cause and effect of black experience, and influencing our thoughts in real time. To harness such power changes reality for the better.

This black networked consciousness generates hope, a charged impulse representing the desire for life, liberty, and knowledge, the essential psychic drive seeding resistance, rebellion, and subversive writing in the coming future of early America—of now in fact. This hope impulse reverberates across time and space, linking past, present, and future as black people continually strive for acknowledgment as human beings. To connect to the black networked consciousness, to experience the hope impulse, we readers create and maintain a transhistorical feedback loop, where we go outside the bounds of today's systematic narrative of past events related to early white America. We overload this control system with new input, original thinking, and innovative ideas, causing a systemwide adjustment and, perhaps, inspiring a response to advance the human condition. Afrofuturism functions as such an idea, generating the necessary intellectual dynamism to jolt the discovery of other truths—a revolutionary power. Enough interconnected feedback loops working together—techno-orientalism, Latinx futurism, indigenous futurism, afrofuturism—can change history's whitewashed narrative.[9]

An afrofuturist reading practice switches between systems by linking with this black networked consciousness through material texts—a technique later demonstrated in this introduction with the autobiographical *Narrative of the Life of Frederick Douglass* (1845)—initiating a transhistoric feedback loop. Our response to an early black text completes the loop, causing us to modify our parameters of thought. Mayhap, black readers can only tap into what the literature accomplishes because we are already plugged into our own historical feedback loop and networked consciousness. We achieve an intuitive feeling, a hope impulse, linked with the text where we become almost indistinguishable from our antebellum counterparts to learn from their painful reality. I say "almost indistinguishable" because we project onto that author notions we already hold about race, about antebellum experience, about hope. This moment is ahistoric. Even so, our explorations of human spirit can be startling, beautiful, and breathtaking, as emotive data unilaterally transfers into our minds from the past to impact the future. The sensate information current flows into the deep sphere of subaltern history, electrifying the circuitry of this feedback loop and running into the future ad infinitum.

When literally circumventing cultural codes embedded within the words of a book to modify our sense of what blackness means, afrofuturist reading practices look like hacking when applied to texts that are not considered science fictional in the first place. Nor, for that matter, should these texts be considered as SF, not without hacking the network and skillfully modifying its textual artifacts with beneficent intent to make political action possible through this reading practice. As a mode of interpretation, afrofuturism unlocks the liberatory potential of blacks who see themselves at the fulcrum of contemporary life—as emotional, spiritual, and technological beings in the body politic. As we wrestle with slavery's many legacies—oppression, racism, prejudice, stereotypes, segregation, colorism, and violence—in the twenty-first century of the United States, we dare to hope. By drawing strength and inspiration from this past, we imagine black worlds and identities differently.

---

9. See David Morley and Kevin Robins's "Techno-Orientalism: Japan Panic" (1995); Rachel Haywood Ferreira's *The Emergence of Latin American Science Fiction* (2011); and Anishinaabe scholar Grace L. Dillon's "Imagining Indigenous Futurisms" (2012).

Science-Fictional Blackness

Now imagine the bulk of social Darwinism falling on people with greater amounts of melanin in their skin. Imagine the significance of pseudoscience in inventing the concept of race to justify racism against these people. Imagine the weight of history, religion, and culture dropping on a dark-skinned people metaphysically marked with social inferiority and the belief that they are somehow less than others, namely, their white counterparts. Dating to the Enlightenment era, a science-fictional blackness comes into being that still remains as part of the world in this contemporary age. Blackness *is* science fictional in the sense that these flights of fancy have used science to create the fiction of race as it is applied to black people—indeed, to all people of color. As Greg Tate perceived about a quarter-century ago, "Black people live the estrangement that science fiction writers imagine" (qtd. in Dery, "Black to the Future" 768). Abducted, chained, and transported to the far side of the world by white people. Cultures stripped away, languages stripped away, and autonomy stripped away by white people. Black women raped, black people brutalized, black children sold by white people. Bastardized, mongrelized, mulatto-ized by white people yet still sold away. Worked to death, animalized, and mechanized simultaneously in the cash crop fields—cotton, sugarcane, and tobacco. The stolen profit of this forced labor today endows the foundation of the United States—government, industries, and universities. Gaslit, brainwashed, and manipulated into questioning reality to the point that they even join in ludicrous debates over whether Margaret Mitchell's *Gone with the Wind* (1936) accurately represents slavery; that slavery was not so bad in hindsight; nostalgic, melancholic, hallucinogenic reminiscences of the past for white Americans only.

Now imagine an unchanging same! Inconvenient truths abound—black people are not as important, their lives and children not as precious, their thoughts and feelings not as vital. Unarmed black people beaten, shot, and slain by police officers unthinkingly supported by the white majority, stirring up in black hearts and minds even more fear of a force meant to protect and serve, despite the existence of contrary evidence: audio, video, and eyewitness accounts. There *is* no equality. As Gerry Canavan declares, "If we are interested in stories about brutal invaders who come in technologically advanced ships from far away, who kidnap, murder, rape, and enslave, we do not need to look to outer space; that is already Earth's actual history" (2). And now afrofuturism has emerged to understand the science-fictional existence that blacks have *always* experienced living in the New World—an unreality driven by economic demands, would-be science, and skin color.

Of course, what seems an ahistorical argument allows us to see that there are similarities as well as clear differences between the present and the past linked by racism and violence. This contention does not so much disregard historical context as it opposes showing how the past bleeds into the future. As William Faulkner opined in *Requiem for a Nun* (1951), "The past is never dead. It's not even past" (73), a sentiment later paraphrased by our future president Barack Obama in his inspiring "A More Perfect Union" speech in 2008 to address the many difficulties faced by America, where black anger and white resentment equal a race divide nearly impossible to cross. In this regard, ahistoricism becomes a strength by looking back with a soberness when unavoidably comparing the past with the present and the disadvantages of blackness and by examining how these things impact the anticipation of future changes for black people. Afrofuturism allows us to experience these changes. In some ways, I mirror the "strategic presentism" now emerging from the V21 collective[10] in that I desire to make political change as afrofuturism shapes future race relations (Freedgood and Sanders 117). Afrofuturist knowledge *is* useful knowledge despite the risk of blurring historical specificity.

All readers must rightfully interpret black existence in the New World through the twin lenses of afrofuturism and SF because of the unbelievable, overwhelming, and damaging contact experiences with whites. This sentiment reflects something akin to the "Blackness of Blackness" dream sermon that Ralph Ellison's narrator hears yet sees in *Invisible Man* while hiding out underground, smoking reefer, listening to Louis Armstrong's song "What Did I Do to Be So Black and Blue" in the novel's prologue, and contemplating violence, reality, and, of course, invisibility (8–9). The narrator questions what is it about blackness that causes white folks to not acknowledge the basic humanity of brown-skinned peoples as being anything more than a delusion or a nightmare; black people never seen for who they really are—invisible. In his daydream, the narrator perceives a layering of black history where skin color and violence coincide from the moment of enslaved blacks setting foot in America. Armstrong's words also signify this violence, prejudice, and racial conflict faced by black people. Black and Blue weigh heavily, but the narrator suddenly grasps that the song also "demand[s] action" (12). But smoking reefer has already hindered any action he might take at present or in the future, even though he deems it necessary for change to come which, is, of course, the reason for his "hibernation" as "a covert preparation for a

---

10. The V21 collective are a group of Victorian scholars who desire to make their field relevant for the present by responding to neoliberalism.

more overt action" in the first place (13). And so blackness squared becomes intangible and intuitive at the same time, physical yet abstract; it perfectly describes invisibility that "'*Black will make you . . .*' '*Black . . .*' '*. . . or black will un-make you*'" (emphasis in the original 10). The narrator has attained a conscious awareness of his own science-fictional blackness. In this regard, science-fictional blackness begins with slavery and the hyperreal violence loop.

The Hyperreal Violence Loop

Slave narratives reveal the truth of the brutal conditions faced by human beings oppressed by other human beings for financial gain because of skin color. As Eric Williams argues in his landmark study *Capitalism & Slavery* (1944), "A racial twist has been given to what is basically an economic phenomenon. Slavery was not born of racism: rather, racism was the consequence of slavery" (7). Put another way, chattel slavery started off as an economic institution and was then justified through racial rhetoric. Fugitive slave accounts go beyond reality because their authors demonstrate the materiality of black bodies and various ways to control them, thus creating a hyperreality. Hyperreality, as described by Jean Baudrillard, represents "models of a real without origin or reality" (1). Violence and the threat of violence become hyperreal in the Baudrillardian sense in *Narrative of the Life of Frederick Douglass* or Harriet Jacobs's *Incidents in the Life of a Slave Girl* (1861), among other texts. They read like SF because contemporary readers are overawed by the visceral reality of a racism stirred by pseudoscientific beliefs. The alien-ness of mirror-shaded officers gunning down black people with little or no evidence because of perpetuated stereotypes disturbs in the present just as much as a white overseer whipping a black slave to a bloody death in the past. The unreality, the outlandishness, the implausibility of it feel science fictional in that readers cannot tell where reality ends and fiction begins. Readers today cannot encounter the physical reality of slavery without reading texts written well over 150 years ago or without viewing objects, such as wrought-iron slave shackles, locked away behind the clear Plexiglas panes of museum exhibits. Violence against black people endures as a repeating copy of the colonial period followed by the antebellum era which has not existed in the United States for more than 150 years. Violence is normalized, mythologized. Reality blends with representation and generates models of a real violence that depends on a sign exchange value placed on black bodies—hyperreality. Reality and simulated reality become impossible to differentiate.

Hyperreality deprives most of today's white folks of any real emotional engagement with black folks. Instead, white people fear the stereotyped images of black men and black women as overtly violent and sexual and do not hesitate to protect themselves from endless reproductions of these black signifiers devoid of real meaning. A simulacrum of meaning develops that becomes truth in its own right by perverting the pretense of black bodies as a dangerous commodity. So from Baudrillard's definition to white disengagement to white projection onto black bodies, past and present realities come together making it impossible to distinguish one from the other, resulting in unending paradigms of violence. Afrofuturism seems an effective countermeasure because it offsets the reality break. Afrofuturism creates new realities by recovering basic reality reflections and projecting them into possible futures. Indeed, afrofuturism challenges a de facto black science-fictional existence.

History records the horrors of the science-fictional blackness produced by slavery in all its brutality through slave narratives, auction records, and ship manifests, among other things. The sheer violence on record, then, looks nearly interchangeable with the ultraviolence against blacks we now see nightly on cable news and local TV. All of it taken together initiates a hyperreal violence loop from an afrofuturistic standpoint because it marks a reality faced by blacks for centuries in its racial stasis. In exploring this hyperreal violence loop through afrofuturism, we can disrupt the repeating pattern with a pragmatic optimism for different futures and new realities starting with the most famous slave narrative.

In terms of violence and the threat of violence, *Narrative of the Life of Frederick Douglass* captures exactly what I mean in Douglass's description of how a slave named Demby is murdered for disobeying Colonel Lloyd's overseer, Mr. Gore. Gore intends to scourge Demby. After only a few whip licks, Demby flees Gore by submerging himself in a nearby creek up to the shoulders while rebuffing Gore's lethal warnings. Douglass states, "Without consultation or deliberation with anyone," Mr. Gore "raised his musket to his face, taking deadly aim . . . and in an instant poor Demby was no more. His mangled body sank out of sight, and blood and brains marked the water where he had stood" (39). I cringe at the gunshot in my mind's ear. Gore simply explained "that Demby had become unmanageable" (39). As proven across time, black lives do not matter when a white man's authority comes under scrutiny, and this is the crux of our hyperreality. Such a temporal loop repeats over and over again throughout American history, exacerbating already strained racial tensions.

Flash-forward to the civil rights era of the mid-twentieth century. The violence under examination is real and historical but feels unreal and science fictional in its invariance. This defines a hyperreality—endless repetition. The hyperreal violence loop amplifies itself. Emmett Till, Medgar Evers,[11] and Martin Luther King Jr.[12] *are* murder victims. Till was a black teenager lynched in Mississippi on August 28, 1955, for supposedly wolf-whistling at a white woman, Carolyn Bryant,[13] in a local grocery store. But the most disturbing part of this hyperreal cycle is the 16th Street Baptist Church bombing in Birmingham, Alabama, on a Sunday morning, September 15, 1963, in which four black girls—Addie Mae Collins, Denise McNair, Carole Robertson, and Cynthia Wesley—were blown up by the Ku Klux Klan.

Flash-forward again to the post–civil rights era of the late twentieth century. The hyperreal violence loops around again in different parts of the country. John Africa, Rodney King,[14] Amadou Diallo,[15] and Timothy Thomas[16] stand out among many black victims. John Africa, the leader of MOVE, a Philadelphia-based black liberation group engaged in a variety of racial protests, along with eleven others, died in the Philadelphia police bombing of their MOVE row house on May 13, 1985, resulting in a fire that destroyed sixty-five other houses and left close to 300 people homeless.[17] Flash-forward a third time to the "postrace" era of the contemporary

---

11. Medgar Evers, the Mississippi field secretary of the NAACP, was shot though the back in his driveway on June 12, 1963, in Jackson, Mississippi, murdered by White Citizen's Council member Byron De La Beckwith, who remained free for over thirty years. Two all-white juries failed to convict him in 1964, but new evidence emerged in 1994 and a third prosecution found him guilty of first-degree murder.

12. Civil rights leader King was assassinated by James Earl Ray on April 4, 1968, on the balcony of a hotel room at the Lorraine Motel in Memphis, Tennessee.

13. In *The Blood of Emmett Till* (2017), when asked about her testimony about how Till "grabbed her around the waist and uttered obscenities," Carolyn Bryant-Donham confesses to Duke historian Timothy B. Tyson—in her only interview sixty-two years later—that "that part is not true" (6).

14. On March 23, 1991, Rodney King was severely beaten by four Los Angeles police officers, an act that happened to be caught on tape. The officers were acquitted on all charges, sparking the 1992 LA riots.

15. Amadou Diallo, a Guinean immigrant, was shot nineteen times by four New York City police officers on February 4, 1999. He died outside his Bronx apartment; the officers were found not guilty.

16. Nineteen-year-old African American Timothy Thomas was shot and killed by white Cincinnati police officer Stephen Roach while resisting arrest for a nonviolent misdemeanor. The shooting ignited four days of rioting in downtown Cincinnati from April 9 to 13, 2001.

17. John Edgar Wideman fictionalizes MOVE and the police bombing of their headquarters in *Philadelphia Fire* (1990) through his fictional writer Cudjoe, who returns home to the "City of Brotherly Love" (a name often used sarcastically today) in the aftermath of the event.

United States. The hyperreal violence loop intensifies. Trayvon Martin,[18] Eric Garner,[19] Michael Brown,[20] Tamir Rice,[21] Jeremy McDole,[22] Alton Sterling,[23] and Philando Castile[24] *are* murder victims too.[25] And now we have elected Donald J. Trump as the forty-fifth president of the United States, who campaigned to "Make America Great Again";[26] who seemingly represents an angry white America; and who promises to turn back the racial clock with a "law and order" slogan harking back to the 1970s antiblack rhetoric.

The necessary information overload here strongly makes my points about the hyperreal violence loop and a science-fictional blackness that can be best understood through afrofuturism. Breaking this repeating loop requires that the *hope impulse* be generated by a *connected black consciousness* capable of transmitting itself along a different *transhistorical feedback loop*—my trifocal afrofuturism lens. Please note that the hyperreal violence loop differs from the transhistorical feedback loop in that the violence loop and

---

18. Seventeen-year-old African American Trayvon Martin was shot and killed by George Zimmerman of the Neighborhood Watch program in Sanford, Florida, on February 26, 2012. Zimmerman was later acquitted of all charges, with the stand-your-ground law of Florida having an impact after he claimed self-defense. The Black Lives Matter social media and activist movement began shortly after the acquittal of Zimmerman in 2013.

19. Eric Garner was killed in Staten Island of New York City on July 17, 2014, when a white police officer restrained him with an illegal chokehold. The officer in question, Daniel Pantaleo, was not even indicted even though he had used a banned restraint method.

20. Teenaged Michael Brown was shot and killed on August 9, 2014, in Ferguson, Missouri, by a white police officer after an altercation. The police officer, Darren Wilson, was later exonerated on all charges.

21. Twelve-year-old Tamir Rice was shot on November 22, 2014, by two white police officers in Cleveland, Ohio, while swinging in a city park and playing with a toy gun. He died the next day. The officers were dismissed but not charged.

22. While in his wheelchair, black paraplegic Jeremy McDole was shot and killed by Wilmington, Delaware, police on September 23, 2015.

23. On July 5, 2016, Alton Sterling was shot several times at point-blank range by two white Baton Rouge police officers while pinned to the ground, an act that resulted in his death.

24. A day later on July 6, 2016, Philando Castile was shot multiple times and killed by a St. Anthony, Minnesota, police officer during a routine traffic stop after Castile stated that he was licensed to carry a firearm and had one in the car.

25. For further reflection, see Houston A. Baker's "The Black Bottom Line: Reflections on Ferguson, Black Lives Matter, and White Male Violence in America" (2016).

26. Octavia E. Butler foresees Trump's campaign slogan eighteen years earlier in her Nebula Award–winning *Parable of the Talents* (1998). Her protagonist Lauren Olamina grows the Earthseed religions in a United States politically dominated by far-right conservatism and President Andrew Steele Jarret's campaign "to make America great again" via the religious intolerance and racial inequality of its earlier days (20).

its hyperreality produce these three things, which can be read only in terms of afrofuturism. These artificial loops differ in that the hyperreal violence loop engages the nonsensical violence inflicted on black people across time and the transhistorical feedback loop provides blended information to readers about the world inside the text and the cultural moment that created it.

Black people *suffer* from this needless repetition of hyperreality. The repetition of stereotypes to such an enormous extent symbolizes a science-fictional blackness and also a hyperreality. It will continue until we reexamine, reprioritize, and figure a way out of this useless cycle. The real, political, polemical force of afrofuturist criticism arises in this darkening moment to provide glimpses of variegated futures, some good and some bad, through the past. In other words, the cultural and material realities of the hyperreal violence loop make it possible to return to the past of African American culture and see these hints of the future; or, said another way, the physical, historical, and economic context of this dangerous hyperrealness generates an afrofuturistic response. This narrative practice, this going back through an afrofuturist lens, allows us to see the futures already there in these classic works of black fiction. We can then utilize the techniques of SF to see our way out. Along these lines, afrofuturism offers hope of breaking this cycle because it permits us to time-travel, to see this dangerous pattern generated by greed, to value *future* black life in the present, and to revel in a successful black presidency despite a racist government, eight full years of an efficacious Obama presidency with a legacy now under threat. Of course, these benefits upload to the networked black consciousness and spread.

Adventures in Afrofuturism

Afrofuturism provides a unique way of reading with respect to canonical black literature because scholars have not previously commented on the strands of futurism that exist in these texts. Novels such as *Their Eyes Were Watching God, Native Son* (Wright 1940), and *Captain Blackman* (J. Williams 1972) reconstruct our sense of feasible political futures in which black people determine their own destinies. Each of my chosen writers counteracts accepted racial histories by forging connections between past, present, and future to help explain a problematic black social experience. Resonating intertextually with earlier nineteenth-century fantastic works such as Martin R. Delany's *Blake; or the Huts of America* (1859–62), all of these texts have in common an aesthetic resistance to segregation, the literal alienation of a black people historically dislocated by Western ideas of progress, a reclamation of both past and future histories, and black uses for technoscience—like a compass to traverse rough geographic terrain while escaping North as the eponymous Blake uses in Delany's novel.

Certainly, it seems odd to elide the civil rights struggle in my account of afrofuturism, but the urgency of the period largely dampened novelistic creation as African Americans seized their future through passive resistance. The speeches, sermons, and poetry of the 1950s and 1960s stand out the brightest in my mind, but writing about that moment's importance demands a different book. Nonetheless, Ellison's *Invisible Man* remains an obvious choice, and I consequently offer substantial readings of key moments in the novel in chapter 6. I strongly considered using James Baldwin's novel *Another Country* (1962) because of its frank portrayals of racial, gender, and sexual difference. However, I think of Baldwin primarily as the finest of essayists, and the examination of one of his book-length essays, such as *The Fire Next Time,* (1963), as science fictional—since it reads during his dinner encounter with the honorable Elijah Muhammad of the Nation of Islam[27]—goes beyond the scope of my book, as does the poetry of the Black Arts Movement.

While Kenneth W. Warren proclaims the death knell of African American literature in his provocative *What Was African American Literature?* (2011), the act of imagining a world without African American literature is itself an afrofuturist application in that he inverts twentieth-century racial politics to create his very own postracial reading theory. Revisiting the black canon in terms of afrofuturism changes what we know about African American historical and cultural conditions and what we know about race as an oppression technology. Hope, optimism, and future-looking visions have always existed in black literature against the backdrop of white supremacy. Afrofuturism teaches us to see these "science fiction" aspects of texts that are not science fiction better than we have before, so a pessimistic text such as *Native Son,* for example, actually contains a lot of hope in its artistry.

I have made three significant decisions in writing this book. First, I have chosen to begin with slavery as afrofuturism's starting point because no one else has comprehensively explored this theory in early America, prompting me to delve more deeply into the literary and cultural history between 1619 and 1903. Since 1619 putatively represents the arrival of the first black slaves on a Dutch warship stopping at Jamestown, Virginia, in colonial North America, this date seems like the obvious starting point.

---

27. I am referring to the second of the two essays—"Down at the Cross – Letter from a Region of My Mind"—contained within the pages of Baldwin's *The Fire Next Time.*

Second, I have decided to discontinue mapping afrofuturist terrain into the twentieth century and to concentrate my writing efforts on single African American authors as case studies. I can say with certainty that African American SF, if not afrofuturism, in the twentieth century *is* already well documented. My first book, *Race in American Science Fiction* (2011) covers much of this territory. I have decided on canonical black texts that most would agree are classics and that have always struck me as being speculative as I am teaching them in my classes. I cannot tell you how many times I thought it fascinating that Janie Starks displayed telepathic ability in *Their Eyes Were Watching God,* just as I found fascinating the metallic description of Bigger Thomas's skin in *Native Son* and the drug-induced time-travel reveries of a badly injured black military officer in *Captain Blackman*. Though none of these novels emphasizes slavery, the peculiar institution's alarming effects are felt in the segregated environments that the characters experience almost as if they were an alien species living on alien planets as white characters would have them believe.

And third, I use technocultural metaphors—such as a network or a feedback loop, among others—to further expand afrofuturist theory throughout this book. Mirroring the language of technoculture—machines, electricity, circuits, hacking, and so on—proves useful to this afrofuturistic study because this language represents the metaphoric discourse currently operating within science fiction, itself the signature literature of our moment. Put another way, I locate science-fictional elements in non-science-fiction texts at the level of language, imagery, and metaphor. This language proves useful for interrogating texts written well before such systems were literally invented because it connects the past with the present as well as the future. And it proves useful in demonstrating the power of race used positively to call for the social action necessary to foster change and transform the world.

In Part I, "1619–1903: The Afrofuturist Vista and the Possibility of Freedom," the first three chapters of the book trace afrofuturism in key figures, historical rebellions, and political moments by challenging and extending boundaries. In Part II, "Afrofuturism and Classic Twentieth-Century African American Novels," the final three chapters function as case studies of single works by noted black authors. In these chapters I apply afrofuturism to classic mainstream novels—works of the highest quality that have an enduring interest.

Chapter 1, "Hope and Freedom Technologies," explores how the hope impulse operates as a core concept in early American afrofuturism which in turn forms a networked black consciousness among slaves galvanizing themselves to endure the science-fictional reality of early America, all of which creates a transhistorical feedback loop. I start with literacy as a kind of freedom technology in the antebellum era as a prelude before diving deeply into American racial history to examine afrofuturism's roots. From this point, I look at conjuring as a spiritual technology; linguistic coding as afrofuturist ciphers in slave songs and quilting; and the colonial afrofuturists Phillis Wheatley, Olaudah Equiano, and Benjamin Banneker. The chapter emphasizes the breadth of what afrofuturism makes possible because its roots lie buried in the past, in the abscess of racial experiences caused by slavery. Through these roots we see the connections made by twentieth-century black writers in tracing a science-fictional blackness whose origins lie in the past.

Chapter 2, "Black Uprisings and the Fight for the Future," traces the hope impulse and a fledging networked black consciousness through historical slave uprisings and conspiracies undergirding the oft-denied potential of a black revolutionary America occupying white antebellum minds. Uprisings and conspiracies under consideration include the Stono Rebellion, the Haitian Revolution, and the German Coast Uprising, as well as Nat Turner's Rebellion and the thwarted conspiracies of Gabriel Prosser and Denmark Vesey. Such a frank desire for freedom, if not parity, impels David Walker to write his *Appeal* (1829) challenging colored people to rise up across the globe, simultaneously anchoring this feedback loop in the past while projecting it into the far future of the twenty-first century. Early black novelists, such as Martin R. Delany, Sutton E. Griggs, and Pauline Hopkins, capitalize on this history by offering distinct and defiant afrofuturist visions such as a pending transatlantic race war, a secret black nation, and a lost heir from America to a mythic African kingdom scenario, respectively.

Chapter 3, "Of Alien Abductions, Pocket Universes, Trickster Technologies, and Slave Narratives," examines slave narratives: their depiction of a black science-fictional existence against the backdrop of the peculiar institution and a demonstrable hope in fugitive flights to freedom. A fully functioning networked black consciousness results from the recollections of slaves like Frederick Douglass and Harriet Jacobs, among many others, that we can figuratively jack into today simply by reading and thinking about their accounts. In addition to the well-known slave narratives of Douglass and Jacobs, I address how Olaudah Equiano, Venture Smith, Solomon Northup, Henry "Box" Brown, William Wells Brown, Henry Bibb, and the Crafts certify afrofuturism's cogency in exposing a science-fictional blackness. Their individual accounts of antebellum politics forge the afrofuturist vista that now exists in terms of black resistance.

Chapter 4, "Black Bodies in Space: Zora Neale Hurston's *Their Eyes Were Watching God*," demonstrates how Hurston used the literalized metaphors germane to science fiction to demonstrate her complex views of racial consciousness, her desire to value and humanize blacks, and her hope for a new and better future. Hurston's protagonist, Janie, explores the parallel black worlds of Eatonville and the Muck, where her self-actualization pivots on seeing a future for herself. Utilizing black folk conventions, Hurston creates these black spaces within the white world in which a networked black consciousness operates and characters get by in the alternate world with vernacular technology—a technology of knowing that weaves together the ocular, oral, and aural involved in storytelling. Extrasensory powers and alien encounters—unrecognized science-fictional elements in the novel— also help create a planetary romance ripe for afrofuturist interpretation as Janie contends with a difficult social existence as a black woman.

Chapter 5, "'Metallically Black': Bigger Thomas and the Black Apocalyptic Vision of Richard Wright's *Native Son*," explains how Wright cannot imagine a future for his notoriously alienated character trapped by racial oppression. Protagonist Bigger Thomas, disconnected from his own humanity, suffers mightily from institutional racism in Chicago and reacts by murdering two women in his attempt to feel alive, relevant, and human. However, Wright impairs his own vision of social protest here by catapulting an extremely noxious black male beast stereotype into our own future, where a hyperreal violence loop seemingly wraps itself around the necks of black men. Bigger suffers from a science-fictional blackness metaphorically configured as a cyborg/alien/monster throughout the novel, unfit to live in either the white world or the black one, severed from the networked black consciousness. Within such a framework, Wright's novel, grasped as an afrofuturist text, signifies a positivistic caution against the maintenance of such powerful racial stereotypes.

Chapter 6, "Racial Warfare, Radical Afrofuturism, and John A. Williams's *Captain Blackman*," investigates how black militancy manifests in an ongoing war between races, creating an alternate world where such a war could happen in the near-future America. Abraham Blackman, a black officer gravely injured by enemy fire on patrol in the Vietnam jungle, experiences drug-induced fever dreams in which he participates in each of America's wars, leading him to seek revenge on white people, ultimately resulting in a black victory. Williams creates a transhistoric feedback loop where Blackman, as a student of black military history, fights as a black man in a white man's army, feeling the racial vitriol of an institution that for so long has not been welcoming to black soldiers. His firsthand experience radicalizes him, and he in turn teaches radicalism to his men at informal meetings. Williams's story illustrates the power of a webbed black awareness encompassing the past and future of a black hope.

Afrofuturism Rising ends with a brief conclusion, "Into the Black-o-Sphere," in which I do two things. First, I expand afrofuturism beyond its American frame by briefly outlining how Chinua Achebe's canonical *Things Fall Apart* (1958) feels like SF when one reads it as a hostile alien colonization story resulting from the contact between the Ibo and the British Empire's representatives. But *African futurism*[28] is probably the more exacting and appropriate term, because European colonization of the African continent gathered steam in the mid-nineteenth century. In this respect, Achebe frees all of the African diaspora to write its own futures, which we now see emerging in the likes of Nnedi Okorafor's *Lagoon* (2014)[29] and Tade Thompson's *Rosewater* (2016),[30] among others. Second, I offer a short afrofuturist reading of Colson Whitehead's Pulitzer Prize–winning novel *The Underground Railroad* (2016) as a link to twenty-first-century black writing demonstrating how mythologizing history reclaims the future as well.

African American literature perpetually reflects the science-fictional reality of blacks in America. In this light, as Samuel R. Delany carefully ruminates in his now classic "Racism and Science Fiction" (1998), "the racial situation, permeable as it might sometimes seem [. . .] is nevertheless your total surround" (391). Delany perfectly expresses the black experience. While first Delany and next Butler become major black figures in SF, I largely leave them on the margins as important personages with the intention of periodizing this "literary prehistory" or "classic" era of afrofuturism by the exclusion of black people from a white publishing genre called *science fiction*. Delany and Butler actually represent a threshold, marking a change in the energy state in afrofuturism at the time it becomes an accepted part of SF. This change clarifies why Delany's "Racism and Science Fiction" is such

---

28. See Nnedi Okorafor's tweet "I am an Africanfuturist. BEFORE you start asking for or debating it's meaning, please call me the name first" from November 4, 2018 (@Nnedi Okorafor, PhD).

29. See Okorafor's first alien-contact novel, *Lagoon* (2014), where shape-shifting aliens land offshore in Lagos, Nigeria, the largest city on the African continent, instead of in places like New York, London, or Tokyo.

30. Thompson provides a new assessment of postcolonialism in his hard-boiled SF first alien-contact/invasion story *Rosewater*.

a key afrofuturist text that makes clear the obstacles black people, not to mention other minorities, face in both real and imaginary worlds with "the concept of race inform[ing] everything" about them (392). We should never forget Delany's point about the "total surround." That is why I use the first-person pronoun so often in my book. My awareness of this racial surround, its entirety, goes bone-deep. It is quite literally everywhere in the physical, virtual, and imaginary worlds we inhabit. Engaging with it, really engaging with its permanence, merely signals one of the reasons I doggedly continue to study race, science fiction, and afrofuturism in all its forms. I live and feel it every day, and I see its presence in the literature I teach, particularly classic texts not thought to contain one iota of speculative content. As this book will show, afrofuturism represents one significant way of grappling with this reality across time and space.

PART I

1619–1903

*The Afrofuturist Vista and
the Possibility of Freedom*

CHAPTER 1

HOPE AND FREEDOM TECHNOLOGIES

AFROFUTURISM PROVIDES a new way to both literally and figuratively decode the dreams of black freedom in a country built on slave labor. As exemplified by Frederick Douglass, the ability to read and write—what I term a *literacy technology*—helps to preserve a resilient and revitalized black heritage, extracted from the existential nadir generated by race and racism, from which future generations draw strength by accessing these archived memories. Literacy, long denied to enslaved blacks, made it possible for them to better interpret white world codings and to survive the social deaths of slavery, segregation, and, now, the prison industrial/complex recently dubbed the New Jim Crow.[1] Likewise, spiritual technologies such as conjuring, clandestine coding through slave song, and the ardent colonial writings of Phillis Wheatley, Olaudah Equiano, and Benjamin Banneker, identified as colonial afrofuturists, represent an embryonic stage of afrofuturism in the sense that these freedom technologies first developed in early America. Technologies are not necessarily Western or mechanical for that matter, but these black secretive technologies functioned as networking systems in which historical figures linked their own cultural production, their own bodies, and their own experiences with others to perform this kind of networking.

---

1. See Michelle Alexander's *The New Jim Crow: Mass Incarceration in the Age of Colorblindness* (2010).

Imagine encountering someone who refused to believe slavery occurred as horrifically as it did in the United States. A slave narrative would immediately teach such persons otherwise, but a deeply embedded racism might prevent them from acknowledging the validity of firsthand accounts. Because terms like *race* and *racism* burst with already learned connotations, the iconic science-fictional feel of estrangement seems common in this moment because most Americans do not want to confront the guilt associated with their antebellum heritage. An unorthodox alternative presents itself to contemporary readers in using the idea of freedom as a technology. Any kind of practical knowledge that helps black people solve problems with their environment and in their society, abetting their escape from physical and psychological bondage and thereby allowing them control of their own actions, qualifies as a freedom technology. For instance, demonstrating literacy as a freedom technology in *Narrative of the Life of Frederick Douglass* makes understanding how afrofuturism combats the power of slavery's vestiges paramount in this context. Afrofuturism as a body of culture and as a critical practice combines science-fictional language and black racial experiences to establish and evaluate a consciousness of cultural projections based on history. Because we live now in what feels like a science-fictional, dystopian world, afrofuturism seems even more relevant when we look backward at historical texts like that of Douglass.

In Douglass's *Narrative*, we fully experience the miserable existence of slaves in the nineteenth century in terms of physical drudgery, bodily torture, and emotional torment as political, spiritual, and economic crises merge in the black body. Douglass suffers from a science-fictional blackness but later discovers the means to breaking free: literacy, the ability to read and write. The importance of literacy cannot be stressed enough here because Douglass learns it is the key to unlocking his mind after overhearing his master Hugh inform his wife Sophia, "If you teach that nigger . . . how to read, there would be no keeping him. It would forever unfit him to be a slave" (48). For blacks, the ability to read historically opened possibilities, both good and bad, to redirect one's very own future, to imagine a future free of slavery. Afrofuturistically speaking, such a powerful realization generated a sense of long-denied personhood for Douglass.

Douglass recalls various risks in gaining literacy from being beaten, sold, or even killed, though he endangered his own life by using a "board fence, brick wall, and pavement" as his "copy-book" (57) after challenging white street urchins in Baltimore to spelling contests and rewarding them with bread as he himself is awarded with a deepening knowledge of letters.

Mimicking his young charge Master Thomas's hand by copying over it in spelling books, Douglass learned to write. His life-drive highlights literacy as a freedom technology, which Douglass later passed on to other slaves by covertly teaching them to read at "Sabbath school" from discarded spelling books (89). As twenty-first-century readers of Douglass's *Narrative*, we figuratively jack into the networked black consciousness, surf the feedback loop backward in time, and connect with Douglass to reiterate the magnitude of hope that literacy as a freedom technology offers black people especially.

In the early twentieth century, Richard Wright shared a similar story with respect to sharpening his own reading ability in his memoir *Black Boy* (1945). Southern whites actively discouraged bright black children from learning and prohibited them from using the local library to borrow books. But one morning, a teenaged Wright arrived early to work at the Memphis optical plant employing him, picked up the *Commercial Appeal* newspaper, and began "his free reading of the press" during which he came across an article condemning H. L. Mencken (244). That the Southern press would offer "furious denunciation" of this Northern literary critic piqued Wright's curiosity, but he had no access to the critic's works (244). Wright actually went to the "library several times to get books for the white men on the job"—only when they wrote notes of permission for him to do so (245). Wright desired to know what Mencken said to infuriate the South, and he devised a plan to gain access to the whites-only library, though he already "knew that [he] would create hostility if [he] went about this business of reading in a clumsy way" (245). In other words, these white coworkers expected Wright to be uninformed and to play the role of a submissive yet happy darky. If we hack American racial history at this point, we can easily discern that the century between the lives of Frederick Douglass and Richard Wright may be different, but racism and prejudice remained the same.

By metaphorically uploading Wright's experience to the transhistoric feedback loop, we can connect Wright with Douglass. We can see how Wright sought out access to a networked black consciousness in hoping for a better future for himself and his race despite sensationalizing the black brute stereotype with his earlier 1940 novel *Native Son*—the topic of chapter 5. Wright utilized his own hard-earned literacy as a technology of freedom to liberate his thinking.

In his narrative, he enlists the aid of Mr. Falk, an Irish Catholic coworker, "who was hated by the white Southerners," by borrowing Falk's library card and signing Falk's name to check out a Mencken book (245). Wright forges a note to the librarian: "*Dear Madam: will you please let this nigger boy*—I used the word 'nigger' to make the librarian feel that I could not possibly be the author of the note—*have some books by H. L. Mencken*" (246). After telling the librarian that he "can't read," she lends him two books by Mencken, and he learns the possibility of "fighting with words" (247). And so Wright forges many more notes and borrows many more books as reading becomes an obsession for him. Reading becomes a passion because Wright believes "that there were feelings denied" him because of his skin color (250). Like Douglass in the antebellum era, Wright became unfit to live in Jim Crow society roughly one hundred years later because he now *"knew"* that "the world about [him] was hostile, killing" (251). Armed with only an eighth-grade education, Wright decided to become a writer in order to address the black condition in America with loaded words reverberating into the future.

If we return to the imaginary slavery apologist or, even more strongly worded, denier, afrofuturistic coding confronts their tragically narrow views—the Civil War was not about slavery but states' rights; or slavery was not as bad as people say it was for blacks because they were fed, housed, and clothed; or only rich whites could afford to own slaves, meaning that actual slaveholders were a low percentage of the population; and so on. Where the Missouri Compromise of 1820, the Fugitive Slave Act of 1850, and the Dred Scott Supreme Court Decision of 1857 could not convince them that slavery was even a bad thing, the power of literature could, and still can—something the abolitionists knew. This contemporary slavery apologist can no longer deny that slavery happened, that it was more than bad, and that it has had a lasting impact still damaging to African Americans as it continues to prop up a white supremacist belief system. Afrofuturistic coding makes white persons conscious of the societal sicknesses of race and racism, and it presents them with a choice—remain ignorant or acknowledge black people as fully human. This is why it is absolutely imperative that we fight against textbook companies, backed by wealthy conservatives, that take advantage of historical memory by manipulating young minds. In 2015, for example, McGraw-Hill Education placed a caption in its ninth-grade geography textbook that reads, "The Atlantic Slave Trade between the 1500s and 1800s brought millions of workers from Africa to the southern United States to work on agricultural plantations" (Fernandez and Hauser).[2] Thankfully, a sharp-eyed black mother and her teenage son spotted this *error,* used their social networks to capture news media attention, and brought awareness to this historical erasure that would have enabled racism to grow unchecked even further. An enlightened citizenry must feel obligated to fight against the sanitization of history to prevent the pattern from repeating itself. Literacy as a freedom technology has always proved itself useful, and tracing

---

2. See Manny Fernandez and Christine Hauser's "Texas Mother Teaches Textbook Company a Lesson on Accuracy" (2015).

its importance through a transhistoric feedback loop demonstrates the difficulty in navigating the emotional grooves of a living history.

As specified in the introduction, afrofuturism's deep history has increasingly fascinated scholars over the past decade. Afrofuturists understand that slavery's terrible legacy represents a science-fictional blackness in which African slaves were abducted, relocated across a vast ocean, and suffered through all manners of abuse at the hands of peculiar white beings. Such a dystopian alien existence intrinsically represents the substance of SF. With slavery as its base, American society relied on the "systematic, conscientious, and massive destruction of African cultural remnants" as declared by Delany (qtd. in Dery, "Black to the Future" 747). Being able to endure the still-oppressive conditions that blacks face on a daily basis going all the way back to antebellum America depends on hope. Delany believes that "if science fiction has any use at all, it is that among all its various and variegated future landscapes it gives us [black people] images *for* our futures" (*Starboard Wine* 31). Our understanding of afrofuturism as a complex historical phenomenon that unfolds across centuries, cultures, and creative practices begins with an exploration of how the central concerns of afrofuturism first emerged in early American scientific and political debates.

This chapter demonstrates how "the hope impulse" functions as a conceptual key in perceiving early American afrofuturism. Black people's desire for a better life, for a better future, and for freedom itself provided the basic intuitive urge powering resistance, rebellion, and subversive writing in early America. Black generational experience encoded in the folklore, native scientific practices, and spiritual beliefs that survived the Middle Passage and reverberated through American history created and later helped a networked black consciousness, the basis of the freedom technologies that help blacks withstand the horrors of slavery. In this chapter I choose to cover a range of historical texts and individuals rather than doing in-depth readings of a few texts, as will happen later in *Afrofuturism Rising,* because I aim to demonstrate how widespread concepts like code-breaking and native science, among other things, have always existed in black creative expression and rhetorical thought. Mapping the hope impulse's evolution and the networked black consciousness it formed among slaves and free blacks allows us to see how black people survived the science-fictional reality of early America.

Native Science and Afrofuturism (Spiritual Technology)

Race, science, and spiritual practices have often come into conflict in American history. But this familiar tension feels different when viewed through the lens of afrofuturism, which focuses on the production of an alternative technology: a spiritual technology that produces knowledge by using different truths that have been arranged systematically to show how the nonphysical world works in tandem with the material world and by applying this information for practical ends such as freedom. Anthropologist Colin Scott declares that the "opposition of science for 'the West' to myth and magic for 'the rest' is far from dissolved" and that "Western self-conception remains profoundly involved with images of rational 'self' versus mystical 'other'" (176). In this regard, afrofuturism does not evoke Western scientific notions that largely follow the politics of appropriation. As an illustration, medical experimentation on black bodies goes as far back as one of the Founding Fathers of the United States, if not earlier. During the summer of 1796, Thomas Jefferson injected 200 slaves with cowpox to prove the validity of English physician Edward Jenner's vaccination techniques before inoculating his own family to protect them from smallpox (Washington 59).[3] In other words, society seemingly trusted that scientists, physicians, and philosophers appeared to have control of the truth, whereas the rest of the world made up stuff. Enlightenment thinkers such as Jefferson discredited the accumulated knowledge(s) expressed as a form of pattern recognition in ritual practices like song, dance, story, art, and other cultural traditions.

Native science per se experiences an odd flattening effect, an inertial dampening of the apparently supernatural or magical, that excludes it from Western notions of science and technology. When thought of only in terms of technoculture, afrofuturism devalues the native scientific practices of enslaved Africans. For that reason, widening afrofuturism's definition to include *fantastic* elements becomes essential.

Conjuring and spirit work involve more of a sense of the supernatural that is dependent upon native scientific practices and the knowledge that goes into root work, potion-making, and exact measuring and mixing of ingredients. Such mythical practitioners construct their own definition of science as a mode of knowledge production about the natural world via method, training, and practice that suggests a repeatability principle to measure observable phenomena. Mark Dery acknowledges this neglected element of afrofuturism and its "mojos and goofer dust . . . lucky charms, fetishes, effigies, and other devices employed in syncretic systems, such as voodoo, hoodoo, santeria, mambo, and macumba, function very much like the joysticks, Datagloves, Waldos, and Spaceballs used to control vir-

---

3. As a more recent example, think of the African American Henrietta Lacks and the theft of her cells for medical research. See Rebecca Skloot's *The Immortal Life of Henrietta Lacks* (2010).

tual realities" ("Black to the Future" 766). But Dery dismisses these spiritual technologies. Scholars, thus far, have failed to investigate this branch of afrofuturism by further exploring the ties between the supernatural and the scientific. Dery, nevertheless, has recently admitted that afrofuturism disputes "the positivist, rationalist, materialist biases of the Enlightenment project by reasserting the value of intuition and the unconscious; of the pre-industrial, mythic modes of modeling the world" ("Afrofuturism Reloaded"). However, this frank concession does nothing to mitigate the critical neglect of afrofuturism's supernatural element fostered through the passage of time. But thinking of this supernatural element as an alternative spiritual technology helps lessen the disregard.

For example, the looming historical figures of Tituba and Marie Laveau greatly enhance the supernatural edge of African American literary culture.[4] From mainstream works such as Toni Morrison's *Song of Solomon* (1977) and Gloria Naylor's *Mama Day* (1988) to speculative fiction works such as Octavia E. Butler's *Wild Seed* (1980), Nalo Hopkinson's *Brown Girl in the Ring* (1998), and Tananarive Due's *The Good House* (2003), among many others, spirit work pervades black fiction.[5] Although the slave Tituba's racial ancestry causes heated debate today, she was one of the first people accused and convicted of witchcraft at the Salem witch trials between February 1692 and May 1693. But Tituba escaped execution claiming to be a witch only after staunchly denying her guilt; accusing her friends Sarah Good and Sarah Osborn of witchcraft; and confessing to flying on a broom and to meeting Satan in various guises while never signing the devil's book with her own blood.[6] As Kameelah L. Martin notes, Tituba used "her wit and subterfuge to evade capital punishment when her white counterparts could not" (27). After thirteen months in prison, Tituba disappears from all public records. Like Tituba, Marie Laveau embodies this supernatural bent as the Voodoo queen of New Orleans during much of the nineteenth century.

Herein lies afrofuturism's paradox: The occult and science both attempt to explain, harness, and exploit the power of nature. Technoculture has

---

4. See Ann Petry's *Tituba of Salem Village* (1964), Maryse Condé's *I, Tituba Black Witch of Salem* (trans. 1992), and Jewell Parker Rhodes's *Voodoo Dreams: A Novel of Marie Laveau* (1993).

5. Pilate, born without a bellybutton, does spirit work in Morrison's novel; Miranda (Mama) Day practices magic to help the people of her small town in Naylor's novel; Anyanwu, an African medicine woman, shape-shifts in Butler's novel; Ti-Jeanne learns spiritualism and root work from her grandmother in Hopkinson's novel; and Angela Toussaint inherits Voodoo powers from her grandmother Marie in Due's novel.

6. See Marilynne K. Roach's *The Salem Witch Trials: A Day-by-Day Chronicle of a Community under Siege* (2003).

come to dominate our world today. "If the sacred is ultimately that which is experienced as absolutely powerful," Richard Stivers claims, "then it was inevitable that technology would replace nature as the object of tacit veneration" (2). Right or wrong, we can directly see this shift in some early African American writings.

Enlightenment thinkers believed in the rational observation of the natural world and had no place for the perceived occult practices of an enslaved population. This clearly European disdain for the supernatural beliefs of conquered peoples shifted to the New World colonies and transferred itself to these very people. According to Jeffery E. Anderson, most of the enslaved community "followed the lead of whites, condemning Hoodoo as a sign of backwardness" (7). Olaudah Equiano demonstrates such condescension in his slave narrative, *The Interesting Narrative of the Life of Olaudah Equiano* (1789), in regard to a reputed conjure woman in Philadelphia whom he meets. Equiano does not "believe in any other revelation than that of the Holy Scriptures," yet Mrs. Davis "astonished" him by accurately "relating many things that had happened" to him and predicting that he would not be a slave for much longer (119–20). Despite his wonder at Mrs. Davis's conjuring ability, Equiano's Christian faith is not shaken by the experience because he does not value the application of a spiritual technology diluted by a white disdain.

Frederick Douglass's thoughts on the special root he received from Sandy Jenkins, along with his advice to always keep it on his right side to prevent the slave breaker Edward Covey from abusing him, provides a stronger example of contempt for the conjuring arts (*My Bondage* 147). Sandy may have been "a genuine African" who "had inherited some of the so called magical powers," but Douglass calls "talk about the root . . . very absurd and ridiculous, if not positively sinful" and "beneath one of [his] intelligence to countenance such dealings with the devil, as their power implied" (146–47). Despite such reactions, "we see the effect of an African religious survival in the African American community in the New World" (Matthews 21). The afrofuturist contradiction fully manifests itself because Douglass denies any power in root work, instead placing his trust in himself and his God. Nonetheless, hope throbs through him, and his ultimately triumphant altercation with Covey proves energizing for later generations across the globe.

Somewhat more positively, the Kentucky slave Henry Bibb sees conjuring as symbolic of hope and protection but ultimately false. Bibb recounts an early experience where he paid a conjurer "a small sum" to prevent being flogged; the conjurer "mixed up some alum, salt and other stuff into a powder" to "sprinkle around his owner" in addition to a "bitter root to chew" (26). Miraculously, he escapes a flogging on this occasion, although the concoction does not work a second time, causing Bibb to seek out a second conjurer for an even more potent blend of "fresh cow manure" mixed "with red pepper and white people's hair" reduced to a powder over a fire (27). This second creation fails as well, convincing Bibb to seek freedom by running away for the first time. Nonetheless, former slave midwife Marrinda Jane Singleton of Norfolk, Virginia, indicates how conjuring "caused so much confusion among the slaves, along wid fear dat the Marsters took steps to drive it out by severe punishment" (Fett 96). Despite these obvious failings, these magic mixtures represent extraordinarily creative ways to resist slavery, and afrofuturism comes into play as slaves grasp at the psychological power to revise their own reality.

For the most part, antipathy for conjuring mirrors the general sentiment of other early black writers like Martin R. Delany. Delany, in his serialized novel *Blake; or the Huts of America,* dismisses conjuring through his protagonist Henry Blake:

> "Now you see boys," said Henry, "how much conjuration and such foolishness and stupidity is worth to the slaves in the South. All that it does, is to put money into the pockets of the pretended conjurer, give him power over others by making them afraid of him; and even Gamby Gholar and Maudy Ghamus and the rest of the Seven Heads, with all the High Conjurers in the Dismal Swamp, are depending more upon me to deliver them from their confinement as prisoners in the Swamp and runaway slaves, than all of their combined efforts together. I made it a special part of my mission, wherever I went, to enlighten them on this subject." (136–37)

Delany rejects any notion of conjuring's spiritual power. Such "African derived spiritual beliefs among the enslaved" within the novel's confines are not appreciated, though "conjuring culture permeated the South" and still managed to infuse early black literature (Martin 59–60).

A spiritual integration of sorts occurs in Charles W. Chesnutt's foundational conjure story "The Goophered Grapevine" (1887). Chesnutt combines trickster and conjuring elements in his protagonist, the former slave Uncle Julius McAdoo, who attempts to convince a Northern couple, John and Annie, not to purchase a vineyard plantation in North Carolina. Uncle Julius questions the couple on "whe'r you b'lieves in cunj'in' er not,—some er de w'ite folks don't, er says dey don't,—but de truf er de matter is dat dis yer ole vimya'd is goophered" (606–7). He spins a tale about how the deceased owner, Master Dugal McAdoo, hired the local conjure woman Aunt Peggy to curse the scuppernong grapevines to prevent the slaves from stealing and eating the grapes. The slaves see Aunt Peggy walking in the vineyard as she works her magic:

> She sa'ntered 'roun' mongs' de vimes, en tuk a leaf fum dis one, en a grape-hull fum dat one, en a grape-seed fum anudder one; en den a little twig fum here, en a little pinch er dirt fum dere,—en put it all in a big black bottle, wid a snake's toof en a speckle' hen's gall en some ha'rs fum a black cat's tail, en den fill' de bottle wid scuppernon' wine. W'en she got de goopher all ready en fix', she tuk'n went out in de woods en buried it under de root uv a red oak tree, en den come back en tole one er de niggers she done goopher de grapevimes, en a'er a nigger w'at eat dem grapes 'ud be sho ter die inside'n twel' mont's. (608)

The curse takes hold of the land, and Dugal makes a great deal of money. He buys a new slave named Henry who eats some of the grapes before learning they were goophered. In Aunt Peggy's attempt to reverse the curse on Henry, he becomes tied to the growing season, strong in the spring and weak in the fall as the grapes grow over the next five seasons. Dugal profits from both the grapes and from selling Henry at a high price in the spring and buying him back for much less in the fall. Henry eventually dies along with the vineyard, though Master Dugal suspects interference from a visiting Yankee that he hires on the Yankee's promise to make the vineyard yield more profitable. Dugal rushes off to kill the Yankee during the war and gets killed himself, leaving no one behind to tend the land. Subsequently, Uncle Julius advises the "marster" not to buy the land because "de goopher's on it yit" (612). John buys the postwar plantation anyway, and it thrives; he also discovers that Uncle Julius has been living off the vineyard for years and hires him as a coachman. He continues the legacy of exploiting black labor for wealth.

In summarizing this story, we can see afrofuturism arising in a few ways. As a storyteller, Uncle Julius functions as a powerful circuit in the black consciousness network in which he relays the experiences of slaves on this land. He connects past, present, and future. The mystical ramifications of storytelling permeate black cultures on both sides of the Atlantic Ocean, shaping an intertextual nodal point from which other folkloric fragments take root and spring forth in black American fictions. Yet Uncle Julius fails as an interface between blacks and whites because John and Annie, as the new landowners, continue to misuse black people as capital-generating engines. They view Julius's tall tales, as related in Chesnutt's *The Conjure Woman* (1899), as mere entertainment. Further, Henry as a natural machine provides one source of income for Dugal and a second revenue stream as tradable property. In turn, Julius tries to relate this maltreatment to John and Annie, who nonetheless "rationalize blacks as inferior and non-human, to be left out of the nation" (Kim 429). Chesnutt demonstrates the prevailing white sentiment—whether from the North or the South—toward black personhood in the postbellum period, and he resists it with the conjuring tradition. Uncle Julius relies on his intellect to survive in true trickster fashion.

In general, conjuring represents a significant aspect of afrofuturism as an alternative spiritual technology that has been ignored for far too long. Conjuring searches for the same truths as more conventional formulations of science do through different systematic methodologies. But its inequality originates in racist European thought, and so its goals shifted to securing freedom for some black people and power for others. It has become a clandestine black technology that exists in whispers which we faintly hear from time to time on the darker web of black consciousness. However, this spiritual technology survives and still throbs with hope in its representation in black literature.

Afrofuturistic Ciphering and Code-Breaking

Afrofuturism *is* a bit like code-breaking in that spoken and written languages can mean very different things in black America across time. Linguistic coding, or wordplay, becomes a key component that ensures black survival. As Henry Louis Gates Jr. stresses:

> Black people have always been masters of the figurative: saying one thing to mean something quite other has been basic to black survival in oppressive Western cultures. Misreading signs could be, and indeed often was, fatal. "Reading," in this sense, was not play; it was an essential aspect of the "literacy" training of a child. This sort of metaphorical literacy, the learning to decipher complex codes, is just about the blackest aspect of the black tradition. ("Criticism in the Jungle" 6)

In this respect, spirituals, maxims, and folktales—their figurative language—contain the beating pulse of hope that black slaves relied upon to endure. Linguistic coding concerns daily survival, a better tomorrow, and multiple future expectations in crisis moments and relates directly to the three features of afrofuturism explored in this book.

A very different sense of afrofuturism emerges when not eliding important aspects of black culture. Instead, as De Witt D. Kilgore reminds us, afrofuturism presents "a challenge to remember a past that instructs a present that can build a future" ("Afrofuturism" 563). That is to say, "afrofuturists are constantly recontextualizing the past in a way that changes the present and the future" (Womack 158). Enslavement, forced migration, oppression, and, ultimately, commodification define the history of African people in the New World, making blacks subjectively inhuman if not mechanical or alien. But afrofuturism reclaims raced space and time, opening up possibilities for cultural analysis by assembling "countermemories that contest the colonial archive, thereby situating the collective trauma of slavery as the founding moment of modernity" (Eshun, "Further" 288).

Spirituals represent an obvious starting place if we expand on the necessity of verbal coding for black subsistence, if not hope. In talking about slaves' singing in *Narrative of the Life of Frederick Douglass,* Douglass notes:

> I have often been utterly astonished, since I came to the north, to find persons who could speak of the singing, among slaves, as evidence of their contentment and happiness. It is impossible to conceive of a greater mistake. Slaves sing most when they are most unhappy. The songs of the slave represent the sorrows of his heart; and he is relieved by them, only as an aching heart is relieved by its tears. At least, such is my experience. I have often sung to drown my sorrow, but seldom to express my happiness." (30)

However, Douglass says something different about spirituals in his second autobiography, *My Bondage and My Freedom,* when he explains the double meaning of a coded slave song that he and his compatriots sing in planning their failed escape from St. Michaels, Maryland. He states, "A keen observer might have detected in our repeated singing of *O Canaan, sweet Canaan, / I am bound for the land of Canaan,* something more than a hope of reaching heaven. We meant to reach the *north*—and the north was our Canaan" (203–4). Then he further clarifies the "double meaning" by declaring that "in the lips of some, it meant the expectation of a speedy summons to a world of spirits; but, in the lips of *our* company, it simply meant, a speedy pilgrimage toward a free state, and deliverance from all the evils and dangers of slavery" (203–4).

Coded messages and double meanings abound in the lyrics of these supposed religious songs used to cope with slavery's miseries. For example, "Follow the Drinking Gourd" allegedly directed fugitive slaves to look in the night sky and follow the Big Dipper constellation which pointed to the North Star and freedom, for this song provided a vernacular map to the Underground Railroad. Clearly, the symbolic drinking gourd contains much more meaning than a mere water dipper. "Swing Low, Sweet Chariot" evidently signals slaves that conductors of the Underground Railroad are near and that those planning to escape should be ready to leave. "Wade in the Water" instructs runaway slaves to use waterways to misdirect bloodhounds. Then and now, such songs provide hope and motivation in an endless afrofuturistic loop for a networked black people just trying to make it through another day.

Nonetheless, some scholars question the authenticity of these speculative claims regarding spirituals. James B. Kelley believes that "the propagation of the claim of a coded message in the lyrics of 'Follow the Drinking Gourd' reflects a propensity of all peoples, not just enslaved African Americans, to organize their past and present through shared, popular stories rather than researched histories; the story itself, not the proof of it, is what makes the story true" (275). True enough, the song itself, its meaning, and the manner in which it has been used by other groups like the National Aeronautics and Space Administration (NASA), the National Park Service (NPS), and the National Security Agency (NSA), not to mention countless educators, establish the credibility of these claims through association.[7] Analyzing these spirituals, where slaves engage with astronomy, geography, and cryptography, gives credit to the ingenuity of enslaved people and their collaborators, something Kelley seems dismissive of in his essay.

Kelley makes a good point concerning actual physical proof from the antebellum era, though Douglass provides such evidence in his autobiographies, particularly his *Narrative*, where he states slaves "would sing, as a chorus, to words which to many would seem unmeaning jargon, but which, nevertheless, were full of meaning to themselves" (29). Why would Douglass purposely reveal coded messages to slaveholders? He would not, and so the double and deep meanings went unrecognized. Douglass and other enslaved blacks lived by the maxim "a still tongue makes a wise head" (34). After all, slaves had to be careful, because a conversation overheard by an

---

7. See the *NASA Quest* website, quest.nasa.gov/ltc/special/mlk/gourd2.html, "Explanation of 'Follow the Drinking Gourd'" and "History of 'Follow the Drinking Gourd'"; the National Park Service's *Network to Freedom* website at www.nps.gov/subjects/ugrr/index.htm; the National Security Agency's website on the nature of ciphers in connection to slave quilts at www.nsa.gov/resources/everyone/digital-media-center/image-galleries/cryptologic-museum/past-exhibits/. Patrick D. Weadon, the Curator of the National Cryptologic Museum, discontinued the patchwork quilt exhibit.

overseer, the wrong field hand, or a house slave trying to curry favor with whites could end in disaster: being sold, whipped, or even murdered.

The networked black consciousness that further developed from such veiled discourse represents other means of communication that slaves used to survive, to hope, and to escape: literally the difference between life and death. As Thomas P. Barker argues, spirituals "provided the US plantation slaves with a space in which the hegemony of the White ruling class could be subverted, adapted, and resisted" (363). The spirituals also "provided slaves with the metonymic tools necessary to air discontent without fear of reprisal, constituting a space of material freedom" (380). Singing together to alleviate the backbreaking drudgery of picking and pulling, weeding and watering cash crops also provided an emotional escape from slavery's material and social conditions, transporting slaves to a timeless place each workday. This togetherness formed a black networked consciousness that allowed coded communications to occur in the first place as a precursor to afrofuturism. At the start of each chapter in his classic *The Souls of Black Folk* (1903), W. E. B Du Bois recognizes this notion and includes "a bar of the Sorrow Songs—some echo of a haunting melody from the only American music which welled up from black souls in the dark past" (42). During the Progressive Era, Du Bois created a feedback loop between past, present, and future, continuing to network a black consciousness in order to imaginatively reclaim personhood for a despised race. And in all cases, in every era, this loop became more important than the scene of past or future that was being imagined.

Another significant way in which slaves used coding covertly involves quilts and quilt patterns to signal times, locations, and directions along the underground railroad. Although facts about quilting ciphers remain hotly disputed among historians, many of whom regard them as mere folklore, to view them as myths from an afrofuturistic viewpoint seems easy because of the hope contained within a *simple* piece of patchwork fabric.[8] While these slave-made quilts provide literal warmth, they also "functioned by stitching literal maps along with instructions on how to obtain provisions, decide which routes to follow, and which steps to take at various connecting points on the railroad through cultural mnemonic devices developed in Black culture through African retentions and American realities" (Banks 124). All a slave would need to know is how to read the code contained within the pattern in order to plan a route to freedom in the North. In *Hidden in Plain*

---

8. For example, quilting historian Barbara Brackman states, "We have no historical evidence of quilts being used as signals, codes, or maps" (7).

View: A Secret Story of Quilts and the Underground Railroad (2000), Jacqueline L. Tobin and Raymond G. Dobard provide a fascinating account of South Carolina quilter Ozella McDaniel Williams—three generations removed from slavery—and all the passed-down oral history of black quilting that she possessed. In her conversation with Tobin and Dobard, Ozella gives an example of the coded meaning of quilt patterns and fence placement on airing days:

> Slaves could nonverbally alert those who were escaping. Only one quilt would appear at any one time. Each quilt signaled a specific action for a slave to take at the particular time that the quilt was on view. Ozella explained that when the Monkey Wrench quilt pattern was displayed, the slaves were to gather all the tools they might need on the journey to freedom. The second quilt placed on the fence was the Wagon Wheel pattern, which signaled the slaves to pack all the things that would go into a wagon or that would be used in transit. When the quilt with the Tumbling Boxes pattern appeared, the slaves knew it was time to escape. (70)

Slave ingenuity, demonstrated in stitching fabric together in covert patterns within an everyday object like a quilt, sometimes undermined white antebellum power by aiding fugitive slaves in their escape, further building a quite literal and functioning networked black consciousness. Even if it is unproven, quilts make a nice tale for afrofuturism and the hope these pieces of art inspire.

Colonial Afrofuturists: Wheatley, Equiano, and Banneker

A few colonial-era black Americans performed well as afrofuturistic coders whose words transhistorically reached across the space-time continuum to inspire new generations of African Americans by constructing the earliest version of a networked black consciousness. They could not keep secret their desire for liberty, projecting it in their writings and seeding a dormant afrofuturism. They had to build their own knowledge base from the detritus of a stolen past and destroyed cultures. Moving forward to a visionary of our time, Samuel R. Delany reflects on how black people "were systematically forbidden any images of our past," which in turn "impoverished . . . future images" because "every effort conceivable was made to destroy all vestiges of what might endure as African social consciousness" (qtd. in Dery 746–47). Yet, somewhat amazingly, survive it does. Delany mentions that "some musical rhythms endured, that certain religious attitudes and structures seem to have persisted" (qtd. in Dery 747). Spirituals, perhaps, best represent this endurance, resistance, and active consciousness—this survivance.[9] Further traces of a latent afrofuturism can be seen in the works of early black Americans Phillis Wheatley, Olaudah Equiano, and Benjamin Banneker, together with the white reaction epitomized by Thomas Jefferson.

Rather than focusing on the merit of Wheatley's poetry, many scholars focus on her place in history as a black female slave poet in Revolutionary America, but her use of irony actually signposts afrofuturism. When analyzing her verse, critics then and now say how dull, unrefined, and worthless her words are because of her brazen religiosity, her mimicry of earlier English poets such as Alexander Pope and his use of the heroic couplet, and her seeming apathy toward slavery.[10] Wheatley's eight-line poem "On Being Brought from Africa to America" (1773) encapsulates a subversive sarcasm.

Henry Louis Gates Jr. brings to our attention how a contemporary freelance writer, Walter Grigo, reveals Wheatley's entire poem as an anagram, where rearranging the letters of the title is the key to unlocking a hidden meaning, "Bitter, Go I, Ebon Human Cargo, from Africa," almost as if the poem's title is an encoding machine (Gates, *The Trials of Phillis Wheatley* 89). Wheatley's poetry forms an intertextual nexus for afrofuturism that we can see in black American poetry across time. We see it in Paul Laurence Dunbar's "Ode to Ethiopia" (1893), Langston Hughes's "I, Too" (1925), and Douglas Kearney's *The Black Automaton* (2009), among many others, but further exploration of this poetical terrain is not the subject of this study, which is overtly invested in narrative prose.[11] Still, such intertextual networked moments embody afrofuturism.

Revealing the subtle double meanings in Wheatley's poem requires a translation of afrofuturistic coding to make them obvious. The opening line,

---

9. See Anishinaabe scholar and author Gerald Vizenor, *Manifest Manners: Narratives on Postindian Survivance* (1999).

10. I agree with Rafia Zafar, who deduces such negative criticism of Wheatley's poetry as "the refusal to recognize the liberating possibilities of Protestant Christianity and the supposition that Wheatley must want to be 'white' because she is a confessed Christian have fostered simplistic critiques of her work" (17).

11. Briefly, Dunbar's "Ode to Ethiopia" prominently displays the hope impulse in the fifth stanza, where he states, "Be proud, my Race, in mind and soul; / Thy name is writ on Glory's scroll / In characters of fire" (lines 25–27). Hughes envisions a better future in terms of race relations in "I, Too," when he speaks of being at the table tomorrow riffing on Walt Whitman's "I Hear America Singing" (1860). In fact, Kearney's entire second installment of *The Black Automaton* evokes SF, if not afrofuturism, with the title alone which suggests the mechanical functions of black racial constructions as he confronts serious issues like politics, race, and class.

"'Twas mercy brought me from my *Pagan* land," seems straightforward in that European slavers believed they were doing her a kindness in transporting her away from a savage place. But *mercy* must be replaced by its antonym *cruelty*. Cruelty enabled and emboldened slave traders to rip a person from the arms of her family living in a supposedly uncivilized landmass and declassify her as human. A phrase from the second line, "benighted soul," seems to suggest that she is primitive, crude, and uncultivated, but the poem itself, evidence of her precocity, rejects such a notion, however humble she may have been in person. The fifth line, "Some view our sable race with scornful eye," rightly suggests the unthinking hatred that white Europeans heaped upon blacks to usher in modernity through power, force, and terror. Even the most naive African slave would not believe the lies of a mass democracy. Wheatley mocks the mock dignity that *sable*—black— bestows on African captives. Another meaning of *sable* gets nearer the truth in that blacks are prized animals, symbols of the material wealth that they procure for their owners, much like the luxuriant "sable" fur of a marten. Her careful cipher requires an afrofuturistic sensibility to crack it.

The closing couplet focuses on her use of irony and wordplay as afrofuturism. Wheatley declares: "Remember, *Christians*, *Negros*, black as Cain, / May be refin'd, and join th' angelic train" (lines 7–8). Remembering something recalls the past, ushers memory into the present, and reflects a course of action for the future. Italicizing *Christians* suggests that Wheatley is largely unconvinced that colonists are practicing the peaceful ways of Christ in the keeping and violent treatment of slaves. Italicizing *Negros* implies her love for her people even if marked by black skin as many white Christians believe Cain was marked for murdering his brother. She reminds these Christians that blacks will also achieve salvation and suggests a future racial equality too. Wheatley goes from being a pagan in the first line to becoming an angel herself in the last line. In the process she soundly rebukes the incompatibility of slave-owner practices and Christianity with the poignancy of her closing proclamation in this highly political poem. Hope exists in this poem only if whites can set aside their privileges, but her poem functions as a clear warning of revolt that other blacks like David Walker and Nat Turner later echo in their writings and their actions.

Wheatley's position as the first black poet in America directly challenges European notions of superiority by fully demonstrating the creative potential of a maligned race, representing the hope of afrofuturism. She shines all the brighter as an icon of resistance to the foolish racism of David Hume and Immanuel Kant. For example, the eighteenth-century Scottish philosopher Hume, one of the leading lights of the Enlightenment Era, avows in his 1742 volume *Essays, Moral, Political, and Literary,* "I am apt to suspect the Negroes, and in general all other species of men . . . to be naturally inferior to the whites" (629). Likewise, the eminent German philosopher Kant maintains a similar racist opinion in his 1764 essay "Observations on the Feeling of the Beautiful and Sublime":

> The Negroes of Africa have by nature no feeling that rises above the ridiculous . . . and . . . among the hundreds of thousands of blacks who have been transported elsewhere from their countries, although very many of them have been set free, nevertheless not a single one has ever been found who has accomplished something great in art or science or shown any other praiseworthy quality, while among the whites there are always those who rise up from the lowest rabble, and through extraordinary gifts earn respect in the world. (58–59)

Phillis Wheatley's 1773 *Poems on Various Subjects, Religious and Moral* debunks the racist twaddle of these otherwise great thinkers. Though Wheatley comes after them, the point is that Hume and Kant most likely ignored the evidence right in front of them, such as their peer Anton Wilhelm Amo, an African from the region now known as Ghana, who earned a doctorate in philosophy from the University of Wittenberg, Germany in 1734.[12]

In fact, the power of Wheatley's words garnered attention from three of the Founding Fathers of the United States of America. Gates proves that Wheatley met Benjamin Franklin in London sometime in 1773 through a letter that Franklin wrote to a nephew: "'I went to see the black Poetess and offer'd her any Services I could do her'" (Gates, *Trials* 34). George Washington actually responded to the poem, "To His Excellency General Washington," written in his honor and accompanied by a letter from Wheatley, with a letter of his own openly inviting her to visit him at Cambridge, Massachusetts, declaring that he "shall be happy to see a person so favoured by the Muses, and to whom Nature has been so liberal and beneficent in her dispensations" (38). As Gates informs us, Washington eventually published the poem in a March 1776 issue of the *Virginia Gazette* after she spent half an hour visiting him in Boston (38–39). However, Thomas Jefferson, seeking to undermine any and all black artistic achievement, wrote in Query XIV of his *Notes on the State of Virginia* (1785) that "Phyllis Whately [sic] [and] the compositions published under her name are below the dignity of criticism"

---

12. See William E. Abraham's "The Life and Times of Anton Wilhelm Amo, the First African (Black) Philosopher in Europe" (1996).

(147). Entirely dismissive of her demonstrable excellence, Jefferson wholeheartedly believed in and feared the pseudoscientific racial beliefs of his day. Apart from Jefferson and others of the peculiar institution's advocates, Wheatley's originality and vision proved inspirational for a second black American poet of the eighteenth century, Jupiter Hammon, who consciously crafted a networked moment via his 1778 poem "An Address to Miss Phillis Wheatley" urging her across space-time to repent.

Like Wheatley, Olaudah Equiano, the second figure in colonial America, experienced a violent dislocation from his native land, present-day Nigeria, only he conveyed his story with an autobiographical account, *The Interesting Narrative of the Life of Olaudah Equiano* (1789). This exemplar of slave narratives in the Americas began in west Africa and recorded his initial encounter with white people on a slave ship, "a world of bad spirits" that "were going to kill" him (57). He noted their skin color, long hair, and language and how very different these features were from his own. Equiano's description of these strange white men, their "horrible looks, red faces, and loose hair," evoked the science-fictional theme of alien contact (57). However, his story became outright afrofuturism when he stated, "If ten thousand worlds had been my own, I would have freely parted with them all to have exchanged my condition with that of the meanest slave in my own country" (57). He used afrofuturism to describe the horrors of slavery that he endured and said he would frankly exchange ten thousand other worlds to be free of slavery's inequities. Equiano provided one powerful example with his description of the slave hold under the ship's decks:

> The stench of the hold while we were on the coast was so intolerably loathsome, that it was dangerous to remain there for any time, and some of us had been permitted to stay on the deck for the fresh air; but now that the whole ship's cargo were confined together, it became absolutely pestilential. The closeness of the place, and the heat of the climate, added to the number in the ship, which was so crowded that each had scarcely room to turn himself, almost suffocated us. This produced copious perspirations, so that the air soon became unfit for respiration, from a variety of loathsome smells, and brought on a sickness among the slaves, of which many died, thus falling victims to the improvident avarice, as I may call it, of their purchasers. This wretched situation was again aggravated by the galling of the chains, now become insupportable; and the filth of the necessary tubs, into which the children often fell, and were almost suffocated. The shrieks of the women, and the groans of the dying, rendered the whole a scene of horror almost inconceivable. (60)

Clearly dehumanized and alienated by the Middle Passage, Equiano somehow survived his first encounter with whites, learned to master their sailing and writing technologies, and fought to abolish slavery in a world not his own.

The twin legacies of slavery and colonialism, which have shaped black cultures in the Americas, produced afrofuturism. The networked black consciousness began here in the misery suffered by captive Africans who survived crossing the Atlantic Ocean. No wonder critics like Greg Tate conceive of how "black people live the estrangement that science fiction writers imagine" (qtd. in Dery 768). Equiano's narrative reads not like a SF novel but as an afrofuturistic work in that it, too, functions as a nodal point. It reminds us of a past echoing into the future, warning us of the inherent dangers of presuming a color-blind future rather than one in which white people continue the practice of cultural appropriation and exploitation.[13]

A third figure in early America—Benjamin Banneker—foretells afrofuturism signs by radiating hope and networking a future black consciousness. Banneker was a free black farmer, inventor, and almanac writer, who was also a self-taught mathematician, astronomer, and surveyor who helped lay out the site for Washington, DC, in 1791. He built a working clock from wood. He published his own *Almanac* annually from 1792 to 1797 that was based upon his own astronomical calculations and that rivaled Franklin's *Almanac*. He created math puzzles and even conducted a long-term scientific study of the seventeen-year cycle of the cicada.[14] Remarkably, Banneker's enduring interests in math, science, and the natural world must have been inherited from his likely Dogon ancestry. The Dogon people of Mali are known for their advanced knowledge of astronomy and math in regard to the star Sirius (Barber and Nkwanta 113). According to biographer Charles A. Cerami, Banneker's grandfather was a Dogon prince captured, sold into slavery, and freed by Molly Welsh, the white woman who bought him and later married him (5).

Somehow the appellation of *scientist* does not seem to do enough justice to the intellect of Banneker. Lisa Yaszek points out, "Perhaps not surprisingly, Banneker used his technoscientific genius to fight what he perceived as the greatest evil of his own day: slavery" ("The Bannekerade" 16). He dared to call out Thomas Jefferson's perfidy on the subjects of liberty and

---

13. Rachel Dolezal resigned from her position as president of the Spokane, Washington, NAACP chapter when her inarguably white parents revealed that she had been "passing" for black. The event instigated a national debate on racial identity in 2015.

14. See Charles A. Cerami's *Benjamin Banneker: Surveyor, Astronomer, Publisher, Patriot* (2002). Also see Barber and Nkwanta.

black intelligence in a personal letter, dated August 19, 1791, to the first secretary of state in George Washington's presidential administration. Banneker's voice for black freedom and equality reverberates into our present and future as he took up and amplified the abolitionist cause on behalf of the millions of enslaved and free black people in the United States. Thus, he validates a networked black consciousness by using his personal agency to publicly disprove the prevalent European beliefs concerning the supposed mental inferiority of black people, a science-fictional reality challenged by afrofuturism then and now.

In his fifteen-paragraph letter, Banneker carefully defers to Jefferson fourteen times throughout the epistle with the honorific "sir" while excoriating Jefferson's beliefs. Fully aware of their difference in social station, Banneker bravely addresses the "general prejudice and prepossession which is so prevalent in the world against those of [his own] complexion" (Banneker 50). Such a rhetorical move immediately aligns Banneker with all black people then and now as he eloquently challenges racial oppression, defies the status quo, and represents the brilliance of African-descended peoples. He offers hope, strength, and wit while activating a networked black consciousness across time and space to fight for freedom by simply using "we" to speak for "a race of beings who have [. . .] long been considered rather as brutish than human, and scarcely capable of mental endowments" (50–51).

In the middle of the letter Banneker appeals to Jefferson's Christianity and asks for help "to eradicate that train of absurd and false ideas and opinions, which so generally prevails with respect to [blacks] since one universal Father hath given Being to us all [, . . .] afforded us all the same sensations, and endued us all with the same faculties" (51). Though Banneker himself is "not under that state of tyrannical thralldom and inhuman captivity to which too many of [his] brethren are doomed," he "cheerfully acknowledge[s]" his race (51). Banneker then wonders how the architect of the Declaration of Independence, a document Banneker greatly admired, could keep slaves himself "detaining by fraud and violence so numerous a part of my brethren under groaning captivity and cruel oppression" (51). He finds the irony of Jefferson's revolutionary ideals, his self-evident truths, contemptible since blacks, who fought in the war on both sides, have been denied their unalienable rights and remain enslaved or, even if freed, reduced to second-class citizenship. He dares enraging a Founding Father by speaking truth to power, and the hope pulsing in Banneker's challenge strongly resonates in the temporally inscribed afrofutures now seen in black writing.

Banneker puts himself forward as a model of black intelligence in the last third of the letter, a living denunciation of Enlightenment philosophies. He includes a handwritten copy of his almanac stating that "this calculation . . . is the production of [his] arduous study [and] unbounded desires to become acquainted with the secrets of nature [. . .] to gratify [my] curiosity" despite "the many difficulties and disadvantages which [he] had to encounter" (52). Of course, it is up to Jefferson to work out the slight here that Banneker succeeded despite the racial intolerance he faced on a daily basis. The almanac and letter combined function as proof positive of an intellectual parity that exists between the races. As Angela Ray infers, "Jefferson himself, fascinated by scientific pursuits, could be expected to view Banneker's astronomical efforts positively" (398). In effect, Banneker fully utilizes writing as a technology to defend black people. Historian Lerone Bennett Jr. says it best: "For men who appeal from the gutters to the stars, for men who stand up and protest, no matter what the odds, the star-gazer remains a persuasive and articulate example" (58). Without a doubt, Benjamin Banneker influenced afrofuturism well before its recognition as a relevant theory for understanding the importance of literacy technologies as a networking mechanism for a hopeful black defiance.

Science fiction is not so special here when the lived reality of black folks *is* science fictional. If we collapsed a lot of variation in the black experience into a single naked assertion about what was thinkable at the time, most enslaved black people in the antebellum era would probably look back and forward and see no beginning or ending for slavery, caught in a time loop, repeating the same day again and again and again. But here a future never glimpsed, let alone realized, develops from native scientific practices retained from the Middle Passage, the slave and work songs capable of separating mind from body, and the few blacks who dared dream freedom for the rest. Freedom technologies manifested, and the afrofuturist vista came to be even in the worst times and places. That is why afrofuturism requires reading non-SF texts as if they were science fiction: because the twinned genres share a common origin in a slow modernity. It becomes necessary to create some kind of separation with new terminologies like the hope impulse, black networked consciousness, and the transhistorical feedback loop.

Not only does afrofuturistic coding unlock older texts like Douglass's *Narrative* or Wright's *Black Boy*; it counteracts the transformation of seemingly familiar historical material—such as the antebellum era as presented in a simple geography textbook—into a lie by rendering a freedom technology like literacy (which many now take for granted) visible to the masses.

Likewise, spiritual technologies such as conjuring become easily discernible. Carefully encrypted slave songs and skillfully constructed quilts are deciphered and meticulously interpreted by afrofuturists today. Wheatley, Equiano, and Banneker, envisioned as architects of the black neural web, also receive the praise and attention they deserve in providing hope to an oppressed race. Providing a broad afrofuturist overview of the United States of America's antebellum era figuratively broadcasts a signal across the networked black consciousness that represents the reality of this ongoing black struggle in to the future.

Afrofuturism as a hermeneutic makes new sense of texts by privileging the networking actions within, among, and around black people. Whether it is the technical knowledge of quilt making developed by slaves, or Equiano's vision of "ten thousand worlds" discussed in this chapter, or Nat Turner's faith in the solar eclipse or even the uses of astronomy in Delany's *Blake* (both addressed in chapter 2), these references evoke explicit scientific phenomena to awaken future possibilities that deepen the afrofuturist mindset. In this respect, the year 1619, the artificial temporal restriction I use, will expand into the multiple and multicolored futures foreseen in black writing of the twentieth century and beyond. But it is so very important to look to the past, acquire feedback data from these collected black experiences, maintain the network, and imagine futures. Going deeper into history, afrofuturism can be found in the slave rebellions of the New World and the literature such rebellions would later inspire, the subject of the next chapter.

CHAPTER 2

BLACK UPRISINGS AND THE FIGHT FOR THE FUTURE

POPULAR CULTURE would have us believe that a black Revolutionary America never existed within antebellum Southern society, squelching whatever sentiment this belief might stir in black hearts. That is, black uprisings in American history have been either intentionally sanitized or effectively erased from popular memory to prevent black people from connecting with a past thought to be lost, beyond the pain of a remembered inferiority and nonhuman treatment. For example, the 2016 film *The Birth of a Nation*, a biopic regarding Nat Turner's rebellion on August 22, 1831, in Southampton, Virginia, grossed only around $16 million in its box-office run, a commercial bomb. The film attempts "to provoke a serious debate about the necessity and limitations of empathy, the morality of retaliatory violence, and the ongoing black struggle for justice and equality in this country. It earns that debate and then some" (Chang n. pag.). But the film-going public[1] did not turn out to see this insightful historical film because of a suspected deep unease with images of blacks killing whites and a discomfort with remembering the horrors of slaveholding prompting such historically neglected

---

1. The film's African American director, Nate Parker, was acquitted of rape charges dating to 1999 during his time as a Penn State student athlete, though these allegations resurfaced in the national media during the film's promotion in 2016. The allegations may have had something to do with the film's poor box-office reception.

uprisings. As Henry Louis Gates Jr. appropriately frames this notion, "One of the most pernicious allegations made against the African-American people was that our slave ancestors were either exceptionally 'docile' or 'content and loyal,' thus explaining their purported failure to rebel extensively" ("What Were the Earliest Rebellions?"). Gates then asks, "So, did African-American slaves rebel? Of course they did" and reveals how scholars have discovered over 300 revolts ("What").

Making such a connection to uncover the liberatory desire to feel and be human fundamentally reboots the future. Afrofuturism, then, requires, if not advocates, another telling of the past where hacking this whitewashed code of political correctness reprograms and remakes black identities for the future. Perhaps that is the reason why segments of the white supremacist South fight so hard to clutch the misplaced glories of genteel farming, honor, and wealth built upon a literally alienated and dehumanized black people. They attempt to recall the Three-Fifths Compromise of 1787, to hold on to their monuments that pay homage to the Confederate past—statues of Robert E. Lee, Jefferson Davis, P. G. T. Beauregard, and the like, as well as various versions of the battle flag—and thereby to prevent a burgeoning black futurism, if not a larger colored future. In this respect, it is imperative to critically revise this oppressed past with afrofuturism, to experience the interconnectivity of past, present, and beyond to enhance a black networked consciousness derived from a transhistoric feedback loop pulsing with hope as black men and women fought for their freedom without much success. This afrofuturistic process works by finding entry points into the transhistoric feedback loop through history and narrative which allows readers to access the networked black consciousness in order to empathically relive this horrifying past and be thankful for the strength of black people's hope.

Ironically, black uprisings disrupted America's Revolutionary ideology. David Walker's 1829 *Appeal* quickly comes to mind and stands in stark protest to the promises made to America's citizens in the Declaration of Independence. From the country's birth as a sovereign nation on July 4, 1776, "self-evident" truths have prevented black people from "certain unalienable Rights . . . Life, Liberty, and the pursuit of Happiness" (Jefferson, *Autobiography* 706). History and politics concerning the fate and futures of African Americans compel afrofuturist revisions to counter white supremacist ideologies that dictate in perpetuity a monolithic whiteness to the United States of America. Afrofuturism provides a color shift into the black-o-sphere, akin to Henry David Thoreau's "realometer" (1021), but with a transcendental, ineffable black in which dreams of freedom imaginatively materialize. Actual and dreamed narratives draw upon different evidentiary sources, reject white authority, and ultimately refer to a black independence by way of resistance. They resist appropriation; they warn against postracial rhetorics; and they counter established hegemonies.

Slave uprisings and conspiracies represent another violent burst of hope, operating with a limited network connectivity that eventually failed in colonial America but necessarily interpenetrated early afrofuturist writings. The Haitian Revolution (1791–1804), led by Toussaint L'Ouverture in the French colony of San Domingo, and Nat Turner's Rebellion (1831) in Southampton, Virginia, are undoubtedly the best-known instances of black unrest bubbling to the surface in New World antebellum societies; these exceptional events were not isolated, but more widespread than history catalogues or admits.[2] In addition to the Haitian Revolution and Turner's Rebellion, I focus on the 1739 Stono Rebellion in colonial South Carolina and the 1811 German Coast Uprising in the Orleans Territory (Louisiana) and also briefly touch on the failed conspiracies of Gabriel Prosser in 1800 and Denmark Vesey in 1822. The chronic atmosphere of fear in which white slaveholders lived went a long way in creating control mechanisms to maintain their own security from a disgruntled black population. Moreover, historian Herbert Aptheker states:

> The masters of the Southern states were not content to depend merely upon social inertia, or the power that their ownership of the means of production gave them in order to maintain their dominant position. On the contrary they called into play every trick, rule, regulation, and device that the human mind could invent to aid them; the attempted psychological, intellectual, and physical debasement of an entire people, the inculcating and glorifying of the most outrageous racial animosities buttressed by theological, historical, and anthropological theories. (*American Negro Slave Revolts* 78)

Aptheker continues with his listing of atrocities:

> the dividing of the victims against themselves, the use of spies and the encouragement of traitors, the evolving of a rigid social code helpful for their purpose, the disdaining, tabooing, and finally repressing of all opposition thought and deed, the establishment of elaborate police and military systems, enacting of innumerable laws of oppression and suppression;

---

2. See Kerry Walters's *American Slave Revolts and Conspiracies: A Reference Guide* (2015).

the developing, in short, of a social order within which the institution of Negro slavery became so deeply embedded that it was true that to touch one was to move the other. This indissoluble linking of one with the other epitomizes the entire method of control, and was at once its strength and its weakness. (*American* 78)

Slaveholders must have been equally distressed by the appearance of *David Walker's Appeal, in Four Articles; Together with a Preamble, to the Coloured Citizens of the World, But in Particular, and Very Expressly, to Those of the United States of America* in 1829. The *Appeal* called for an uprising by colored people across the globe and was a sustained, impassioned, and intelligent critique of the ignoble institution by a black man, something that was thought to be impossible and that repudiated Jefferson's endorsement of slavery in *Notes on the State of Virginia* (much like Banneker's "Letter to Thomas Jefferson"). As James Turner indicates, "A group of wealthy planters offered a ten-thousand-dollar reward for [Walker]—dead or alive"; the Georgia and Louisiana governments "passed laws against circulation of the *Appeal*"; and "North Carolina made it a crime to teach a slave to read" (13–14). In fact, Walker presented an explicit afrofuturist vision for black people that resonates across time and perpetually informs monumental speeches such as those of the Reverend Doctor Martin Luther King Jr., Malcolm X, and President Barack Obama.[3] His *Appeal* simultaneously punctuates the hope impulse and networked consciousness by linking together the revolts, slave narratives (the subject of chapter 3), and early fictions in African American history and culture. Indeed, early black novelists such as Martin R. Delany, Sutton E. Griggs, and Pauline Hopkins offer future visions of a burgeoning revolution, the rise of a separate black nation, and a return to Africa, respectively, that I will explore at chapter's end. By creating a legacy of resistance to racial oppression, all of these black freedom fighters engender the afrofuturist vista from America's colonial beginning into the twentieth century.

---

3. See King's 1963 speech "I Have a Dream" in which he declared that "the whirlwinds of revolt will continue to shake the foundations of our nation until the bright day of justice emerges" (107). Consider Malcolm X's 1964 speech "The Ballot or the Bullet" in which he proclaimed exactly how "the government has failed" blacks via "political oppression," "economic exploitation," "and social degradation" to the point where "You can't swing up on freedom. But you can *swing* up on some freedom" (119). Finally, refer to President Obama's 2008 speech "A More Perfect Union" in which he stated that our country has "to continue the long march of those who came before us, a march for a more just, more equal, more free, more caring and more prosperous America . . . to move . . . towards a better future for of children and our grandchildren" (238).

The Real New World Rebellions and Revolutions

Regarding acts of slave rebellion in relation to afrofuturism, the first conduit into the transhistorical feedback loop must be the Stono Rebellion of 1739, the earliest recorded uprising in colonial North America occurring before the American Revolution. At the time, South Carolina whites feared losing their slaves because of political propaganda coming from Spanish Florida. The Spanish established a maroon[4] community for any blacks who escaped from English territory, and British subjects suspected Spanish missionaries of spreading the word of freedom (O'Dell 41). The promise of freedom may have induced dozens of slaves to attempt to escape on September 9. They were led by a literate slave named Jemmy, sometimes called Cato, who guided the group southward toward the city of St. Augustine. Jemmy and his core group may have been captured soldiers from the Angolan kingdom of Kongo according to historian John K. Thornton (1102). The fugitives burned plantations, killed white folks on their trek south, and used drums to attract other slaves along their path. Somewhere near the Stono River, the South Carolina militia caught up to the slave party, which numbered close to ninety blacks, and killed, captured, or scattered the runaways. Most of these slaves "were put to death, after which the whites 'stuck their Heads upon Poles in the Path-way as a Terror to the other Slaves'" (O'Dell 42). As a consequence of this uprising, preventive edicts such as outlawing the teaching of slaves how to write, forbidding slaves to assemble in groups, and banning the use of drums to communicate were adapted into law by the South Carolina Negro Act of 1740.

Providing as much of this fading history, creating an overload of historical information as it were, remains a key to confronting an early instantiation of science-fictional blackness, because enough people, especially black people, do not know about this particular rebellion, not to mention other, untold rebellions. One of afrofuturism's mandates involves visiting the past to help the future. In this regard, the historical dimension amplifies afrofuturism's literary dimension, as will be discussed later in the chapter. From an afrofuturist perspective, the most fascinating outcome of this early rendition of a pulsing networked black consciousness was that by using such draconian measures, the colonial government partially succeeded at disrupting communication channels between slaves and plantations. Whites stifled

---

4. Maroons were escaped slaves who banded together in independent communities throughout the Americas and survived through subsistence farming, stealing from surrounding plantations, and help from other slaves.

black hopes with such a ruling by keeping them chained in ignorance, but black ingenuity arose time and time again in blacks' quest for a future free from slavery.

The successful establishment of the first black republic in the New World remains the utmost example of such a black initiative. When the Saint-Domingue (Haiti) slaves rose up against their masters in April of 1791, as Nick Nesbitt claims, they "invented decolonization" and laid the groundwork for the "unqualified human right to freedom" (56, 159). The Haitian Revolution actually epitomizes the highest ideals of Enlightenment thought—liberty and equality. Under the leadership of Toussaint L'Ouverture, the former slaves withstood repeated invasions by "French, British, and Spanish imperialists" throughout the twelve-year struggle (C. L. R. James 271). Consequently, Haiti became "the first postcolonial state" on January 1, 1804, when Governor General Jean-Jacques Dessalines, L'Ouverture's primary lieutenant and successor, declared Haitian independence and later ordered the massacre of the white minority, an estimated 4,000 people, throughout Haiti between February and April (Nesbit 9)—an independent black world freed at such a terrible price.

Imagine how the networked consciousness operated between the United States and the Caribbean. Communication channels and social gatherings helped enable these revolts and spread the word through time and space because slaves who were traded between the two regions brought word of the Haitian Revolution—notes supposedly from L'Ouverture himself carried by black sailors to ports on all sides of the Atlantic. Black ears at keyholes overheard white anxieties in parlor room discussions too: gossip, verbal exchanges at religious meetings, or perhaps legends/memories of other revolts. Delany's *Blake* definitely imagined such broadcastings in interesting ways. Hope pulses from the past to present for afrofuturists along the transhistorical loop and filters into the literature being produced then, now, and yet to come.

The Haitian Revolution rightfully frightened the Southern United States because it had such large slave populations and whites could not prevent their slaves from learning about the Haitian Revolution, further agitating their yearning for freedom. The revolution fundamentally short-circuited the institution of slavery.[5] Such fears legitimized a practically self-fulfilling

---

5. In fact, noted Historian David B. Davis believes that "the Haitian blacks' defeat of the best armies of the British, the Spanish and the French inspired black rebels [. . .] and hovered like a weapon of mass destruction in the minds of slaveholders as late as the American Civil War" (7).

prophecy because the Enlightenment myth of a black subhumanity supported the Southern way of life in its entirety. A fully attained networked black consciousness functioning as early as 1791 subverted white supremacy and provided hope to the enslaved Africans of the New World. Afrofuturism was realized and a black world was set free. For a black leader like Toussaint L'Ouverture to emerge must have seemed impossible to white supremacists, though all manners of excuse could be found for the successful uprising, such as a black penchant for violence, the aforementioned exploding black populations, or, perhaps, the rigors of tropical warfare. Anything but a strong black leader who defied European empire could be accepted. Early African American writer Frank J. Webb captures this exact feeling in his novel *The Garies and Their Friends* (1857) in a dialogue between the wealthy black Philadelphian Mr. Walters and the white Georgia planter Mr. Garie:

> "So you, too, are attracted by that picture," said Mr. Walters, with a smile. "All white men look at it with interest. A black man in the uniform of a general officer is something so unusual that they cannot pass it with a glance."
>
> "It is, indeed, rather a novelty," replied Mr. Garie, "particularly to a person from my part of the country. Who is it?"
>
> "That is Toussaint L'Ouverture," replied Mr. Walters; "and I have every reason to believe it to be a correct likeness. It was presented to an American merchant by Toussaint himself—a present in return for some kindness shown him. This merchant's son, not having the regard for the picture that his father entertained for it, sold it to me. That," continued Mr. Walters, "looks like a man of intelligence. It is entirely different from any likeness I ever saw of him. The portraits generally represent him as a monkey-faced person, with a handkerchief about his head." (122–23)

Looking back from a twenty-first century afrofuturist standpoint, we can feel the sense of wonder that accompanies the best SF because the Haitian Revolution reads like a future history that actually happened. Indeed, the rightfully celebrated Jamaican-Canadian SF writer Nalo Hopkinson named an entire planet after him in her novel *Midnight Robber* (2000).

Unfortunately, this appeal for freedom and egalitarianism, qualities the Haitian Revolution clearly symbolizes, went unheeded. Blacks in North America could hardly sustain hope, let alone an afrofuturist vista, when whites immediately snuffed each and every revolt, rebellion, and act of resistance before they could burgeon into something revolutionary. The enslaved blacksmith Gabriel's 1800 conspiracy to revolt in Richmond, Virginia, and the self-purchased carpenter Denmark Vesey's 1822 plot in Charleston,

South Carolina, both failed because the local white communities acted swiftly in response to rumors of uprisings that never even had a chance to happen.[6] Inevitably, both men were hanged along with many of their alleged followers.

In Gabriel's case, tolerance for slave movement between Richmond and its surrounding plantations made it possible for him to socially engineer an operational networked consciousness from the start.[7] His plan called for setting a fire on one side of Richmond, taking the state armory, and holding the governor hostage while killing whites. But Gabriel suffered a network failure when two of his closest men divulged the plan to their owner, ending the largest slave conspiracy to never materialize as historians speculate. That, and a terrible rainstorm that caused local flooding in the area, prevented the black would-be rebels from meeting up to carry out their plan.

The full extent of Vesey's insurrection plans would have shocked anyone in the country. As described by David Robertson, Vesey planned "to seize the United States arsenal and ships at the harbor in Charleston," assassinate South Carolina's governor, kill the entire white population, and sail captured ships to Haiti or Africa (4–5). To do so, he recruited a guesstimated 9,000 slaves, some from the city, some from the surrounding plantations, and some from the Emanuel AME church, which he helped found. The botched uprising certainly would have been the largest in US history.[8] Vesey's network crashed because two of his accomplices revealed the plot to their master, just like Gabriel's. And just like Gabriel, Vesey was caught, tried, and executed for an insurrection plot. Because Vesey admitted nothing while on trial, Charleston officials, like James Hamilton Jr., created a counterfactual account of the conspiracy, one involving violence, secret informants, and San Domingo; his account of events helped to secure the death penalty and assuage angry white anxieties.[9]

---

6. See Arna Bontemp's *Black Thunder: Gabriel's Revolt: Virginia 1800* (1936) as well as John Oliver Killens's *Great Gittin' Up Morning: A Biography of Denmark Vesey* (1972).

7. As James Sidbury observes, "In an odd way, Black men traveling the roads in and out of Richmond found in that most public of spaces an escape from the danger of observation. . . . In that space they could forge the community necessary to cooperate in an effort to overthrow slavery" (87).

8. Ironically, in this 200-year-old church that Vesey helped found, twenty-one-year-old Dylann Roof committed a hate crime by shooting to death nine black people attending a prayer service on the evening of June 17, 2015, hoping to provoke a race war.

9. Carrie Hyde believes that "an alternative version of history—with the city in ashes and soaking in blood" substantiates an anticipated yet unproven guilt and paves the way for "preemptive" execution because "the act of imaginative description is the only way of making the conspiracy concretely available" (47).

Though these planned insurrections failed, dimmed the hope impulse, and damaged a burgeoning networked black consciousness, the legends of these men live on in the black imagination. We have to look no further than Martin R. Delany's serialized novel *Blake, or the Huts of America* (1859–61) for verification of my claim. In brief, Delany writes about his slave protagonist Henry Blake's encounter with two High Conjurers in the Great Dismal Swamp, Maudy Ghamus and Gamby Gholar, and describes how these men revere the names of "Nat Turner, Denmark Veezie [sic], and General Gabriel . . . whom they conceived to be the greatest men who ever lived" (113). Delany connects this rebel past with his present and projects it into the future where Cuba's slave population is on the eve of a rebellion led by Blake as the novel ends unfinished. For Kodwo Eshun, "Afrofuturism therefore stages a series of enigmatic returns to the constitutive trauma of slavery in the light of science fiction" ("Further" 299). And Eshun *is* right in that these historical returns offer futurological healing acts.

The averted rebellions of Gabriel and Vesey actually sandwich the largest and little-known rebellion on American soil—the 1811 German Coast Uprising in what is now Louisiana. Very little is known about this rebellion because Governor William Claiborne, hand-selected by Thomas Jefferson to manage the territory, suppressed information in the papers.[10] The administration truly feared what news of such a large insurrection could do to further galvanize the black hope for freedom and to destabilize the confidence white citizens had in the carefully constructed fallacy of white supremacy. Just imagine the panic whites would have experienced facing an estimated 500 angry slaves led by the mulatto overseer Charles Deslondes, who himself was uprooted from San Domingo as his French family fled to Spanish-controlled New Orleans at the start of the Haitian Revolution in 1791 (Thrasher 70).

The slaves chose to rise up on January 8. Although the revolt was crushed by January 11, the slaves, joined by maroons from the swamps, burned several plantations, killed two whites, and created chaos among the fleeing whites "who told [of] having just escaped from 'a miniature representation of the horrors of St. Domingo'" (Aptheker, *American* 249). The slaves were defeated, and Governor Claiborne wasted no time in labeling them criminals to justify the violent punishments meted out: "Around 100

---

10. This slave rebellion is the largest recorded in US history, but Daniel Rasmussen indicates that "the longest published scholarly account runs a mere twenty-four pages" and predates the 1995 publication of Albert Thrasher's *"On to New Orleans!": Louisiana's Heroic 1811 Slave Revolt* and the 2011 publication of his own book, *American Uprising: The Untold Story of America's Largest Slave Revolt* (2).

dismembered bodies decorated the levee from Place d'Armes in the center of New Orleans forty miles along the River Road into the heart of the plantation district" (Rasmussen 147–48). Tri-narratives of crime, punishment, and white authority still plague blacks in America today; the disproportionate numbers of blacks in the contemporary legal system amounts to the continuation of generational racial warfare. Though the failed rebellion was largely hushed in historical accounts, it powerfully symbolizes how blacks would organize and fight for their futures in America as social networks both passive (civil rights movement or Black Lives Matter) and aggressive (Black Panther Party for Self-Defense). Looking to past rebellions across the transhistorical feedback loop, plugging into this networked blackness, imparts a pragmatic anticipation as fact and fiction become entangled.

Black Radicals: David Walker and Nat Turner

While Charles Deslondes and his slave compatriots remain virtually unknown in American history, David Walker's revolutionary *Appeal* grants him notoriety in the antebellum world. Walker attended the AME church of Charleston in the early 1820s, where Vesey likely planned his revolt in which Walker may have been involved himself even if he "was not directly acquainted with Denmark Vesey" (Hinks 39). Regardless, Walker "seems to have become the radical evangelical activist he would remain for the rest of his life" at this church before leaving for Boston (40). In today's afrofuturist terms, this radical association granted Walker political cachet because of the combined and continuing revolutionary impact on future generations of African Americans.

In his *Appeal* Walker provides a complex and unrelenting critique of slavery on social, religious, and economic grounds and calls for resistance by any means. He further dispels the established racialist notion that black intelligence is innately inferior to that of whites as championed by Thomas Jefferson and other apologists. Walker recognizes that slaveholders "are so afraid [slaves] will learn to read, and enlighten [their] dark and benighted minds" (84). A few years later, Frederick Douglass realizes this very thing in his own *Narrative* when overhearing his new master, Mr. Auld, tell his wife how reading would make Douglass "become unmanageable, and of no value to his master"; that reading would cause him "a great deal of harm" in making him "discontented and unhappy" (48). As Douglass reflects, "These words sank deep into my heart" and "I now understood what had been to me a most perplexing difficulty—to wit, the white man's power to enslave the black man. . . . From that moment, I understood the pathway from slavery to freedom" (48). Simply put, literacy was the key to freedom for both men. In effect, in his demand for freedom on behalf of all colored peoples around the globe, Walker used writing as a black creative technology to claim white political power for blacks. No wonder that "once the *Appeal* began circulating, officials arrested anyone who possessed copies of the document." As Kevin Pelletier explains, "Laws were enacted quarantining Northern black sailors in order to prevent them from disseminating Walker's polemic," and "prohibitions against black literacy were reinvigorated and earnestly enforced" (257). His *Appeal* functioned as a beacon of determined hope and literally wove webs of black consciousness together on a time continuum from an afrofuturistic standpoint. Walker's words directly impacted the future as he envisioned a new society.

As a foundational text for afrofuturism, Walker's *Appeal,* in its four articles and preamble, insists on a future for black people and describes how they can achieve a future as emancipated citizens. In the preamble, Walker establishes a prophetic vision through a series of questions regarding how the conditions of slavery cannot be worsened without setting off a race war. He states that slave owners "are afraid to treat us worse, for they know well, the day they do it they are gone" (22). Entreating heaven, he then provides his motive for writing as the desire "to awaken in the breasts of my afflicted, degraded and slumbering brethren, a spirit of inquiry and investigation respecting our miseries and wretchedness in this REPUBLICAN LAND OF LIBERTY!!!!!!" (22). Furthermore, Walker wants whites to set aside their "prejudice long enough to admit that we [blacks] are *men*" (24–25). In this respect, Walker seeks to establish a brave new world in which he undermines the pernicious effects of slavery, overcomes racism, and establishes black equality. However, he also offers an ephemeral hope for white redemption if wholesale manumission occurs expeditiously. Otherwise, whites should expect violent black resistance to oppression.

In Article I, "Our Wretchedness in Consequence of Slavery," Walker highlights and denounces slavery's viciousness in maintaining a racial farce where blacks are animals and should be treated as such with no hope of ever attaining freedom, all in the name of white material enrichment. He then directly spurns Jefferson's justification for slavery—that blacks have descended "originally from the tribes of *Monkeys* or *Orang-Outangs*"—since "Mr. Jefferson declared to the world, that we are inferior to the whites, both in the endowments of our bodies and of minds" (30). Jeremy Engels makes a good point: Jefferson, "endowed with the power of authorship, more than anyone else . . . perpetuated this system of slavery" (53). Walker understands this authorial power and rightfully challenges Jefferson's abuse of it in order to uphold slavery.[11] At the right time in the perfect moment, rejecting Jefferson's opined views on slavery in itself represents a black triumph for Walker that appears simultaneously strange and threatening to various visions of America as a white nation. Walker next visualizes a black self-governed future, insisting that "God will not suffer us, always to be oppressed. Our sufferings will come to an *end*, in spite of all the Americans this side of *eternity*. Then we will want all the learning and talents among ourselves, and perhaps more, to govern ourselves" (35). This instant *is* profoundly science fictional for some and afrofuturist for others because very few writers, if any, have ever imagined a black-determined future world in the postmodern era, let alone the early nineteenth century, with education as a key. By *science fictional*, I mean that a white reader of the antebellum era would think of any black person writing as being a weird future tale. On the other hand, a contemporary readership might think of the successful black counter-response offered by Walker as afrofuturist since he engages the past, present, and future of both races while developing a black distribution network to get his work out there: indeed, a powerful network, since his prophetic words are anthologized and taught today.

In Article II, "Our Wretchedness in Consequence of Ignorance," Walker emphasizes the necessity of education and religion in breaking three centuries of bondage. Blacks "have to prove to the Americans and the world, that [they] are MEN, and not *brutes,* as [they] have been represented, and by millions treated" (50). Learning and faith provide the requisite knowledge to defeat a white-imposed ignorance and to achieve freedom. Next, Walker attacks religious hypocrisy on the part of white Christian slaveholders in Article III, "Our Wretchedness in Consequence of the Preachers of the Religion of Jesus Christ." Likewise, he pronounces doom to white Americans: "But I tell you Americans! that unless you speedily alter your course, *you* and *your Country are gone!!!!!!* For God Almighty will tear up the very face of the earth!!!" (59). His plea for sympathy from his likely white readership falls on deaf ears because whites simply cannot identify with slaves' terrible

---

11. Hypocritically, Jefferson himself envisions a coming race war in Query XVIII of his *Notes on the State of Virginia.* He writes:

> Indeed I tremble for my country when I reflect that God is just: that his justice cannot sleep for ever: that considering numbers, nature and natural needs only, a revolution of the wheel of fortune, and exchange of situation, is among possible events: that it may become probable by supernatural interference! The Almighty has no attribute which can take side with us in such a contest. (169)

circumstances; they would rather believe in myths of happy and contented slaves before abolitionist efforts take hold.

Finally, in Article IV, "Our Wretchedness in Consequence of the Colonizing Plan," Walker strongly objects to the idea that black American slaves should be returned to Africa and recolonize there. Many afrofuturists would certainly agree with Walker's way of thinking on this African repatriation plan that "this country is as much ours as it is the whites, whether they will admit it or not, they will see and believe it by and by" (75). Walker justifiably continues:

> America is more our country, than it is the whites—we have enriched it with our *blood and tears*. The greatest riches in all America have arisen from our blood and tears—and will they drive us from our property and homes, which we have earned with our *blood*? They must look sharp for this very thing will bring swift destruction upon them. The Americans have got so fat on our blood and groans, that they have almost forgotten the God of armies. But let them go on. (84)

Fascinatingly, Walker says America is our country, a black country more than a white, but then he refers to the whites as Americans. He expresses the paradox of science-fictional blackness in the sense that black contributions to building the country are invisible. In fact, Walker predicts the Civil War in the Article IV, about issues of emancipation and equality; points out duplicity in The Declaration of Independence, except for the part about throwing off a despotic government; and talks about God's judgment on white American society without immediate liberation and a national apology for the wrongs committed against black people. "Given the failure of America's revolutionary history as it bears on slavery," Pelletier asserts, "it stands to reason that Walker would adopt an alternative world-view in order to theorize new modes of resistance" (261). Walker also questions why slaveholders search ships to prevent copies of his *Appeal* from reaching his fellow slaves. He recognizes they fear the power of his words just as he knows that literacy is crucial to freedom and that Southerners must prevent its spread. He specifically evokes technology and uses afrofuturist language to indicate how "there is a secret monitor in their [white] hearts which tells them" blacks are people and "that there can be nothing in our hearts but death alone" for whites "when we see them murdering our dear mothers and wives" (80). In this way blacks covertly look inside white minds, gauging threat levels; whites only see a black mask: blacks watching whites watching them.

Metaphorically speaking, this built-in network receiver allowed blacks to navigate slavery and prepare for freedom by keeping track of white folks and transmitting warnings to the webbed consciousness. Race war seemed the obvious consequence of chattel slavery and genocide. As Thulani Davis writes, "The whole problem of emancipation or extermination becomes, in fact, cultural," and Walker's vision of what could happen presents a viable solution (19). Mixing prescient vision, rhetoric, technology, and the supernatural, Walker does an amazing thing in shaping an empowered black consciousness. It survives, it rebels, and it imagines necessary futures.

Though many scholars, critics, and writers have speculated on Nat Turner's having read Walker's *Appeal,* no evidence exists today that suggests he did, other than a gut feeling. Nat Turner's famous/infamous uprising in Southampton, Virginia, commencing on August 22, 1831, remains the bloodiest slave revolt in US history, claiming the lives of roughly 60 white men, women, and children and resulting in the deaths of an estimated 200 black people, including Turner himself after evading capture for two months. Turner was hanged, his corpse was beheaded, his skin was flayed, and his limbs were quartered on November 11, 1831 (Gibson).[12] Vincent Woodard even accounts for "whites who tried to coerce them [blacks] into consuming Nat Turner's boiled-down flesh and entrails" in addition to whites' themselves using it "as a panacea for all ills . . . known as 'Nat's Grease'" according to oral accounts gathered in *The Delectable Negro: Human Consumption and Homoeroticism within US Slave Culture* (6, 92).

To this day, Turner remains a hero to black people and an anathema to whites—a racially polarizing figure. Black scholars took particular umbrage against William Styron's depiction of Turner in his Pulitzer Prize–winning novel *The Confessions of Nat Turner* (1967). They responded with a critical volume, *The Second Crucifixion of Nat Turner* (Clarke 1968), assaulting Styron's book if not Styron himself. Kyle Baker's award-winning graphic novel *Nat Turner* (2008) goes a long way in re-lionizing Turner for a new generation of readers in the twenty-first century. Taken together, Styron and Baker shatter the historical space-time bubble surrounding Nat Turner by presenting alternate views of the revolt. Freddie Gray's death in Baltimore and the civil unrest it caused highlight a prolepsis of white fear of contemporary uprisings by the downtrodden. This future already exists, reverberating forward

---

12. See Christine Gibson's "Nat Turner, Lightning Rod" (2005) for a full account of how his body was treated.

and backward in time and always recurring.[13] White *fear* and black *rage* are real. Critical and popular responses by African Americans reveal the development of a networked black consciousness, manifested not only in Baker's graphic adaptation but in the various lyrics of hip-hop groups such as Public Enemy, the Wu-Tang Clan, and The Roots.[14] Afrofuturists use this repetition and reverse the prolepsis of Turner mythology to expose artificial constructions of black reality.

In a very real way, Nat Turner's revolt crystallized the differences between North and South and breathed life into the abolitionist movement. He wanted to free his people, and the local slaves trusted him because of his natural gifts: precocity, religious fervor, and foresight. Such trust became apparent while Nat Turner was making his jail-cell confession to lawyer Thomas R. Gray, who took notes, wrote them up, and later published Turner's own account of the insurrection.[15] Turner recalls a moment in his childhood "when [he was] three or four years old," his mother overheard him mention something to his friends: that he could not have possibly known which led to his enslaved brethren, saying in his hearing that he "would surely be a prophet, as the Lord had shewn [him] things that had happened before [his] birth" (Aptheker, *Nat Turner's Slave Rebellion: Including the 1831 "Confessions"* 133). Though Turner himself denied conjuring as a prophetic source, as opposed to communing with the Holy Spirit, such mystic power is a kind of "African virtuality . . . a transitory space wherein syncretic African epistemologies and Christianity were neither fully separate or completely merged" (Martin 57). The essence of this spiritual interface, whereby Turner conveyed information to his followers "by signs in the heavens," symbolically functioned as downloadable, wireless programming to revolt (Aptheker, *Nat* 138). Turner's observation of the solar eclipse as a heavenly sign to begin his revolt must be interpreted as a scientific phenomenon through supernatural means, qualifying him as a native scientist. Regardless, his name powerfully reverberates across the transhistorical feedback loop and connects black people, wiring them with hope and determination to fight.

---

13. The arrest, the neck and spine injuries, and the death of Freddie Gray while in police custody lead to the 2015 Baltimore protests against police brutality and the resulting April riots.

14. See Public Enemy's song "Prophets of Rage" (1988), the Wu-Tang Clan's "The City" (1997), and The Roots' "Somebody's Gotta Do It" (2004).

15. See Thomas R. Gray's *The Confessions of Nat Turner; The Leader of the Late Insurrection in Southhampton, VA* (1831). This lone interview serves as the primary source of evidence regarding Turner, although many historians question its veracity since Gray may have embellished it in order to make a profit.

Early Afrofuturist Novels and Imagining Resistance

Just as Turner connected to the past to guide his own prophetic visions, postbellum black novelists did so as well, only using Gabriel, Vesey, and Turner as their own access points to a networked black consciousness. In turn, African Americans today connect to a past replete with real science-fictional metaphors, creating a transhistorical feedback loop directly tapping into a networked black consciousness. Postbellum black novelists helped to upgrade this system in their stories by asserting black agency as a new horizon of possibility. These writers provided alternative vision modes that challenged a hegemonic whiteness while simultaneously recalibrating the future by traversing the divide between fantasy and reality and suggesting "black bodies and lives as valid terms for imagining the future" (Stringer 204). New modes of being came into existence, not alien or mechanical but human, fully exhibiting dignity, genius, and potentiality. Much good, both personal and political, could be accomplished in showing black people such liberating images heading into the future and wresting back control of the black body at the official end of black skin-trading in America.

Underneath the skin, a powerful discontent existed within artificial and highly policed black bodies, even if slave rebellions were uncommon, near-impossible to sustain, and snuffed out with alacrity. Opposition, if not defiance, existed in early African American literary endeavors. Black writers penning poetry (think Phillis Wheatley), missives (think Benjamin Banneker), plays (think William Henry Brown and his lost play *The Drama of King Shotaway*) [1823],[16] pamphlets (think David Walker), autobiographies or slave narratives (think Frederick Douglass or Harriet Jacobs discussed in the next chapter), and, finally, novels, all expressed the hope impulse and imagined freedom or rebellion. Although each and every slave rebellion was crushed in American history, the memories of black insurgent heroes like Gabriel Prosser, Denmark Vesey, and Nat Turner live on in the pages of Delany's *Blake; or, The Huts of America* (1859–62). Their concepts, like intranations, live on in the pages of Sutton E. Griggs's *Imperium in Imperio* (1899). And their response to popular back to Africa debates lives on in the pages of Pauline Hopkins's *Of One Blood: Or, The Hidden Self* (1903).

These black authors wrote against the backdrop of the Jim Crow era, newly sprung from the antebellum period during which lynching, propaganda, and the Ku Klux Klan, not to mention race riots—terrorism, in fact—

---

16. For definitive information about this play, see George A. Thompson Jr.'s *A Documentary History of the African Theater* (1998).

were used as methods to regulate emancipated black bodies.[17] Delany,[18] abolitionist and Black Nationalist; Griggs,[19] Baptist minister and integrationist; and Hopkins,[20] black feminist editor, all dared to create afrofutures in their writing despite the roiling racial tensions. They further established a practical interface with a networked black consciousness, translooping time forward and backward with depictions of revolution, separatism, and social ancestry laws governed by blood, boosting the hope impulse into the twenty-first century. Using the technology of writing itself, they disproved pseudoscientific beliefs regarding the subhumanity of black people, adapting a largely white tool to benefit their race and hence redefining the future. "Proof of the common humanity of bondsman and lord," as Gates suggests in *Figures in Black: Words, Signs, and the "Racial" Self*, reading and writing "as measured against an eighteenth-century scale of culture and society, [were] an irreversible step away from the cotton field toward a freedom larger even than physical manumission" (4). Using science-fictional language to describe the next three centuries, Gates continues, the "urgency and fundamental unity of the black arts became a millennial, if not precisely apocalyptic, force" (*Figures* 4). Gates means that black literature and art as creative forces represent a longstanding and continuing sociopolitical mission to demonstrate equality and dismantle long-held white beliefs of their own superiority. This would at least poke a hole in the notion of the collective greatness of white civilization—if not destroy it—and produce something new in the process, perhaps a pan-racial world. As Sheree R. Thomas writes, "For their day, these works were extraordinarily courageous, imagining in the wake of ruins and ashes a people who boldly forge alternate states for Black liberation and freedom" ("And So Shaped the World" 5). Accordingly, I will spend a bit of time writing about the afrofuturist content in Delany's *Blake*, Griggs's *Imperium in Imperio*, and Hopkins's *Of One Blood* to ruminate further on the relationships among race, science, and society.

The first twenty-six episodes of the serialized *Blake; or the Huts of America* first appeared in *The Anglo-African Magazine* (January–July 1859) before the

---

17. In fact, Ida B. Wells-Barnett bravely and carefully documented the propaganda behind white racial violence in *The Red Record: Tabulated Statistics and Alleged Causes of Lynching in the United States* (1895). In her work she provides three white excuses—to prevent race riots, to suppress black political activity, to stop the rape of white women—to justify their violence. Appallingly, the same propaganda lives on unchanged in the twenty-first century.

18. See Cyril E. Griffith's *The African Dream: Martin R. Delany and the Emergence of Pan-African Thought* (1975).

19. See Finnie D. Coleman's *Sutton E. Griggs and the Struggle against White Supremacy* (2007).

20. See Lois Brown's *Pauline Elizabeth Hopkins: Black Daughter of the Revolution* (2008).

Civil War. Those installments plus the remaining fifty-four chapters were then published in *The Weekly Anglo-African* (November 1861–May 1862) during the Civil War itself, which may account for the novel being largely forgotten until Floyd J. Miller's rediscovery of it in 1970 at the height of the Black Power Movement. However, it must be noted that only seventy-four chapters of the eighty-chapter novel exist. Nobody knows what happened to Blake's concluding chapters. In fact, Beacon Press would probably pay handsomely for information concerning the missing *Blake* chapters from the now-lost May 1862 issues of *The Weekly Anglo-African*. Probably forever unfinished for readers, the novel ends on the eve of protagonist Henry Blake's uprising in Cuba. We simply do not know if Blake triumphs in Cuba and if his success spreads to the Southern United States, where he meticulously develops a sleeper network to carry out his "deep-laid scheme for a terrible insurrection" (85). While Andy Doolen feels "safe" in saying that "the missing revolution deflates many readers' enthusiasm for the novel" (173–74), afrofuturists more likely agree with Eric J. Sundquist, who sees this specific "hemispheric African American cultural history" in the Americas as "among the most compelling statements of black transnationalist ideology in the nineteenth century" (206). In not so many words, Sundquist envisions the networked black consciousness that existed between slaves in the black Atlantic.

The extant novel relates to Henry Holland, "a pure Negro—handsome, manly and intelligent . . . having been educated in the West Indies, and decoyed away" into slavery (Delany, *Blake* 16). Purchased by Colonel Stephen Franks of Natchez, Mississippi, and renamed Henry Blake, Blake endures as a slave until his wife Maggie is sold to the Ballard family, Northern relatives with holdings in Cuba, while Blake is away from the plantation on his master's business. Because of this betrayal, Blake frees himself, traveling extensively throughout the South as a fugitive and harbinger of revolution. Depending on a loose but far-reaching underground information network composed of slaves, Blake goes "from plantation to plantation . . . sowing the seeds of future devastation and ruin to the master and redemption to the slave," using science and skill to evade capture (83). He then liberates his immediate family (his son and in-laws), helping them escape to Canada before going to Cuba to reclaim his wife. Before settling in Cuba to begin his war, Blake travels to Africa and back onboard the slaver *Vulture*. As tension builds on the Spanish island among the rightly paranoid white slaveholders, Blake gathers his Cuban retinue together as "the Leader of the Army of Emancipation" and continues building his transatlantic network, laying the foundation for a black empire in the Western hemisphere (251). Blake's final speech at chapter 70 in the available text urges violence: "'You know my errand among you; you know my sentiments. I am for war—war upon the whites'" (290). The novel ends with several of Blake's confidantes attacked by fearful whites on the island and Blake's ally General Montego shouting for revenge. About 112 years later, *Blake* serves as a clear precursor to John A. Williams's novel *Captain Blackman* (1972), which I discuss at length in chapter 6.

Rather than offer any further extended analysis of *Blake*, I now focus my afrofuturistic reading on three key features of the text—networking, alternate space, and science. With the first feature, Henry Blake expands on an already existing networked black consciousness as he travels from Texas to North Carolina's Dismal Swamp, and from Mississippi to Canada, Canada to Cuba, Cuba to the Guinea Coast of West Africa, and back to Cuba, preparing for a black revolution larger than the world has ever seen. In the first part of the novel, "Delany establishes the possibility of an extensive underground network of communication among the enslaved"; in the second part, "his overarching vision of a distinct transnational black culture—a new nation—begins to emerge" (Biggio 449). In Galveston, Texas, for example, Blake meets a black body-servant named Sampson and develops a deliverance plan for black people. Through his interaction with Aunt Rachel and Uncle Jerry, who have long been looking for a leader, he learns that Arkansan slaves are "pretty well organized already" (89). Later, he joins the High Conjurers of the Dismal Swamp and finds fugitive blacks, maroons "in sufficient number to take the whole United States" (114). In Richmond, Virginia, he secrets himself at his friend Mr. Norton's house and "immediately rekindle[s]" the freedom fight sparked by Nat Turner in Southampton (116). His conspiracy proves easy to organize in Nashville, where his "subject was like the application of fire to a drought seasoned stubble field" (122). Blake readily finds people committed to taking liberty into their own hands. He gives them hope and feels its pulse throughout the South.

In such a manner, Delany capitalizes on the white fear that Blake taps into on his recruitment drive, where "the slave holders are beholden . . . to the rebellious desires Blake gives voice to . . . black-on-white violence" (Havard 532). Blake's carefully guarded plotting unites the black South during his travels while also widening the existing network, which eventually becomes transnational.[21] Delany openly likens Blake's planned revolution to the actual Haitian Revolution (1791–1804) led by former slave Toussaint

---

21. As Britt Rusert asserts, "*Blake* registers, and exploits, international preoccupations with the threat of Southern expansion into the new territories of the United States as well as the annexation controversy of the 1850s, in which Southern slaveholders rallied for the conquest and annexation of Cuba as a US slave state" (814).

L'Ouverture to capitalize on white anxieties. Affectingly, we, as readers, never have the blueprints to Henry Blake's plan, thus intensifying the real-world tension for his likely white reading audience. This move demonstrates Delany's cleverness in actually showing a networked consciousness even if his serialized novel did not reach the still-enslaved, largely illiterate black audience.

The second feature combines this fear with the creation of an alternate space within the novel. Some of this worry about conspiracy relates to how Delany invokes the living ghosts of Gabriel Prosser, Denmark Vesey, and Nat Turner throughout the first part of the novel, initiating a transhistoric feedback loop that energizes the webbing of this black consciousness, particularly in the Dismal Swamp setting. The swamp itself becomes a black-o-sphere, as I term it, an area of influence beyond the touch of white supremacy; in this case the peculiar institution is governed by blacks, a seemingly timeless and supernatural alternate space from which to launch a revolution. As Mark Bould claims, "*Blake* also postulates a fabulous other space-time in which revolution might occur" ("Revolutionary" 56).

This alternate space resonates across the current time continuum because Gabriel, Vesey, and Turner are simultaneously mythic heroes to black people and larger-than-life villains to white people. The High Conjurers, men who make use of folklore and magic spells, led by Gamby Gholar and Maudy Gamus, claim to be "the old Confederates of . . . Nat Turner, Denmark Veezie, and General Gabriel," with their names regarded "in sacred reverence" to these "oldest of black rebels" (112–13). Doolen makes a good point here: "That Delany sees these men as part of a revolutionary history marks an estrangement from American history, since they are unintelligible within its framework" as replacements for the likes of Washington, Jefferson, and Adams (160). Undeniably, the Founding Fathers of the United States were revolutionaries, even if two of three were slavers who actively oppressed black people; but history refuses to see their black counterparts in the same light in the fight for freedom. Thus, Delany makes history strange in a science-fictional sense.

Time seemingly overlaps in the Dismal Swamp because these seers have foreseen the coming of Blake—rather a return of these mythic black heroes in the form of Blake—to lead and finish the race war. In fact, Gamby has been waiting over thirty years for Blake's arrival, stating, "'I been lookin' fah yeh dis many years' . . . 'an been tellin' on 'em dat yeh 'ood come long, but da 'ooden heah dat I tole 'em! Now da see! Dis many years I been seein' on yeh!" (112). That is to suggest Gamby, in his capacity as a conjurer, sees the future in sync with past aborted revolutions and maintains the networked black consciousness by projecting it into his future as he waits for Blake. He takes the loop onward with hope, bridging the past, present, and future of the text—an afrofuturism conductor. Blake himself may scoff at the idea of "spells" being cast by the conjurers, but he joins their order after their insistence (114). He realizes that "the more ignorant slaves have greater confidence in, and more respect for, their headman and leaders" and that he "must take the slaves, not as [he] wish[es] them to be, but as [he] really find[s] them to be" (126). In afrofuturistic terms, Blake combines conjuring's superstition, popular among slaves, with scientific practice in pursuit of freedom.

The third feature relates to how Blake navigates multifold spaces—physical, cultural, and alternate—using science and technology to avoid the entrenched surveillance mechanisms to prevent such a massive revolt conspiracy from happening. Simply put, Blake utilizes astronomy and a compass to travel through the Southern nights as a fugitive. For example, Blake remarks on the beauty of the evening moon while in New Orleans, noting how the celestial body "is always an object of impressive interest to the slave as well as those of enlightened and scientific intelligence . . . to impart inspiration" (98). Clearly, this inspiration relates to freedom and escape. He later teaches his wife's family celestial navigation to aid their escape by showing them how to locate the North Star in the night sky, "the slave's great guide to freedom" (132). Blake explains that they must locate the pointer stars in the Big Dipper and extend an imaginary line from them to point out the tip of the handle of the Little Dipper, the North Star. He pragmatically instructs them on how to use a compass as well since "the little box" with "a face almost like a clock" and its magnetic hand that "always points in one direction, and that is to the north" no matter how you move the box is "all that's necessary to guide you from a land of slavery and long suffering, to a land of liberty and future happiness" (133, 134). According to Rusert, the compass becomes "an absolutely essential tool for conducting fugitive science" (816), an opinion that confirms Yaszek's thought about Henry Blake as a "creative engineer" in "using his scientific and technical knowledge" ("Bannekerade" 19). Onboard a Mississippi steamer, Blake has a moment much like Nat Turner, only instead of a solar eclipse signaling the bloody revolt, he witnesses:

> A meteor, then seemingly shot a comet, again glistened a brilliant planet which almost startled the gazer; and while he yet stood motionless in wonder looking into the heavens, a blazing star whose scintillations dazzled the sight, and for the moment bewildered the mind, was seen apparently to vibrate in a manner never before observed by him.

At these things Henry was filled with amazement, and disposed to attach more than ordinary importance to them, as having an especial bearing in his case; but the mystery finds interpretation in the fact that the emotions were located in his own brain, and not exhibited by the orbs of Heaven. (Delany, *Blake* 124)

Human beings have always placed emphasis on astrological signs and how such signs have an influence on our dealings. Such celestial objects inspire Blake as he encounters them throughout the novel to reflect on slavery, if not blackness, and to dream of redeeming his race. As SF staples, these timeless, mystical objects extend from the past and penetrate the future, existing in the alternate space of a networked black consciousness because they pulse with the hope of liberty.

Blake is no different from other human beings in that astronomy and astrology help him negotiate space-time in addition to his environment. He disappears and reappears almost at will in this southscape[22] where time behaves strangely in that he can cross a state in a single day. (Movement and visibility are discussed a bit more in chapter 3.) It helps knowing that Blake "carefully kept a record of the plantations he passed" during the day, just in case he has to pass himself off as a local slave in pursuit of his master's missing livestock "when accosted by a white, an overseer or patrol" (68). Mental cartography helps him remain invisible since he knows the name of every owner and their holdings. As Rusert notes, these "empirical observations" form "part of [Blake's] larger project of collecting data on the status and condition of enslavement across the United States and in Cuba" to help him spur revolution (815). Without this map and the network he built along the way, his revolution fails, even if we do not know the ending. But the map enables us to comprehend the deep unrest seething between the races between points on the map. At its most comprehensive dimension, then, afrofuturism helps us understand that *Blake* functions as a scientific and political meditation on race and freedom as well as a fantastic fugitive adventure that complicates our understanding of antebellum America. In this respect, Delany creates a new horizon for black readers with his radical vision—one that Griggs later explores in *Imperium in Imperio*.

Griggs offers his own far-flung afrofuturist concept in his novel, in which a secret black nation arises in late nineteenth-century Texas. The basic premise of this separatist novel involves the dark-skinned Belton Piedmont and

---

22. Thadious M. Davis intends her term *southscape* to engage "the natural environment and social collective that shapes that environment out of its cultural beliefs, practices, and technologies" (2).

his mulatto friend and rival Bernard Belgrave working together to establish the Imperium, even though their philosophical differences remain. A fascinating miscegenation side plot develops when Bernard's mulatta fiancée, Viola Martin, commits suicide rather than weaken the black race because she cannot dare to love him. As she explains in her suicide note, she once read a book substantiating that "the intermingling of the races in sexual relationship was sapping the vitality of the Negro . . . slowly but surely exterminating the race" (Griggs 118). She could not let the white race win the war by falling in love with Bernard and raising mongrelized children. In fact, she asks Bernard to look more deeply into the matter of racial intermingling and charges him with erecting "moral barriers to separate them" and, failing this, to "make the separation physical" (119). As Bould claims, "Viola's absurd solution to her dilemma, along with the absurdity of her reasons, possess a tone akin to satirical-dystopian [SF] in which rational conclusions are developed from unreasonable premises" ("Revolutionary" 57). Fear of miscegenation and of dilution of black blood by white—an actualization of white pseudoscientific claims about racial purity—results in her death.

Belton recruits the grieving and radicalized Bernard to helm the Imperium. As the Imperium grows in the intervening years, an exceptionally shocking lynching of a black South Carolina postmaster,[23] an Imperium member, compels Bernard to call for a revolution against the United States. But Belton provides the solitary voice of dissent against open war and reveals the existence of the black nation despite surviving an attempted lynching of his own. Bernard later devises another plan to overthrow the US government, a plan that the Imperium accepts. Belton, refusing to consent to this new plot, resigns from the Imperium even though it means death by firing squad. Bernard, corrupted by his power, orders Belton's death, making his friend into a martyr. With the telling of this tale, the novel's narrator, Berl Trout, the Imperium's Secretary of State, betrays the Imperium's existence "in the interest of the whole human family," but only after executing Belton and only in going to his own death having written and delivered these papers to an outsider (6).

Griggs chooses to frame the novel as real, since Trout's papers and Trout's personal reflections on the two men were handed over to Griggs himself to write. In a similar observation, Eric Curry mentions that the Trout

---

23. Griggs clearly based this scene on the February 22, 1898, mob attack on Frazier B. Baker and his family in Lake City, South Carolina.

treachery plotline of "Bernard Belgrave's plans for race war" is "the very reason Sutton Griggs comes into possession of the documents" in the first place; that Griggs "claims to have collected together and circulated rather than conceive of and write" (23). Such a framing device generates the necessary estrangement to be considered science fictional and afrofuturistic in the sense that Griggs surely safeguards his true political feelings as a Progressive-era black preacher in wanting a world where black lives matter in their immediacy. From his pulpit, Griggs could not say such a thing to his Houston, Texas, congregation, where it would be much safer in multiple ways to expound a slow assimilation—safer financially, socially, and physically—while maintaining a Christian veneer. Nevertheless, Griggs links his people together even more through demonstrating a sublimated dream in an ever-receding future.

That the rivals had different philosophical outlooks on the race problem requires a bit more attention. Belton, dark-skinned and deprived, struggled until aided by a white benefactor to attend college, whereas Bernard grew up in luxury, favored by others because of his light skin, and sent to Harvard by his white father who could not openly recognize him. On the political spectrum Belton represents accommodation while Bernard symbolizes an early manifestation of Black Nationalism. As Pavla Veslá sees it, "The heroes represent two irreconcilable ways of bettering the status quo: to assimilate, patiently struggle with racism, or to separate and rely on harsh violence" (274). Griggs, in this respect, mirrors both the popular and the clashing leaders of his time, with Belton Piedmont masquerading as Booker T. Washington and Bernard Belgrave as a stand-in for a young W. E. B. Du Bois. A desired Black Nationalism wins out in the novel, something that strongly forecasts the future Black Panther Party of America. The Imperium, ensconced in Waco, Texas, represents an alternative future where blacks get their own justice for civil rights abuses. In afrofuturistic terms, there is a triweaving of the networked black consciousness through *Blake* and *Imperium in Imperio*, since both novels end on the verge of race war as black people take hope into their own hands to build a future out of the remnants of an enslaved past.

While Griggs utilizes a miscegenation subplot as one of Bernard's motivations in agitating an open race war to announce the Imperium's ascension as a black nation in America, Pauline Hopkins, in her serialized *Of One Blood: Or, The Hidden Self*, more fully examines the phenomenon of racial passing in her depiction of an imaginary lost African kingdom of Telassar reminiscent of the nineteenth century's lost race tales best represented by H. Rider Haggard's *She* (1887).²⁴ Hopkins's novel truly amazes because she clearly had been reading Victorian-Era proto–science fiction with its depiction of lost races, evolutionary themes, and technology in a twisted colonial/imperial context related to the great African land grab, infamously represented by King Leopold II of Belgium and his Congo Free State.²⁵ Twisted into the story is a black woman who explores and intervenes in a fictional terrain reserved for white men such as Joseph Conrad in *Heart of Darkness* (1899).²⁶ Through Hopkins's depiction of an incestuous love triangle among Reuel Briggs, Dianthe Lusk, and Aubrey Livingston, she counters the white men's racist arguments with the creation of a back-to-Africa utopian story to undermine the one-drop rule and the complexities of a blackness that is dependent on optical reasoning. As previously mentioned, the novel concerns an ancient African city state in Ethiopia and its lost American mulatto heirs.

To aid understanding, I will provide a brief outline of the melodramatic story before discussing a couple of its afrofuturistic qualities. *Of One Blood* traces the life of the impoverished Harvard medical student Reuel Briggs, who passes for white. When he and his best friend, the wealthy Aubrey Livingston, meet the beautiful, light-skinned singer Dianthe Lusk at the same time, they both fall in love with her. However, she falls into a coma, and Briggs uses his mesmeric science to revive her. She has amnesia when she awakens, and Briggs allows her to believe she is white. Livingston becomes the secret enemy of Briggs in his attempt to win Dianthe, even though he already has a fiancée, and, as Briggs's enemy, Livingston impedes all of his professional and financial prospects. Livingston makes sure the only money-spinning opportunity that Briggs has will take him to the African continent on an archaeological dig in Ethiopia. Briggs marries Dianthe the night before he sails but unwisely leaves his wife in his false friend's care. Livingston drowns his own fiancée and then blackmails Dianthe into marriage by threatening to reveal her race to Briggs.

---

24. *She* offers the first-person account of Ludwig Horace Holly, who journeys with his ward Leo Vincey to the lost African Kingdom of Kôr, a land populated by a lost cannibal race and ruled by the apparently immortal African queen, Ayesha, "'She-who must-be-obeyed'" (87).

25. Leopold II was the founder/owner of the Congo Free State, a private commercial enterprise lasting from 1885 to 1908. In the name of wealth and empire expansion, the native black population was brutally oppressed and exploited in the removal of the land's natural resources (ivory and rubber) where the present-day Democratic Republic of the Congo exists. Approximately ten million Congolese died in slavery over twenty-three years. See Adam Hochschild's *King Leopold's Ghost: A Story of Greed, Terror, and Heroism in Colonial Africa* (1998).

26. See my *Extrapolation* essay "Reframing *Heart of Darkness* as Science Fiction" (2015).

In Africa, Briggs discovers the lost city of Meroe and gets abducted by agents from the hidden city of Telassar, but not before being told that Dianthe has died in a boating accident. In Telassar he hears of an ancient prophecy: "that from lands beyond unknown seas, to which many descendants of Ethiopia had been borne as slaves, should a king of ancient line . . . return and restore the former glory of the race" (101–2). In fact, Reuel learns that he *is* its royal heir, that these hidden people practice advanced science and use amazing technologies, one of which reveals Livingston's duplicity. Shocked, Briggs returns home too late to rescue Dianthe from poisoning, but he induces Livingston to commit suicide through mental compulsion. But the surprises keep coming as Briggs learns from Aunt Hannah, his grandmother, that Aubrey and Dianthe are his brother and sister "of one blood," born to a former slave. It is Hannah who swapped Livingston for the dead baby of their white master for him to live free and white. Reuel Briggs takes his grandmother back to Africa, where he will rule as king in Telassar alongside their Queen Candace, wakened from a long sleep, the spitting image of Dianthe.

Unlike in *Blake* and *Imperium,* Hopkins creates an image of Africa as the birthplace of civilization: Africa as representative of the past, present, and future for blacks in America, if not the world—certainly a different vision of Pan-Africanism than we saw in Delany's novel. Hopkins uses the lotus-lily birthmark of Reuel Briggs as a genetic map linking him to a long line of Ethiopian kings. This past propels the future as it ironically "challenges the mythology of European superiority" (Gillman 72). Briggs, initially trained in Western sciences, seeks to "discover the broad highway between this and the other world" by strengthening his "mental insight" to erode factual boundaries between these worlds through supernatural activity (459). "That Reuel concerns himself with the paranormal does nothing to detract from his scientific orientation," Melisa A. Daniels argues, since novels "such as *Frankenstein* (1818), *The Strange Case of Dr. Jekyll and Mr. Hyde* (1886), and *Dracula* (1897) all make clear, nineteenth-century science can be every bit as fantastic" (166). Briggs discovers his hidden self as he digs into his own African and American ancestry, blending his scientific acumen in mesmerism with the Telassaran "abstract science of occultism" (143). Not only does this blended science show him the past and the importance of blackness for the future as a practitioner of the "knowledge of Infinity"; it also substantiates his royal claim (143). In a convoluted fashion, Hopkins rewrites American racial history, placing great emphasis on the speciousness of the one-drop rule as Reuel Briggs moves twice from the United States to a hidden city in the African interior as she explores the issue of miscegenation through genetics and archaeological excavation.

Hopkins inverts the miscegenation issue by contesting the pseudoscientific theories of race prevalent in her day. By daringly placing Africa at the center, she forces us to consider what blood means in terms of genealogy by suggesting that we are all descended from a single African source as opposed to the polygenetic idea of separate ethnic origins that are inherently unequal. Hopkins uses the character of Professor Stone to voice her own opinion "that black was the original color of man in prehistoric times"; and she pushes the proverbial button by having Stone ask the question, "What puzzles me is not the origin of the Blacks, but of the Whites" (88). From an afrofuturistic perspective, Hopkins takes a natural step toward a world of equality with this question pinging around the transhistoric feedback loop. This binary inversion, though not progressive, necessarily moves us toward a world without binaries.

Hopkins flips racial science on its head in her deconstruction of racism with this back-to-Africa fantasy. During his expedition, Briggs feels ashamed of his African blood and, through his ability to pass, hides it in America due to the social exigencies of white reality. But he can no longer deny it when explaining his embarrassment to a questioning Ai, his Telassaran advisor. Reuel clarifies the "deep disgrace to have within the veins even one drop of the blood" a bewildered Ai seems "so proud of possessing" (129). Of course Hopkins reverses this American social convention, making this one-drop of African blood royal in Telassar, an advantage beyond belief, and undermining a couple hundred years of black social conditioning that supported white supremacy.

Hopkins dares to contest the prevailing racial sciences of her day with her lost-race tale. Sundquist indicates that "to go 'back to Africa' in Hopkins's patently escapist fiction meant to flee the brutality and racism of American history in favor of a lost history of great wealth, material achievement, and intellectual superiority" (569). Martin Japtok calls this tactic "ideologically dangerous" as a "'Darwinist trap'" because Hopkins seemingly associates a people's value with "material, technological accomplishments [as] the standard by which any people should be measured, allow[ing] technology and pseudo-scientific racism to come together as a world view" (403). But such a danger seems negligible as Hopkins desires to restore pride in a black racial identity then, now, and in the future—a pride that has been factually eroded by slavery and Jim Crow and presently corroded by erroneous notions of a postrace America that allows racism to further hide and embed itself in a continually whitewashed world. She springs the trap presuming to believe in a black scientific genius equal to that of whites by writing in a white, not to mention male, genre.

Instead, an African past connects with the African American present of Hopkins's era through Reuel Briggs's blood. A hope impulse feeds into a new black destiny in which black people connect across continents and cultures in a networked consciousness potentially capable of solving the race problem. As Daniels notes, "One of the psychological implications of this merger is that the solution to racism might live in the development of a Pan-African consciousness" (169). Hopkins compromises the American-ness of African Americans. Her utopian vision of the possibility of such a future "opens up the prospect of a radically re-ordered future" (Bould, "Revolutionary" 63). Despite its romantic excesses in occultism, Egyptology, and pseudosciences, *Of One Blood* transforms our notions of afrofuturism. It demonstrates a demand, or at least a desire, for this connection that we see revealed time and again in contemporary SF by Octavia Butler, Steven Barnes, Nalo Hopkinson, Nnedi Okorafor, and Nisi Shawl.[27] In Yogita Goyal's words, "Hopkins counters the notion of Africa as the heart of Darkness, imagining it instead as the source of a proud black destiny" (42). In doing so, Hopkins inverts the romantic image of Africa to enact this colorism story in a sense restoring the African continent to the black American imagination, seeking to afrofuturistically reboot the networked black consciousness and reconnect lost pathways by twisting the transhistoric loop.

Along with *Of One Blood*, *Blake; or, the Huts of America* and *Imperium in Imperio* stand as proof positive that antebellum and postbellum black culture encouraged itself with radical future visions attuned to lasting racial problems. In other words, revolutionary thoughts stirred the minds of Black America in response to the predicable sanitation of racial history by white institutions. Both deeds and storytelling revise and retell an inspiring black Revolutionary America. How Delany imagines a militant uprising throughout the South and Caribbean might be terrifying for white people in the

---

27. Butler's *Wild Seed* (1980) intertwines her enduring fascination in genetics with occultism in the figure of Anyanwu. Steven Barnes uses the power of racial allegory to provide his counterfactual account of antebellum America in his Insh'Allah series—composed of *Lion's Blood* (2002) and *Zulu Heart* (2003)—in which Africa and Islam influence the Deep South in this plantation saga. In *The Salt Roads* (2003), Hopkinson crosses time and space as the goddess Lasirén experiences the world by embracing the lives of three black women in different centuries on different continents and immersing her consciousness with theirs. In *Who Fears Death* (2010), Okorafor mixes speculative elements into the postapocalyptic, far-future Saharan Desert setting, where the young, mix-raced sorceress Onyesonwu reshapes the world. With *Everfair* (2016), Nisi Shawl presents a counterfactual history of the Congo in which the indigenous population develops steam technology, forms the country of Everfair, and resists the horrors of enslavement by Belgium's King Leopold II. Each of these novels conveys afrofuturism's promise of a different, if not better, tomorrow for black people.

antebellum era, but his novel is a true reflection of the desperate hope that seeds the consciousness of black people everywhere. This hope imbues the postbellum writing of Griggs and Hopkins during the nadir of black existence in America between 1877 and 1915, even though, I must admit, their depictions of revolution drastically depart from the open war that Delany calls for in his novel. Griggs combines Black Nationalism, the desire to live apart from whites, as a solution to the race problem, with a negative reflection on miscegenation. On the other hand, as one of Africa's stolen descendants returns, Hopkins turns this discouraging view of race-mixing inside out to reflect the power, intelligence, and beauty of Africa and its people, potentially providing in turn a way to expand afrofuturism.

The textual and nontextual dimensions of early afrofuturism enabled the creation of these more literary works at the end of the nineteenth century. The fact that Delany knows of the earlier insurrections suggests a certain level of black memory, even though whites tried to quash it. The various revolts depended on networking and passing information, including Stono, Haiti, Prosser, and the rest. Rather than just putting elements of afrofuturism into the texts, this approach might help readers to think in new ways about how the literature itself is an afrofuturist experiment: for example, *Blake* as a novel less about the rebellion itself than the weird, serialized representation of the networked consciousness; *Imperium* less about post–Civil War segregation than the functioning of this network; and *Of One Blood* less about miscegenation than opening the African continent to afrofuturistic investigation. Essentially, these writers revolt against accepted modes of thought by transhistorically challenging white normativity on three different fronts of the race war.

Ultimately, the revolution to which Delany, Griggs, and Hopkins belong is in showing white folks that blacks are just as good as whites: creating worlds, using writing as Wheatley did in her earlier revolution, to demonstrate an equivalence to whites in thought and spirit if not body. This manifestation of the race war continues, and we fight today because some whites still do not believe that blacks are their equals in every way, particularly in the South. But hope springs eternal, and a connected community will see the war won.

CHAPTER 3

OF ALIEN ABDUCTIONS, POCKET UNIVERSES, TRICKSTER TECHNOLOGIES, AND SLAVE NARRATIVES

HAPPILY, in light of all the high-quality and cutting-edge scholarship being done, it can no longer be said that science fiction largely ignores the study of race and racism in its narratives.[1] In this regard, slavery has become an important subject with Octavia E. Butler's *Kindred* (1979) as well as Samuel R. Delany's *Tales of Nevèrÿon* (1979), both of which have led the way for forty years, not to mention Steven Barnes's underappreciated *Lion's Blood* (2002).[2] These important novels have a basis in the truth of collective trauma's impact on black people in America. This truth makes these novels different from strong, white-authored speculations in this area, for example, Terry Bisson's *Fire on the Mountain* (1988) or Ben H. Winters's recent *Under-*

---

1. Reynaldo Anderson and Charles E Jones's *Afrofuturism 2.0: The Rise of Astro-Blackness* (2015), André M. Carrington's *Speculative Blackness: The Future of Race in Science Fiction* (2016), and Sami Schalk's *Bodyminds Reimagined: (Dis)ability, Race, and Gender in Black Women's Speculative Fiction* (2018) are pertinent examples.

2. In Butler's *Kindred*, twentieth-century African American Dana Franklin is repeatedly and inexplicably pulled into the past by her nineteenth-century slave-owning white forefather Rufus in order to preserve her own future by keeping him alive. Delany's *Tales of Nevèrÿon* is the first of four fantasy novels that feature slavery in an overt manner as Gorgik the liberator incites slave rebellion across an entire realm regardless of color. In Barnes's *Lion's Blood*, featuring dual protagonists, the Irish slave Aidan O'Dere and his Black Muslim owner Kai ibn Jallaleddin, Africa colonizes the New World and enslaves white Europeans.

ground Airlines (2016),[3] both of which rely on "empathic fallacy" to engage readers to utilize an idea from critical race theory (Delgado and Stefancic 32). Lived racial experience versus vicarious living has definite bearing in this context. It is invisible perception along the lines of Ralph Ellison's *Invisible Man* (1952) of which I speak here—science-fictional blackness. Thus, our minds fill with heavy thoughts every time we read Frederick Douglass, Harriet Jacobs, Solomon Northup, and many others. But hope still exists for the future of black people in their stories, and the future of white people too. Afrofuturism helps us discern in a new light how enslaved black people survived the peculiar institution: the strength they demonstrated in the face of a powerful, blind, hate embedded deep in American culture to such a point that it still influences the country today. What good can come from using afrofuturist motifs such as the networked black consciousness, the transhistoric feedback loop, and the hope impulse to predicate colored futures,[4] to remix black identity beyond the artificial boundaries of race safeguarded by real prejudice, factual racism, and genuine violence cemented in US history?

This chapter explores the hope impulse expressed in the writings of enslaved black people as a core concept of afrofuturism in antebellum America. This desire for a better life, for a better future, and for freedom itself provides the central force for broadcasting opposition and perseverance in the early United States while disrupting the white intellectual geographies of economics, politics, and history such as those represented in Thomas Jefferson's *Notes on the State of Virginia* (1785). In that book, Jefferson draws upon Enlightenment-Era pseudoscientific beliefs about the biological basis of race to create the technological fantasy upon which slavery hinges, where treating black bodies as objects rather than subjects configures them as natural machines. Among other preposterous claims, Jefferson contends that blacks "require less sleep . . . after hard labour through the day" and suggests that the black imagination is "dull, tasteless, and anomalous" (146). Jefferson completes the machine analogy in noting how "slaves [are] distributable

---

3. Bisson's *Fire on the Mountain* relates a successful raid on Harper's Ferry by John Brown in 1859 and shows how history changes with the emergence of an African American country named Nova Africa. Winters's *Underground Airlines* tells the story of a twenty-first-century America where the South did not lose the Civil War. Victor, the black bounty-hunter, chases the fugitive slave Jackdaw into "the Hard Four" states where slavery remains intact (12).

4. I don't mean only black futures here. I am invested in exploring all racial binaries in SF as well as helping others do this kind of work in maintaining and extending SF's colored wave, whether it be techno-orientalism, indigenous futurism, Latinx futurism, and so on.

... as other moveables" when based "on a principle of economy" that sells them like "old wagons, old tools" (144, 148). As natural machines, with race operating as a labor-based technology, blacks are figured as artificial persons such as robots, cyborgs, and clones. For example, Jacobs refers to slaves as "God-breathing machines" in her 1861 slave narrative, *Incidents in the Life of a Slave Girl* (11). But while Jefferson used this equation between machines and black bodies to justify slavery, his obvious dehumanization of slaves is the reason they needed hope. The emblematic move from machine to god-breathing machine to a cyborg capable of plugging into a networked consciousness depends entirely on black generational experience encoded in the folklore, native scientific practices, and spiritual beliefs that somehow survived the Middle Passage. These African cultural remnants have reverberated throughout American history and have created a networked black consciousness, the basis of the freedom technologies that helped blacks withstand the horrors of slavery. In short, then, mapping the evolution of the hope impulse and the network it formed among slaves and free blacks allows us to see how black people survived the science-fictional reality of early America.

Consequently, slave narratives highlight the hope impulse in action through the sometimes-daring flights of these fugitives. They also demonstrate an operational networked black consciousness, since we still read them well over 150 years later provided we truly connect with the fugitive slave experience. That is, our connectivity to this existing network remains because these texts are still being read, powering up every time a book is cracked open or taught in a classroom, testifying to a basic human need for hope. I discuss how Olaudah Equiano, Venture Smith, Solomon Northup, Henry "Box" Brown, Harriet Jacobs, Frederick Douglass, William Wells Brown, Henry Bibb, and the Crafts attest to afrofuturism's validity as each one lays bare a science-fictional American existence. Each of these black freedom fighters engenders the afrofuturist vista from antebellum America to the twenty-first century by creating a legacy of resistance. They provide a necessary neural link to the past and the way fugitive slaves imagined different futures. In other words, they complete a transhistorical feedback loop in which contemporary black authors critique ongoing racial politics. In this respect, afrofuturist readings of these texts go beyond authorial intent in reappropriating science-fictional tools like alien abductions, pocket universes, and trickster technologies to thereby offer cultural critique and liberation. These SF terms activate my own afrofuturist notions (transhistoric feedback loop, black networked consciousness, and hope impulse) as creative alternatives.

Analogous to Nat Turner's plugging into the past to guide his own prophetic visions, African Americans today connect to a past replete with real science-fictional metaphors. This connection energizes a transhistorical feedback loop directly interfaced with a networked black consciousness: one that escaped slaves helped to preserve and amplify in their narratives, offering hope in combination with the authority of their firsthand experiences of the peculiar institution. All enslavement narratives have in common their hope of achieving a future freedom and their courage exhibited in attempting to attain it. The slave narratives we now read provide a necessary neural link to the past and how fugitive slaves imagined different futures that in turn have influenced African Americans across time-space and how we critique the never-ending racial politics of America. Enslaved black people generated their own power, creating the lasting potency of their tellings, and spawning and maintaining an afrofuturist aesthetic particularly legible to us.

In trying to think about how to describe the feedback loop and networked consciousness, I talk about how this connection works across time, reaching out from the present to touch the past and vice versa. Yet it would also be helpful to think about how these texts are not just transhistorical but even ahistorical—that is, to think about not only how we can somehow bridge the time gap, but also how the narratives articulate a hope impulse that is always *presentist* no matter when we "access" it. It is not just that these texts influence across time in that we see how they did it and can follow their insights to do it too, but it may just be the hope impulse that makes it about our time. From a different perspective, what is afrofuturist about these texts is not their futurism but rather that their futurism is actually a presentism that remains present whether it's 1819 or 1919 or 2019—something "For My People" as esteemed African American poet Margaret Walker would have said (1937).[5]

---

5. The first stanza of Walker's poem reads:

> For my people everywhere singing their slave songs repeatedly: their dirges and their ditties and their blues and jubilees, praying their prayers nightly to an unknown god, bending their knees humbly to an unseen power; (lines 1–4)

The tenth and final stanza of Walker's celebrated poem announces the future:

> Let a new earth rise. Let another world be born. Let a bloody peace be written in the sky. Let a second generation full of courage issue forth; let a people loving freedom come to growth. Let a beauty full of healing and a strength of final clenching be the pulsing in our spirits and our blood. Let the martial songs be written, let the dirges disappear. Let a race of men now rise and take control. (lines 43–48)

Science-Fictional Slavery

Encrypting slavery's numerous ordeals, science-fictional ideas—such as different worlds evoked by Olaudah Equiano's "ten thousand worlds" lament from 1789—abound in slave narratives. To be free of slavery's malevolence, Equiano would trade ten thousand other worlds. With this powerful metaphor, Equiano demonstrates the necessary fluidity of mind to counteract prevailing European prejudices regarding black intelligence and creativity. His narrative becomes afrofuturistic in its castigation of America's perfidy regarding chattel slavery for its black citizens and in its other-worlds metaphor as an appeal for equality in the New World. Such an appeal underscores the hope impulse.

This sentiment is echoed in *A Narrative of the Life and Adventures of Venture Smith, A Native of Africa: But Resident Above Sixty Years in the United States of America, Related by Himself* (1798), in which Venture Smith tells about his hardships as a slave in colonial New England through an unknown white amanuensis. This white agent attests that "it may perhaps, not be unpleasing to see the efforts of a great mind wholly uncultivated, enfeebled and depressed by slavery, and struggling under every disadvantage.—The reader may here see a Franklin and a Washington, in a state of nature, or rather in a state of slavery" (170). Smith, the son of an African king, was captured as a young child in Dukandarra, Africa, somewhere between present-day Senegal and Nigeria; was forced to march 1,000 miles to the coast; and survived the Middle Passage, during which more than sixty other captives died of smallpox. Smith was purchased by Robertson Mumford for "four gallons of rum, and a piece of calico" (175), thrice sold after acts of defiance such as attempting to escape with the enslaved Irishman Heddy,[6] and took a whip from his second mistress, Mrs. Stanton, and then tossed it in the fire to prevent his wife Meg from being beaten. Mr. Stanton then threatened to have him sold to the West Indies, to which Smith replied, "I crossed the waters to come here, and I am willing to cross them to return" (179). After he was pawned to a Mr. Edwards before being sold a third time, his final owner, Colonel Oliver Smith, allowed Smith to hire out his own spare time and to purchase his own freedom for "seventy-one pounds two shillings" (181). He then proceeded to purchase his wife and children from slavery over the course of several years; to acquire land; to, paradoxically, buy his own slaves (who ran off or were freed);[7] to make money at logging, whaling, blacksmithing, farming,

---

6. See Noel Ignatiev's *How the Irish Became White* (1995) or Mathew Frye Jacobson's *Whiteness of a Different Color: European Immigrants and the Alchemy of Race* (1998).

7. I certainly understand why readers might feel that such purchases by Smith would generate despair rather than hope among black people.

and trading, all while getting swindled in business by various white men and defeated in the courts when he pursued just reparations. Though he amassed substantial wealth, Smith's less-renowned slave narrative served as an afrofuturist warning to African Americans who pursued respect, autonomy, and equality in America. Despite the unusual nature of Smith's cautionary tale, he demonstrated a sense of dignity in surviving slavery and the New World he inhabited afterward that inspired hope.

In Venture Smith's narrative, we experience slavery in what is now the northeastern United States of America—New England (Rhode Island and Connecticut) and New York. It is not exactly SF since slavery was also practiced throughout the thirteen colonies, but Smith's tale defies what is commonly taught in America's primary schools today. His tale depicts a series of alien interactions with white people (and, not surprisingly, black people) both as a slave and as a free person of color. In his final paragraph, Smith states:

> My freedom is a privilege which nothing else can equal. Notwithstanding all the losses I have suffered by fire, by the injustice of knaves, by the cruelty and oppression of false hearted friends, and the perfidy of my own [black] countrymen whom I have assisted and redeemed from bondage, I am now possessed of more than one hundred acres of land, and three habitable dwelling houses. It gives me joy to think that I *have* and that I *deserve* so good a character, especially for *truth* and *integrity*. (185)

His account of such alien interactions continues into the present and represents a science-fictional black experience: a time paradox of sorts where we repeat and re-experience the tragedies caused by the invention of race through Venture Smith's recollections. It is also a paradox in the sense that the United States, as the putative leading country of the world, has yet to break away from this ever-looping cyclical violence against black people as evinced by works such as Alexander's *The New Jim Crow* (2010), by the rise of the Black Lives Matter movement in 2013 on social media at the acquittal of George Zimmerman in the 2012 homicide of African American teenager Trayvon Martin, and by the upsurge of white intolerance sparked by the Trump presidency as exemplified by the violent Charlottesville, Virginia, white nationalist rally on August 12, 2017. Although race was not yet a fixed biological category in the eighteenth century, Smith's experiences represent both a return and a departure: a literal return to a black man living among white folks dispossessed of his culture and heritage, and a departure for afrofuturistic thoughts on liberation, revolt, and healing— that is, future possibilities.

As previously discussed in the introduction, slave narratives delve into the hyperreality of violence inflicted upon black people, reducing them to objecthood, in fact a science-fictional existence. Recall the murder of Demby by Colonel Lloyd's overseer, Mr. Gore, in *Narrative of the Life of Frederick Douglass*. The scene becomes a powerful exemplar of the underlying point that black lives do not matter in a racist world. So the scene does not just describe a single historical event that we can relate to by analogy alone. Rather, the scene makes Demby (and Douglass, and everyone else) a presentist example of the situation. Demby has not been killed in the past; he is *always* getting killed, not just every time we read the narrative, but all the time in one form or another. And so Venture Smith is not just one story about one exceptional man, but rather a kind of personalized abstraction of what every black person goes through. Slave narratives warp the time-space of analogy along these lines; you are like Demby because his experiences are actually your experiences. Our hyperreality, where no concern for black lives exists when juxtaposed to white male authority, expands from moments like this one. In this respect, the hope impulse represents a counter-simulacrum of realities offered by afrofuturism.

Douglass's *Narrative* reads like SF in a second way. When it comes to slave management, perhaps the most insidious control mechanism is the creation of a natural panopticon based on fear, exhaustion, and constant surveillance. The slave maxim "every shut eye ain't asleep" exists for this reason. This panopticon could make slaves do strange things, for example, spy for the master, or turn on one another for food, or feel superior because of a lighter skin tone gained through the rape of an ancestor, or any number of other things. Frederick Douglass's time in the care of the slave breaker Edward Covey exemplifies my meaning of *panopticon*:

> Covey would be out with us. The way he used to stand it, was this. He would spend the most of his afternoons in bed. He would then come out fresh in the evening, ready to urge us on with his words, example, and frequently with the whip. Mr. Covey was one of the few slaveholders who could and did work with his hands. He was a hard-working man. He knew by himself just what a man or boy could do. There was no deceiving him. His work went on in his absence almost as well as in his presence; and he had the faculty of making us feel that he was ever present with us. This he did by surprising us. He seldom approached the spot where we were at work openly, if he could do it secretly. He always aimed at taking us by surprise. Such was his cunning. (72)

Virtually undetectable, Covey spies with hostile intent and creates paranoia among the slaves, who are not deluding themselves about the monstrous qualities of this man. None of them are safe in that he knows what work should get done and punishes them accordingly if their work is not completed. Covey's surveillance delivers the menace necessary to keep his slaves in line. He breeds what Daphne Brooks terms "Afro-alienation," whereby slaves have been "encoded with the traumas of self-fragmentation resulting from centuries of captivity in subjugation" (5). Dehumanized, defamiliarized, and utterly alienated, Douglass breaks under Covey's pressurized surveillance. Covey utilizes such monitoring techniques to better control his slaves, psychologically impacting them to generate higher productivity, something akin to thought control from a science-fictional perspective or a literal body snatcher who uses paranoia to suppress their identity and humanness. But Douglass somehow manages to reverse his own breaking. He uses his stolen education to free his mind and then to liberate his body and in the process becomes a powerful writer, a thrilling speaker, and a leader for black people. His move to cache and weaponize words pulses and emotionalizes hope across the entire black network in perpetuity.

Alien Abductions

Using afrofuturism to re-interpret black literature enables us to travel in time and across space to better understand this black utopian impulse, to create counternarratives, and to illustrate the many challenges we face. It shifts the power dynamics at work in analyzing cultural history. As De Witt Kilgore argues, "Afrofuturism can be seen as less a marker of black authenticity and more a cultural force, an episteme that betokens a shift in our largely unconscious assumptions about what histories matter and how they may serve as a precondition for any future we may imagine" ("Afrofuturism" 564). As a combination of cultural history and SF, afrofuturism potentially intensifies black artistic production in such a way as to shift conversations on black experience. Solomon Northup's *Twelve Years a Slave* (1853) provides a case in point. His experience in bondage reads like an alien-abduction story.[8]

But first, a straightforward interpretation of Northup's life, as told to his white amanuensis David Wilson, indicates how Northup was born free in upstate New York; married a loving mixed-race wife; had three children; and

---

8. See Ashley Clark's "Alien abductions: 12 Years a Slave and the past as science fiction" (2013).

was a successful farmer, a raftsman on Lake Champlain, and a much-sought violinist. With his wife and children out of town, the industrious Northup tried to earn a bit of extra income in 1841 by going off with two alleged circus men, Merrill Brown and Abram Hamilton, who convinced him to play music in New York City, to get his free papers sorted out, and to accompany them south on a quick trip to Washington, DC, to make more easy money. In the capital, these men drugged Northup, kidnapped him, and sold him to a slave trader named James Burch, who arranged for Northup to be shipped to Louisiana in the dreaded Deep South, despite Northup's insistence that he was a free person of color. In New Orleans, the kindly cotton planter William Ford purchased Northup at auction, renamed him Platt, and sold him six months later to the abusive carpenter John Tibeats, who in turn sold him to the diabolic and stormy planter Edwin Epps. Northup spent the next ten years laboring in the heat and humidity of the cotton and cane fields on Bayou Boeuf of the Red River region in Avoyelles Parish, most of these years as a slave driver for Epps when not hired out.

Northup chanced to meet Samuel Bass, a traveling Canadian carpenter, who was contracted to help build a house for Epps with Northup's assistance. Quietly and slowly convincing the unorthodox Bass of his lost freedom, Northup placed his trust in Bass. And Bass wrote a series of letters on Northup's behalf in August 1852, one of which eventually reached his wife in Glens Falls, New York, by September, effecting his rescue from slavery on January 3, 1853. Unlike Frederick Douglass, who in his first narrative left unexplained how he escaped, Northup and Wilson decided to divulge essential details like dates, specific names, and places in Northup's story to counteract any disbelief of its veracity. In fact, contemporary scholars use *Twelve Years a Slave* as an indispensable source on antebellum culture. Valerie Smith implies that the book "resonates with" readers today "because of what it has to say about the fragility of black freedom" in "the era of supposed postracialism" ("Black Life in the Balance: *12 Years a Slave*" 365). Smith qualifies this suggestion through "the range and frequency of assaults on black life in the early decades of the twenty-first century [that] undermine national narratives of racial progress from slavery to Emancipation, the civil rights revolution, and the so-called Age of Obama" ("Black" 365). Contemporary fears of a regression in racial politics mingle with the extreme example of Northup's steadfast hope projecting across American history.

With black lives at the crux, an afrofuturist interpretation helps to clarify exactly how the web of black consciousness operates across time. It focuses attention on the nonlinear progression of color-line politics, forcing a purposefully constructed awareness of continuing racial disparities in terms of health, education, wealth, and other public perceptions of the American dream. Afrofuturism should be recognized as a cautious optimism. Northup survives to write about his abduction and transforms his victimization into a triumph from which future blacks in America benefit.

Of course, Northup's abduction and return have been thoroughly authenticated, but adding the alien-abduction twist allows new meaning for contemporary readers—writing as a resistance technology. An alien-abduction narrative relates the alleged experience of a person who claims to have been secretly captured and taken away by extraterrestrial beings. Encounters of the fourth and fifth kinds, as classified by the close encounters scale in the pseudoscience of ufology, were first developed by respected scientist Joseph A. Hynek in *The UFO Experience: A Scientific Inquiry* (1972).[9] Hynek describes how the kidnapped person is imperiled by a variety of invasive tests and practices. While Hynek's original close encounters scale only went up to the third kind, his scale was later extended by his colleague Jacques Vallee to include encounters of the fourth through fifth kinds in the peer-reviewed *Journal of Scientific Exploration* (1998). Vallee contends that a four designates "cases when witnesses experienced a transformation of their sense of reality (often corresponding to the popular characterization of the incident as an 'abduction')," and a five represents "cases of lasting physiological impact such as serious injury or death" (360). To be clear, in five on the scale, the abductee is first captured, then examined, communicated with, transported to undisclosed location(s), suffers through time displacement, and eventually returned home, where he or she experiences a deeply felt sense of well-being or peace at being home before coming to grips with the social, physical, and mental consequences of the encounter.

As in an alien-abduction narrative, Northup awakens in a holding pen, feet chained, with no recollection of how he got there, right in the heart of Washington, DC. He reveals that "there was a blank of some indefinite period, preceding my awakening in that lonely place, the events of which the utmost stretch of memory was unable to recall" (Northup 38). Burch, alien to him, beats Northup with a paddle as he insists on his freedom and then whips Northup as he persists. This moment reminds me of all the stories regarding alien probing because Burch does not believe Northup and continues to test Northup both physically and psychologically by locking

---

9. On the close encounters scale, a "one" represents an unidentified flying object (UFO) sighting; a "two" represents witnessed physical effects caused by the UFO such as electronic interference, paralysis, or scorched earth resulting from arrival or departure; and a "three" signifies an alien sighting, whether biological or mechanical.

him in the dark, still chained, "all on fire," while "it seemed that the lacerated flesh was stripped from my bones at every stroke" (45). Northup's interrogation by Burch results in such anxiety that "a human face was fearful to [Northup], especially a white one" after enduring such a severe flogging (46). Clearly, this infernal session softens Northup for sale and predicts his fate of being transported by steamer to Norfolk, Virginia, and then on to New Orleans. After being renamed Platt in a New Orleans slave pen, he questions if "the events of the last few weeks [were] realities indeed," or if his "passing [were] only through the dismal phases of a long, protracted dream" (77).

This twelve-year odyssey, as such, depicts an entirely different world, one in which Northup experiences the emotional harshness and physical rigors of forced labor by a more savage species of white man, vastly alien to what he knew in New York. Northup suffers slavery's full range: beatings, hounds, auctions, near-lynching, slave songs, betrayal, insurrection talk, foul and abusive language, slave-driving, and even witnessing the brutal flogging and flaying of Patsey. Northup becomes a natural machine just like the other slaves going up and down rows picking cotton or cutting cane. Time slows under such pressure exerted by the peculiar institution and "through the thick, black cloud, amid whose dark and dismal shadows I had walked . . . , broke the star that was to light me back to liberty" (298). Northup can hardly believe his own eyes when his old white friend, Henry B. Northup, arrives to take him home.

Solomon Northup returns home the way he had come—with stops in New Orleans, Washington, DC, and New York City to attempt prosecution of his abductors—but the time loss truly hits home when he enters his youngest daughter Margaret's cottage in Glens Falls, New York, and she does not recognize him while standing next to Northup's namesake grandson whom he did not know he had. As he remarks, "She was grown to womanhood—was married, with a bright-eyed boy standing by her side" (319). The hope impulse arises when he describes how "the violence of our emotions had subsided to a sacred joy" as all of the family had gathered, including his wife and three children, to talk of their individual experiences "during the long separation" (320). Regarding his unjust enslavement, Northup proclaims that his account "is no fiction, no exaggeration" and that he is "thankful to that good Being through whose mercy I have been restored to happiness and liberty" (321). In the aftermath of this traumatic abduction, Northup feverishly works on this account, publishing it within two years of his restored freedom. It becomes a best seller in his lifetime, but he disappears into obscurity while attempting to rebuild his life.

Whereas most alien-abduction tales are questionable hearsay at best, featuring little gray men or some such concoction, Solomon Northup's account is beyond contestation: lured away by the false promise of work made by two white men; drugged, chained, beaten, whipped, and tortured; shipped to New Orleans; renamed and repeatedly sold; and finally returned home, free but different, after an incredibly heartrending journey. Perhaps our emotional and psychological response to *Twelve Years a Slave* should be to hang on to our own freedom—freedom to go where we like, when we live as free citizens of the United States despite our racial history without taking this networked black consciousness for granted, prepared to fight for our continued deliverance. In fact, Solomon Northup's resilience flashes as a beacon of hope across generations.

Pocket Universes

While Northup accomplished the seemingly impossible in returning from the Deep South to independence, Henry "Box" Brown mailed himself from slavery to freedom—from Richmond, Virginia, to Philadelphia, Pennsylvania, over twenty-seven hours—and Harriet Jacobs achieved the same without escaping anyplace, hiding from her pursuer, Dr. Flint, in plain sight for nearly seven years in an attic crawlspace above her grandmother's shed in Edenton, North Carolina, before booking passage on a ship for Philadelphia. Brown's and Jacobs's resistance to slavery provokes a uniquely afrofuturistic vibe when their separate experiences are framed as self-engineered individual pocket universes. Conceptualizing these narratives as existential proof of pocket universes, as the afrofuturist vista itself, alters our construal of these slave narratives. The fullness of their separate realities shrinks into constricted extradimensional spaces. They exist outside history, unobserved by all except their readers: victims of slavery determined to escape from their artificial worlds, from a slave world designed to consume them, to live free in the free world.

A pocket universe, whether natural or artificial, exists within the boundaries of another universe—a space within a space governed by its own rules. The larger world envelops this isolated space, this miniature universe. For instance, as his biographer Charles Stearns states, as told by Brown himself, Brown arranged to have himself shipped to freedom in a wood crate measuring "three feet one inch long, two feet wide, and two feet six inches deep" for $86.00 on March 29, 1849 (Stearns 91). He stood 5 feet, 8 inches tall and weighed 200 pounds. His world collapsed into that confining box for more than a day, with the box becoming a pocket universe because of a "heavenly vision" requiring him to "go and get a box, and put yourself in it." But first he had to burn one of his fingers to the bone with vitriol to get out of working in William Barret's tobacco fields overseen by Joseph F. Allen (59). Brown put himself in that box because his pregnant wife, Nancy, and his three children were sold to North Carolina a year earlier by their owner, a different master from Brown's. With nothing else to lose, Brown chanced his life on this venture, stating that "if you have never been deprived of your liberty, as I was, you cannot realize the power of that hope of freedom, which was to me indeed, 'an anchor to the soul, both sure and steadfast'" (60). This direct appeal speaks to readers then and now, helping to create the interstices where the networked black consciousness exists, a network activated by the hope impulse of which Brown speaks.

His world was reduced to a box, one that contained a water bladder and three small breathing holes that did not exactly provide fresh air, Brown went upside down for parts of the rough journey despite "this side up with care" directions on the box (60). Of "this dreadful position," Brown writes:

> I began to feel of my eyes and head, and found to my dismay, that my eyes were almost swollen out of their sockets, and the veins on my temple seemed ready to burst. I made no noise however, determining to obtain "victory or death," but endured the terrible pain, as well as I could, sustained under the whole by the thoughts of sweet liberty. (60–61)

Transported by wagon, railroad, steamboat, and ferry, Brown endured: He emerged from the box twenty-seven hours later before his abolitionist friends and became a legend on the antislavery lecture circuit. He reminded sympathizers to help free "the three millions of crushed and mangled ones who this day pine in cruel bondage" from "baby-stealers and women-whippers . . . wicked men, all covered with the clotted gore of their mangled victims" (63). No light, no food, little water and air, nailed into a claustrophobic and stultifying space, unable to see the outer world and to hear only snatches of conversations between transporters, Brown determined his own freedom, and his journey resonates across time and space. As Hollis Robbins points out, "Henry 'Box' Brown's *Narrative* has re-emerged to enjoy a kind of academic second act in African American Studies" over the last decade because it "focuses primarily on the symbolic value of Brown's confinement" (5–6).[10] For Daphne Brooks, Brown "exemplifies the role of

---

10. See Martha J. Cutter's "Will the Real Henry 'Box' Brown Please Stand Up?" (2015).

the alienated and dislocated black fugitive subject, and the repetition of his escape 'act' before audiences abroad provided a heightened and alternate expression of conditional and fleeting liberty 'on the run' in the 1850s" (67). And for me, Brown's astonishing tale reads in an afrofuturistic vein as his being explodes from the box like a big bang that reaches new readers in the twenty-first century. On one hand, I sound a bit hyperbolic, and yet, on the other, another black man, Charles McKinley, tried to ship himself in an air-freight box via the United Parcel Service from Newark, New Jersey, to Dallas, Texas, on September 5, 2003.[11] This strange truth, of course, was about saving a buck, not achieving freedom, and resulted in McKinley doing jail time. Conversely, "Brown is a peculiar cargo, not yet man, no longer slave, but something else," as Samira Kawash claims, because "there is not a name or a category to represent Brown in this liminal space" (68). Kawash gets it wrong when she calls the box a liminal space, for it contains an unnameable material hope. Better to think of the box as being interdimensional. In truth, this box became Henry Brown's entire world for more than a day, a universe unto itself.

His desperate attempt to achieve freedom produced inspiration, and he technologized his own freedom by packing himself into that self-containing box and shipping it. Brown escaped the confinement of slavery by passing through this self-constructed pocket universe into the larger world, eventually traveling to England and Canada to share his story. Unshackling himself, Brown's pocket-universe experience altered reality for millions of future African Americans who came to inhabit a larger world created by his audacity—namely, the boldness of his hope pulses across the networked consciousness that we can access through our textual experience of his ordeal. Just the possibility of access produces hope.

Harriet Jacobs offers a second, perhaps stronger, example of a pocket universe created by slavery in *Incidents in the Life of a Slave Girl* (1861), the best-known slave narrative written by a woman. While Brown endured his pocket universe for little more than a day, Jacobs survived in her own "loophole of retreat" for seven years, remaining in stasis as life and slavery continued all around her without her actually going anywhere (95). As Miranda Green-Barteet insists, "Jacobs consciously positions the garret as a border space, one that exists betwixt and between other more clearly defined spaces" (53). It is interstitial much like Brown's crate, and this indeterminate position will help her escape like Brown as well. Likewise, Gloria T. Randle praises Jacobs for "her ability creatively to construct sites of temporary ref-

---

11. See Patty Davis's "Man shipped from New York to Texas in crate" (2003).

uge where none exist; to discover space where there is no space; to identify, over and over again, the narrowest wedge between the rock and the hard place" (43). And this spatial awareness, at least for Valerie Smith, galvanizes Jacobs "to redirect her own and her children's destiny" ("'Loopholes of Retreat'" 213). For me, the pocket universe of Jacobs, a physically and psychically constructed space, offers hope to its readers by mixing a manifold space with racial and sexual politics, thereby proving a revolutionary afrofuturistic connection between past, present, and future.

Before her time of self-confinement, Jacobs recounts her life in slavery. She learns to read and write; she is bequeathed as property to the five-year-old daughter of Dr. Flint; she falls in love with another slave, only to have the relationship disrupted and disavowed by Flint. She also witnesses slaves beaten, overworked, starved, deprived of sleep, dehumanized, and sold away to other masters and locales. Likewise, we see firsthand how white men sexually abused black slave women from bribes to beatings in order to sleep with them and then selling their own children from these crude couplings. Because of their husbands' betrayals, jealous white wives took their own pain out on the slaves. Jacobs herself violated the ideals of antebellum womanhood—piety, purity, domesticity, and submissiveness[12]—and broke her grandmother's heart in the process by sleeping with a different white man, Mr. Sands, and having two illegitimate children with him, just to avoid Flint's repeated and unwanted sexual advances. Yet none of these things explains how Jacobs spent so much time in the cramped attic space, her pocket universe, because she felt resigned to slavery and the space provided an escape.

Flint triggers her desire to run by threatening to bring her young children to his plantation. He retaliates against her disappearance by selling her son and daughter, albeit to Mr. Sands, who promptly places them in Jacobs's grandmother's care. Even after she escapes North by boat with her fugitive friend Fanny, Dr. Flint and his family continue their hunt for Jacobs in the North, managing to get close a few times.

Jacobs hides in a series of places in and out of town before going into her grandmother's garret. She stays at a black friend's place and then some bushes where she is bitten by something poisonous. Next, Jacobs stays in a white woman's house in town for several months while her brother and children are thrown into jail in an attempt to force her out of hiding. Meanwhile, Flint heads to New York to look for her. She ends up in Snaky Swamp when the search intensifies. Her final hiding place above her grandmother's shed

---

12. See Barbara Welter's essay "The Cult of True Womanhood: 1820–1860" (1966).

becomes a pocket universe, a space "only nine feet long and seven wide [with the] highest part . . . three feet high, and sloped down abruptly to the loose board floor" (96). Here in this garret, "some boards . . . laid across the joists at the top . . . between these boards and the roof" (95), Jacobs endures bug infestations, rodents, illness, stifling heat, chilling cold, and extreme loneliness without light or air circulation for seven long years, all the while awaiting her chance to seize liberty. Katherine McKittrick calls the garret a "usable paradoxical space" because of how it provided "a different way to observe slavery," with Jacobs multiply positioned as "a witness, participant, and fugitive" (43).

Jacobs chooses this highly dangerous subterfuge, surviving in the garret and its overwhelming darkness, sitting or lying "in a cramped position day after day . . . rather than [her] lot as a slave" (96). In fact, her enslavement ends here as she takes up her long residence.

The garret allows Harriet Jacobs to think about her time as a slave. Jacobs was

> never cruelly over-worked . . . never lacerated with the whip from head to foot . . . never so beaten and bruised that I could not turn from one side to the other; I never had my heel-strings cut to prevent my running away . . . never chained to a log and forced to drag it about, while . . . toil[ing] in the fields from morning till night . . . never branded with hot iron, or torn by bloodhounds. On the contrary, I had always been kindly treated, and tenderly cared for, until I came into the hands of Dr. Flint. I had never wished for freedom till then. But though my life in slavery was comparatively devoid of hardships, God pity the woman who is compelled to lead such a life! (96)

Despite the totalizing dehumanization inflicted by slavery, this pocket universe also allows her to express her yearning for independence. Such longing strongly represents the hope impulse. She finds a gimlet her uncle Phillip providentially left behind years ago and bores a hole "about an inch long and an inch broad" from which, hopefully, to watch her children (97). Though she sees Dr. Flint first, Jacobs now has a window to the world outside her pocket universe without anyone knowing she resides there with the exception of her grandmother, uncle, and a few others. She cannot take part in the town's activities or participate in her children's lives; but she can see and hear them, and that is enough for her to subsist and to endure the torment of "hundreds of little red insects" (97). Through this peephole, Jacobs witnesses slaves running, slaves captured, and slaves punished.

From this null space, she hears of Dr. Flint's continual search for her because of the town's expressed opinion that she must be in the North. Jacobs manipulates Dr. Flint into believing this rumor by having her friend Peter post letters from New York to her grandmother and to Dr. Flint himself. Flint even intercepts the false letter meant for Jacobs's grandmother Martha, a letter indicating that Jacobs stays in Boston and visits New York only on occasion. He rewrites the letter and delivers the fake one to Martha stating how Jacobs wants to return home for her children's sake. Nonetheless, Jacobs forces Dr. Flint to waste time, energy, and resources in visiting the Free States more than a few times, looking for her there in his desire to possess her. Jacobs pulls off the feat of existing for Dr. Flint "everywhere and nowhere, north and south" (McKittrick 42). Regardless of physical discomfort and compulsory family separation, Jacobs manages to see, know, and influence the larger world from her pocket universe without being discovered—an invisible existence, doubly ironic in her metaphoric invisibility to antebellum society and physical invisibility to the Flints, an invisibility that also provides her with surveillance opportunities. Her story functions as an afrofuturist node of resistance aiding the "two millions of women at the South, still in bondage, suffering what I suffered, and most of them far worse" (2–3). Readers discover that this pocket universe is a space already inhabited by themselves too when time-linked to the networked consciousness. In fact, Jacobs takes us into her pocket to clearly observe the difference that gender makes in terms of how slavery created a strongly black feminist influence on early afrofuturism.

Free of her loophole, Jacobs displays an uncanny consciousness of future generations of readers when she reaches across time. Jacobs both compels and disturbs us simultaneously by challenging us to consider that she was "a human being *sold* in the free city of New York! The bill of sale is on record, and future generations will learn from it that women were articles of traffic in New York, late in the nineteenth century of the Christian religion. It may hereafter prove a useful document to antiquaries who are seeking to measure the progress of civilization in the United States" (163). Imagine a slave being sold in a Free State with respect to the Fugitive Slave Act of 1850.[13] New York itself was complicit in the flesh trade. Likewise, the United States *was* not progressive then or even now in the twenty-first century. Freedom has always been an unalienable human right. Her use of italics ironizes

---

13. See Stanley W. Campbell's *The Slave Catchers: Enforcement of the Fugitive Slave Law, 1850–1860* (1972).

the moment because she should have been free from birth. Jacobs remains ahead of our time, pinging hope across the networked black consciousness.

Viewing these science-fictional pocket universes through an afrofuturism lens helps us better understand these particular slave narratives. Our knowledge of resistance and political action through physical and aesthetic means changes as Brown and Jacobs liberate themselves. They override their own personal slave experiences by anticipating their future lives in full color, queering monochrome white visions in the process and, while outside history, further expanding the networked black consciousness with each sentence, page, and chapter. Their words allow future blacks to figuratively insert themselves into the network, to self-reify, and to construct their own counternarratives in pocket universes like Twitter, Facebook, or Instagram.

Trickster Technologies

A third speculative locus exists alongside the alien-abduction and pocket-universe scenarios already laid out, where folklore and mythology combine with technology writ large to imagine, if not to actualize, the liberated futures of afrofuturism. I identify this source for hope as trickster technology, whereby slaves pragmatically applied biopolitical knowledge to manipulate their environment to their own benefit. Blackness itself provided an effective counter to the "racializing assemblages" of the antebellum South that produced "a conglomerate of sociopolitical relations that discipline humanity into full humans, not-quite-humans, and nonhumans" (Weheliye 3). Simply changing one's name represents the most basic of trickster technologies to claim a denied humanity. To illustrate my point, Frederick Bailey became Frederick Douglass and Hannah Bond became Hannah Crafts.[14] These one-time fugitive slaves deceived their pursuers with a fresh appellation while simultaneously anticipating a new existence. Such ingenuity lives at the heart of all trickster technologies, though blacks at the time were thought not to have the intelligence or guile to utilize such a fundamental ruse—that is to say, until they escaped. Instead, the general white distrust for blacks related to acquiring food, water, and sleep. If a name change signifies a trickster technology, what about simulation?

William Wells Brown affords an entirely different example of a trickster technology in the *Narrative of William W. Brown, A Fugitive Slave* (1847),

---

14. See Crafts's fictionalized account of slavery *The Bondwoman's Narrative: A Novel* (2002).

whereupon his escape from slavery depends on his ability to fool Captain and Mrs. Enoch Price. Brown promises to marry one of their enslaved women, Eliza, specially purchased for that purpose, and pretends antipathy for the Free States. Brown convinces them of his fidelity by claiming to have "never liked a free State," hence securing passage to Ohio with them on Captain Price's steamer, *The Chester* (90). While onboard the ship, Brown has an epiphany that "the trials of the past were all lost in hopes for the future" (91). He later picks up another passenger's trunk upon landing, walks up the wharf with the debarking crowd, keeps on walking directly into the woods, hides until night, and then follows the North Star to Canada and freedom. Playacting—his tricksterlike ability to dissemble—enables him to win his freedom.

Like Brown, environmental manipulation empowered Frederick Douglass himself to secure his own freedom. In his third and final narrative, *Life and Times of Frederick Douglass* (1881), which he even revised once (1892), Douglass finally provides details on how simulation aids his escape in less than twenty-four hours. In true trickster fashion, he writes, rewrites, reworks, and then revises his final slavery account, to safeguard his escape method for other potential runaway slaves and also to protect those who assisted him. About forty years pass in his carefully built and maintained simulacrum. His ability to change the self yet remain the same supports the presentism of my analysis. Douglass could well transform into us, and we could transform into him, because there is a networked black consciousness underlying the historical differences.

Without sentiment, Douglass reveals how he borrowed a sailor's protection from a friend. This protection document featured an American eagle's head and certified that its bearer was a "free American sailor" while also providing a brief physical description (*Life* 246). Douglass relates how he was fairer-skinned than his sailor friend and would not have survived close scrutiny by a white official. As Douglass states, he "relied upon [his] skill and address in playing the sailor as described in [his] protection, to do the rest" (*Life* 246). Confident in his ability to perfectly mimic sailors after having worked in the Baltimore shipyards, he hops a train for Philadelphia dressed as a sailor and fools the railroad conductors. Douglass feels secure in his "knowledge of ships and sailor's talk" enough to appear "like an 'old salt'" (*Life* 247). With words and costume only, Douglass bests the ticket-taker, who asks for freedom papers. Instead, Douglass provides the Eagle's head document and states that it carries him around the world and that he never heads to sea with his free papers. The conductor gives it a fleeting look, collects Douglass's fare, and moves on to other blacks in the segregated car. While there are other harrowing encounters on his freedom journey (a black ferryman Nichols; a man he worked for in the shipyards named Captain McGowan; and a German blacksmith who knows Douglass well and intensely eyeballs him on the second train), Douglass takes two boats and three trains as he navigates between black worlds and white worlds on the way to New York City. Ultimately, imitating a free sailor is the trick that frees Douglass. If pretending symbolizes a second trickster technology, what of the black body itself?

Thinking in terms of a black body as a third trickster technology, a raced and gendered material form performs like unconventional machinery. The objectified black body operates as a natural machine supposedly devoid of an inner life. Recall how, as noted earlier in the chapter, Harriet Jacobs insists on this very same analogy in naming slaves "God-breathing machines" (11). Such a strange cyborg metaphor uttered by an escaped slave provides the nearly invisible moment where technology and culture produce a trace of the technological trickster. It seems that Donna Haraway's metaphoric cyborg is an unrecognized trickster, with its "potent fusions" of human/animal/machine, that "transgress[es] boundaries" and introduces "dangerous possibilities" to our understanding of American slavery (295). The antithetical convergences of myth and science, nature and technology, male and female, flesh and metal, even human and animal create the eugenic cleavage from which the trickster technology emerges in afrofuturism. To be precise, the God-breathing machines function as cyborg vehicles into which any part of the networked black consciousness could just as easily be downloaded or uploaded.

The black slave who, like Frederick Douglass, exploits a "joint kinship with animals and machines" learns the power of transformation (295). Although Mr. Covey successfully breaks Douglass and we see "a man transformed into a brute," Douglass somehow overcomes his own damaged spirit, resolves to fight, and breaks free from his mental bondage by physically standing up to the slave breaker (73). His material body will follow later in this metaphoric shape-shift which demonstrates the survival tactics necessary for a trickster to resist and disrupt the systemic victimization inflicted by the South. These early cyborg instantiations feature the shape-shifting metaphor, where "partial identities as contradictory standpoints" become useful to a trickster figure (295). This trick, in itself, whereby kinds of technologized flesh subvert oppression, demonstrates the need for a science-fictional understanding of body politics.

Flesh itself becomes a trickster technology with its softness and plasticity, whether all natural or biopolitically constructed. Flesh becomes anachronistic for a shape-shifting being engaged in surviving the chaos of slavery's identity politics. In short, shape-shifting provides evidence of a trickster technology likely still in use today. Escaped slaves such as Henry Bibb and William and Ellen Craft best represent the possibilities of a trickster technology whereby this mutable and mythic figure triggers the breakdown of race and gender anxieties leading to freedom. Whatever else the trickster might be—shape-shifter or disrupter of the status quo—they are also a disassembler of meaning in our future images, translating and transferring the hope impulse into afrofuturistic code.

As a primary example, Henry Bibb shape-shifts from a black slave into a white man by utilizing his very own skin as a trickster technology. *Narrative of the Life and Adventures of Henry Bibb* (1849) demonstrates how the mulatto slave Henry Bibb recognizes the repugnant nature of the ignoble institution early in his life as a Kentucky slave. He does not know his father, only that his mother Mildred was raped by the white James Bibb, who happened to be a state senator. Taken from his mother, Bibb is lent out to work at an early age, receives multiple floggings, and is often denied enough food, sleep, and clothing as well as being forced to go barefoot on multiple occasions no matter the weather. Denied a formal education, Bibb learns and perfects the "art of running away" so well as to make "a regular business of it, and never gave it up until making it safely to Canada" where he could be a man as opposed to a thing (16–17). He continually runs and hones this skill by taking items, for example, a bridle, with him into the woods to fool white people he chanced to meet by claiming to be searching for his master's old horse. As Bibb states, his "only weapon of self defence . . . was that of deception" (17). He manipulates his social environment by practicing simulation and develops this technical ability to a fine degree.

Bibb's greatest challenge to his desire for freedom arises when he falls in love with and marries a mulatta slave named Malinda who resides on a plantation a few miles away from his own. However, determined to be free, Bibb escapes as far as Canada multiple times but returns to free his family. He is captured, escapes, is recaptured, is betrayed by both blacks and whites, and is sold, and yet always and continually he escapes many times over. As Bibb tells it, he was "notorious for running away" (95). Though I am fascinated with Bibb's unique ability as an escape artist, what most interests me concerns his first escape when he passed as a white man.

Racial passing[15] represents a deeper manipulation of social codes pertaining to black bodies *still* in existence, for example, the one-drop rule. The

---

15. For examples, see James Weldon Johnson's *The Autobiography of an Ex-Colored Man* (1912), Nella Larsen's *Passing* (1929), or a more contemporary novel such as Emily Raboteau's *The Professor's Daughter: A Novel* (2005). Likewise, see Allyson Hobbs's *A Chosen Exile: A History of Racial Passing in American Life* (2014) for relevant recent scholarship.

one-drop rule dictates that a person with one black ancestor somewhere in their family line is considered black in the United States of America. A great many blood-quantum terms such as *mulatto, quadroon, octoroon,* and *decadroon,* symbolize these blacks of mixed background, as do more popular terms such as *high yella, caramel, or redbone* to name a few more. Consequently, we should think of these terms as a hackable technology developed by prevalent nineteenth-century racial scientists. For instance, the famed Louisiana physician Samuel A. Cartwright invented "imaginary 'black' diseases whose principal symptoms seemed to be a lack of enthusiasm for slavery" (Washington 36). In "Diseases and Peculiarities of the Negro Race" (1851), Cartwright coins "drapetomania" to explain how "mental alienation" caused blacks to "abscond . . . from service" and prescribes whipping as a cure based in biblical scriptures (*Africans in America*).

Combining the absurdities of racial science and social codes, the black skin trade was entirely undercut by racial passing. In a sense, technologized skin potentially became the easiest avenue of escape. That is to say, the artificiality of this blood and tissue economy granted skin a mechanical-like texture as a racial assemblage of cultural and pseudoscientific proportions. Some blacks who were visually undistinguishable from various white ethnics because of their multi-ethnic ancestries had an advantage over their masters in that these slaves had most likely observed them all of their lives from close quarters and could impersonate them well. From such a position, anyone might see how hope and desperation, highlighted by an afrofuturist reading, impelled the drive for freedom.

In this case, Henry Bibb symbolizes one such figure. He transcends his black flesh and becomes white throughout his first successful flight to Canada. He leaves his wife and baby daughter behind—ignorant of his departure—during the Christmas period in 1837, pursuing his own liberty by first crossing the Ohio River into Madison, Indiana. While in this Free State, Bibb finds a hiding place, changes into nicer clothing, waits for nightfall, and boldly boards a Southern steamer headed further North for Cincinnati, though he "was struggling against a thousand obstacles which had clustered around [his] mind" (47). Nevertheless, Bibb "count[s] the cost, and [is] fully prepared to make the sacrifice" by "forsak[ing] friends and neighbors, wife and child" (47). At night onboard this steamboat, "surrounded by the vilest enemies of God and Man, liable to be seized and bound hand and foot by any white man, and taken back into captivity" (48), he consciously fades into the background among the deck passengers and successfully passes for a white man. Bibb declares:

This was one of the instances of my adventures that my affinity with the Anglo-Saxon race, and even slaveholders, worked well for my escape. But no thanks to them for it. While in their midst they have not only robbed me of my labor and liberty, but they have almost entirely robbed me of my dark complexion. Being so near the color of a slaveholder, they could not, or did not find me out that night among the white passengers. (49)

He manipulates his environment through deception and skin tone and makes it to Cincinnati, where he comes into contact with the Underground Railroad which then helps him reach Canada. While free in Canada, Bibb finds work, saves money, and returns to Kentucky to attempt to rescue his family, but he fails and hence initiates the recurring cycles of escape and recapture that take him all throughout the South. Bibb's spirit and his determination to be a free man radiate across time and space, "lighting up the path of freedom and revolutionizing public opinion" (204). Certainly, this single moment of racial passing demonstrates how this type of trickster technology endangers the institution of slavery for those courageous enough to exploit their own color for liberty's sake. Bibb's hope distorts the simulacrum of reality and transhistorically uploads itself onto the networked black consciousness that readers perceive and experience vicariously.

A second, perhaps stronger, model of this trickster technology at work exists in the form of a married fugitive slave couple from Georgia—Ellen and William Craft—who escaped over the Christmas season in 1848. By traveling as a white man with his black valet, hiding in plain sight, over the course of four harrowing days Ellen and William manage to take the train and ferry all the way to Philadelphia even though they are illiterate. They account for this amazing journey in their slave narrative, *Running a Thousand Miles for Freedom; Or, the Escape of William and Ellen Craft* (1860). To be clear, Ellen Craft passes for an aristocratic white man by cross-dressing while William Craft poses as his/her body servant. Utilizing the one-drop rule, the fair-skinned Ellen would be classified as a quadroon, having three white grandparents and one black grandparent. Her own white father treats her as a slave, alongside the black woman he raped, Ellen's mother, because the peculiar institution allows such situations to occur. In fact, Ellen finds herself given away "as a wedding present" at the age of eleven because her mistress "became so annoyed" at Ellen's being "frequently mistaken for a child of the family" (1). Even more peculiar, Ellen and William profess to "have known worthless white people to sell their own free children into slavery" without many people wondering "at such inhuman transactions" (4). This point of antebellum history rarely materializes, but it feels right in its abnormality and depravity. No wonder Ellen and William, and a thousand more slaves, dared to escape. They even placed their lives at risk to write about it for posterity's sake.

William first formulates the escape plan when he notes "that slave holders have the privilege of taking their slaves to any part of the country" and that his nearly white wife could "disguise herself as an invalid gentleman" attended by his slave (16). But Ellen initially thinks it "almost impossible for her to assume that disguise, and travel a distance of 1,000 miles across slave States" (16). However, she acknowledges that "the laws under which [she] lived did not recognize her to be a woman," and this recognition helps her determination to escape with her husband (16). In preparing for their jaunt to freedom, the couple buy her disguise piecemeal, while Ellen also makes her own trousers. They also acquire holiday passes from their separate masters, although they cannot read, and decide to place Ellen's right hand in a sling since travelers must sign registries for hotels and trains. Convinced that her beardless face might betray them, William ties a poultice around her head to fool white people and finally adds a pair of "green spectacles" (19). Cutting Ellen's hair represents the final step in her transformation, but none of it would have worked without her light coloration and role-playing aptitude.

Race, gender, and class all come into play during their escape. Onboard their first train, the Crafts mingle with the upper tier of Southern society and take part in the strangest of conversations. The discussion hinges on "Niggers, cotton, and the Abolitionists" (24). One stranger offers to buy William from the triple-passing Ellen during the train ride, and a second, a young military officer, gives advice on how not to spoil slaves by behaving in a mannerly way toward them as Ellen does to her husband on the second leg of their journey by steamboat. This very same officer will later unwittingly tell a crowd at the custom house that he knows that Ellen is passing as William Johnson. This claimed friendship convinces a steamboat captain to sign the register in Charleston, South Carolina, hence enabling the masquerading duo to make it to Wilmington, North Carolina, and board a second train bound for Richmond, Virginia. On the second train, the Crafts stay in a car for invalids and exchange pleasantries with an old gentleman and his three marriageable daughters. Ellen's disguise remains impenetrable as she successfully appears white, male, and genteel. Passing as a trickster technology mixes nature with performance.

On a third train, the Crafts encounter a Southern white lady who believes that "the very worst thing" for slaves is to set them free (33). The perfidy of this so-called lady astounds the Crafts because she had her slaveholding husband's will altered after his death to retain the slaves, claiming that he was not "in his right mind" in emancipating them (33). Aside from a Yankee officer giving them a bit of trouble as they board a fourth train in Baltimore, the Crafts experience little more adversity on their journey. William falls asleep in the baggage car from all of the tension and nearly misses the ferryboat across the Susquehanna River to the final train as a frantic Ellen tries to enlist train attendants to find him. They arrive in Philadelphia early in the morning on Christmas Day; lodge in a house on the Underground Railroad, where they get their first lesson in reading; and move on to Boston a few weeks later. Two years later Congress passes the Fugitive Slave Act of 1850, and the Crafts flee to England for the next twenty years. In traditional trickster fashion, the Crafts profit from their innovative escape to liberty by repeatedly performing it for abolitionist audiences on both sides of the Atlantic. They laugh best at this racial joke.

The technology of passing as a trickster creates an opportunity for us to think of free worlds for some black people if not others. Passing allows for the possibility of shape-shifting as a matter of biology, fortitude, and situational intelligence, whereby a person socially defined as black, like Henry Bibb or Ellen Craft, can disappear from sight as a survival strategy. Passing establishes a trickster technology to disrupt man-made systems of oppression like race, gender, and class. Once these identity markers become mutable through a reinterpreted technological sense, which can be imagined only through afrofuturism, this trickster technology has license to effect societal change, to perhaps release humanity from the constraints of identity politics, and to practice being human.

To reiterate, afrofuturism makes a trickster technology possible. Scholars and folklorists identify the trickster through mythologies produced by the oral traditions of various cultures throughout the world. Such recognition places this global figure squarely in the realm of fantasy, a genre in terms of how we think of literature today as being separate from SF because it focuses on magic and monsters in juxtaposition to science and technology. Subsequently, African-descended peoples enslaved in the United States developed their own trickster tales based on remembered African folk traditions which are passed down generations by word of mouth—tales in which weak (animal/human) characters overcome their more powerful opponents by outthinking them. While being "a source of humor" around campfires after long hours in the fields, trickster tales also convey "serious commentary on the inequities of existence in a country where the promises of democracy were denied to a large portion of the citizenry, a pattern that becomes even clearer in the literary adaptations of trickster figures" (T. Harris, "The Trickster in African American Literature").

For example, Henry Bibb and Ellen Craft dupe other people, shape-shift, and use their minds to outwit white society to escape their dystopian existence as slaves. They make use of their epidermal layer, a prohibited alternative identity generated by the pseudoscientific beliefs of the day related to the idea of racial contamination through sex. This trickster instantiation results in a *skin technology* that further melds the human and the machine into a miscegenation of a black cyborgian body capable of temporarily (or permanently) crossing the artificially erected racial boundary. In effect, the body becomes so plastic that anybody's consciousness could be uploaded into it. Bibb and Craft literally separate their race from their bodies to steal themselves away North for their own benefit, if not black posterity. They assume the default whiteness, defining the United States in a national sense irrespective of antebellum regions and manipulating the biological machineness ascribed to their flesh by owners for control and for profit. In fact, they *afro-engineer* themselves.

Skin technology supplies the trickster with exchange mobility, yet such argumentation still does not designate the narrative as SF. This liminal being, the trickster, cannot cross over into rigid definitions of SF governed by notions of today's technoculture. Therefore, the trickster cannot exist within SF. But afrofuturism describes "both an artistic aesthetic and a framework for critical theory [that] combines elements of science fiction, historical fiction, speculative fiction, fantasy, Afrocentricity, and magic realism with non-Western beliefs" (Womack 9). This expansive definition, offered by Ytasha Womack, recognizes how black writers use science and technology in ways different from a technocultural understanding, thus opening up the SF genre for inclusion of contemporary black writers like Tananarive Due and N. K. Jemisin, among others,[16] who all make afrofuturistic worlds. But this inclusion does not stop in the twenty-first century; it stretches back across time and space, linking to the transhistorical feedback loop. This updated afrofuturism challenges the weird diminishment that happens with Dery's original definition, a strange leveling effect caused by American perceptions

---

16. The acclaimed horror writer Tananarive Due's *My Soul to Keep* (1997) introduces a secretive group of undying Ethiopian men with advanced science, technology, music, and knowledge in her African Immortals series. Magic and science coexist in N. K. Jemisin's *The Fifth Season* (2015), in which a geologically unstable supercontinent experiences catastrophic seismic activity on a frequent basis and her characters terrifyingly navigate the volatile land looking for sanctuary from a xenophobic society and for control of the earth-science/magic orogeny.

of technoscience and its influence on our contemporary culture, perceptions that thereby exclude things deemed the fantastic. As fanciful as it sounds, racial passing demonstrates factual shape-shifting as the ultimate trickster technology.

The various slave narratives explored here present types of shape-shifting as a trickster technology that revises ideologies of difference with respect to race, gender, and class. This trickster technology repeatedly and reflexively violated strict codes of antebellum society governing how blacks were to live and experience difference. Quite simply, passing induced fear, particularly a fear of miscegenation which was not legally dispelled until the Supreme Court's 1967 *Loving v. Virginia* verdict. Put another way, the racial optics of passing fueled white and black anxieties well before the enactment of legal segregation by the Supreme Court's 1896 *Plessy v. Ferguson* decision as evinced by slave narratives and mid-nineteenth-century fictions featuring passing, such as Lydia Maria Child's "The Quadroons" (1842), Harriet Beecher Stowe's *Uncle Tom's Cabin* (1852), and William Wells Brown's *Clotel; or the President's Daughter* (1853). The combination of myth and science produced this technology that, in turn, helps us understand the painful trajectory of humanity in a world divided by pseudoscience and religion. No wonder the adaptable identity politics necessary to live in these separate, artificial black worlds and white worlds provoked, and continue to provoke, black writers to construct mythologies that converge in a technospiritual world. Trickster technologies continue to challenge a white patriarchal and supremacist culture and supply us with hope through the networked black consciousness.

Though the nineteenth, twentieth, twenty-first centuries occupy different interims in time, race and racism continue to define American reality. In this respect, afrofuturism, interpreted as a black science-fictional experience akin to alien-abduction and other SF metaphors, remains deeply entrenched in New World history, particularly that of the United States. "The great force of history," according to celebrated black writer James Baldwin, "comes from the fact that we carry it within us, are unconsciously controlled by it in many ways, and history is literally *present* in all that we do" (*The Price of the Ticket* 410). As such, afrofuturism draws attention to racial difference to better address the past and present of black/white race relations in order to imagine different and multiple black futures. This historical past is the prerequisite to these imagined futures. The hope offered by afrofuturism might also be construed as utopian. Without negating the material, historical, and cultural conditions under which black identities have been manufactured, afrofuturism suggests, or perhaps produces, new meanings for this difference: a new blackness itself by hoping and healing, by voicing the unspeakable and unthinkable—black sovereignty and being—into future worlds with future technologies.

This chapter maps a few of the ways an afrofuturist reading can reappropriate science-fictional tools and apply them to cultural critique and liberation. The value of reading slave narratives through an afrofuturist lens rests in demonstrating how such science-fictional metaphors can operate as technologies of resistance. Retroactively applying an afrofuturist lens onto slave narratives is useful in opening up the science-fictional context of antebellum America for deeper exploration and in making a new case for afrofuturist readings that go beyond authorial intent (and beyond the usual, sometimes kneejerk, sorts of politics these readings often produce). Specifically, value can be found in reading slave narratives as part of a larger networked consciousness in order to emphasize the "transhistorical" reach of afrofuturist thought, to repeat my earlier contentions in my *performing* this chapter's very argument. By reading these early black writings through an afrofuturist lens, the chapter *creates* a transhistorical feedback loop between past, present, and future, essentially signal-boosting this black networked consciousness, this afrofuturism.

To conclude, we cannot appreciate afrofuturism without a deep understanding of early America because it safeguards "peoples of African descent, their ways and histories, [and ensures they] will not disappear in any credible future" (Kilgore, "Afrofuturism" 569). Throughout the first half of this book, I have examined colonial and antebellum writing in order to extend afrofuturism's literary history backward in time—to reflect the afrofuturist vista and the possibility of freedom. Afrofuturism's lineage is significantly lengthier than Mark Dery admits, with its roots extending as far back as the seventeenth century. A dark energy of sorts, to evoke the physics concept, permeates all that is the United States of America from its beginning to its present. This hope impulse dates back to the August 20, 1619, arrival of the first black slaves in British North America. Tracing and tying this hope impulse to key historical rebellions, figures, political moments, and slave narratives allows us to witness how black people, networked together, emerged from the brink of slavery's slow apocalypse in the United States. This hope impulse results in the literature to come, where twentieth-century black writers display the courage to look past the tragedy of slavery, present visions of potential Americas, and envision a future for their people.

PART II

Afrofuturism and Classic Twentieth-Century African American Novels

CHAPTER 4

BLACK BODIES IN SPACE

Zora Neale Hurston's *Their Eyes Were Watching God*

ZORA NEALE HURSTON'S novel *Their Eyes Were Watching God* (1937) concerns the thrice-married Janie Crawford-Killicks-Starks-Woods. In her story she navigates the color line from Eatonville to the Everglades and back, seeking love and acceptance in places where dozens and blues get played on porches and in jook joints. Described by literary scholars as a black feminist text, a model of Southern literature, and a folk romance,[1] the "folk romance" designation is highly appropriate. At the same time, however, the novel is more than the sum of its parts. In fact, Hurston's novel also incorporates many of the elements of afrofuturism. This incredible notion depends on accepting that in afrofuturism we have a present-day mode of folklore, a tool for interrogating black existence, its dark matter, its reality, and its alternatives. In this respect, afrofuturism sternly exhorts us to bring our racial memories into the future as Hurston does. Hence, I am rethinking *Their Eyes* as a classic in regard to afrofuturism.

Hurston is not readily associated with SF, even though she was a social scientist in her own right who conducted ethnographic research as a partici-

---

1. As representative examples, see Carla Kaplan's "The Erotics of Talk: 'The Oldest Human Longing' in *Their Eyes Were Watching God*" (1995), Martyn Bone's "The (Extended) South of Black Folk: Intraregional and Transnational Migrant Labor in *Jonah's Gourd Vine* and *Their Eyes Were Watching God*" (2007), and Ann duCille's "The Intricate Fabric of Feeling: Romance and Resistance in *Their Eyes Were Watching God*" (1990).

pant-observer, research that resulted in works such as *Mules and Men* (1935) and *Tell My Horse: Voodoo and Life in Haiti and Jamaica* (1938).[2] As early as 1935, in addition to a camera she used a tape recorder, a new technology in the early twentieth century, to store audio on a magnetic tape for many of her folkloric explorations.[3] Hurston's scientific training transformed her fiction because the recordings helped with the sense of authentic orality she captures in her writing. In this way, Hurston embraced an afrofuturist methodology to record folklore and forge it into fiction for future generations to hear.

Although long read as a folk romance, *Their Eyes Were Watching God* can be usefully recast or repositioned as an afrofuturist romance. After all, while she was attending Columbia University, Hurston was formally trained as a folklorist with the famed anthropologist Franz Boas; thus, she mirrors another early afrofuturist, W. E. B Du Bois,[4] who blends social science and creative writing "to generate counter-histories that reweave connections between past, present, and future," counter-histories that affirm a black vitality in American culture that has long been ignored (Yaszek, "An Afrofuturist Reading of Ralph Ellison's *Invisible Man*" 299). In other words, the value of reading *Their Eyes Were Watching God* through the critical lens of SF and SF theory is that doing so repositions the novel as an exploration of a utopian horizon of possibility that takes the reader beyond history into something new—an afrofuturist condition wherein folklore and futurity are at the center of black imaginings.

Such a reading constitutes a valuable and necessary intervention into Hurston studies and afrofuturism, two fields that otherwise have had little to say to one another. In fact, no interaction between scholarship on Hurston and scholarship on afrofuturism has occurred because most scholars believe that afrofuturism only concerns black uses for technology. Perhaps this is why Hurston's contemporaries Du Bois and George S. Schuyler garner critical attention from academics in SF circles—their use of fantastical imagery in *Dark Princess: A Romance* (1928) and in *Black No More* (1931), respectively.[5]

---

2. See Lori Jirousek's "Ethnics and Ethnographers: Zora Neale Hurston and Anzia Yezierska" (2006).

3. See Laura K. Crawley and Joseph C. Hikerson's "Zora Neale Hurston: Recordings, Manuscripts, Photographs, and Ephemera" in the Library of Congress's American Folklife Center (2014).

4. See Du Bois's *The Quest of the Silver Fleece* (1911).

5. In *Dark Princess,* Du Bois expands color-line politics by using fantastical imagery, in which his black protagonist, Mathew Towns, seeks to unite the darker races of the world to end imperialism. In *Black No More,* black scientist Dr. Junius Crookman solves the American race dilemma, but not without consequences, by inventing a skin-whitening process that turns black people white.

While Hurston keeps use of traditional technology to a minimum in *Their Eyes Were Watching God*, she directly taps into black people's desire for a better life and a better future and thus provides an essential urge to challenge oppression, which is also essential to afrofuturism. Revisiting Hurston's novel in terms of afrofuturism changes what we know about African American historical and cultural conditions and what we know about race as an oppression technology. Hope, optimism, and future-looking visions have always existed in black literature against the backdrop of white supremacy. Afrofuturism teaches us to see these things in texts like *Their Eyes Were Watching God* better than we have before. Therefore, this chapter describes and defines the ways in which afrofuturism illuminates how the novel turns to folklore to transform black historical being. I contend that in Hurston's novel, not only does folklore function to record and preserve aspects of a black cultural past, but it is also central to projecting into the future.

While afrofuturism's originator stresses technoculture and recognizes Samuel R. Delany as its first practitioner,[6] the theory "does have a literary pedigree that is rather longer than [Mark] Dery acknowledges" according to De Witt D. Kilgore ("Afrofuturism" 563). Kilgore offers Sheree R. Thomas's *Dark Matter: A Century of Speculative Fiction from the African Diaspora* (2000) as convincing proof while suggesting that "a core value of afrofuturism" is "to imagine futures directed by the survival and even the resurgence of black people and their cultures, experiences, and designs" ("Afrofuturism" 563). *Their Eyes Were Watching God* displays the futurist—nay, the afrofuturist—perspective that has come to define SF, but it merely deploys these longings in a text now more readily accepted as mainstream American fiction. These leanings are perhaps nowhere more evident than in the framing tale when utopian longing, a longing that is at the core of much SF, emanates from the interrelated images of ships, horizons, and the future.

The cosmic opening paragraph of *Their Eyes* establishes a future-oriented vision with its imagery of ships and horizons: "Ships at a distance have every man's wish on board. For some they come in with the tide. For others they sail forever on the horizon, never out of sight, never landing, until the Watcher turns his eyes away in resignation, his dreams mocked to death by Time. That is the life of men" (1). Switching to the dreams of women, this futurist theme continues: "Now, women forget all those things they don't want to remember, and remember everything they don't want to forget. The dream is the truth. Then they act and do things accordingly" (1). Hurston suggests the horizon is ever unattainable for most men and women.

---

6. See Delany's early work such as *The Jewels of Aptor* (1962), *The Ballad of Beta-2* (1965), or *Babel-17* (1966).

For black folk, however, weighed down by stereotypes and oppression in a white world, obtaining this vista is nigh impossible. But Janie sees her dreams and goes after them anyway. A future horizon exists in this novel that has not been explored, where literalized metaphors, characteristic of SF, help explain a problematic black social experience. African Americans, who seemingly have no future, turn to folklore to create one, breaking the protocols of a raced reality.

Drawing on Delany as a theorist helps explain how Hurston's novel can be retroactively read through an afrofuturist lens using such metaphors. Delany's theory allows us to see figurative language in the novel as science fictional, allowing the much-studied novel to do things that it otherwise could not do, namely, reading Janie's travels as a version of planetary romance[7] in which she shuttles between different imagined versions of black community and its future. While this thought seems to be in contrast to folk romance, I mean to suggest a way of thinking about folklore as a mode through which this afrofuturist vision is enabled.[8] Delany models a literalized metaphor with the sentence "the red sun is high, the blue low" in his classic essay, "About 5,750 Words," by examining each word of a sentence in his line-by-line corrective reading process called subjunctivity (*The Jewel-Hinged Jaw* 7). As Delany claims, "The particular verbal freedom of SF, coupled with the corrective process [subjunctivity] that allows the whole range of the physically explainable universe, can produce the most violent leaps of imagery. For not only does it throw us worlds away, it specifies how we got there" (*Jewel* 12). Consequently, subjunctivity captures the style

---

7. An adventure story set on one or more alien worlds, a planetary romance features a distinctive physical sociocultural environment between which a heroic protagonist quests, often by a spaceship or by other means such as astral projection. Edgar Rice Burroughs's eleven-novel Barsoom series (1912–43), beginning with *A Princess of Mars* (1917), quickly comes to mind as a relevant example of the genre. Likewise, Tobias Buckell perhaps provides the best afrofuturistic example with his Xenowealth series, opening with *Crystal Rain* (2006), showcasing the black cyborg mercenary Pepper and his world-hopping. Inasmuch as Janie travels between black spaces and white spaces searching for a better tomorrow, Hurston's novel functions like a planetary romance.

8. I must stress that SF itself is a form of romantic fiction. Mark Rose insists that "we expect to hear of marvels and adventures in strange places populated" by strange beings and that "science fiction achieves the distancing of romance by setting its narratives in the future" (8). And Janie certainly has such adventures as she navigates the black worlds and white worlds of her time-space as Hurston "fuse[s] history and myth into a new reality that enshrines blacks' efforts to maintain their humanity despite the forces acting on them" (J. Campbell ix). For me, at least, reading *Their Eyes* as a planetary romance is not off the mark for afrofuturism.

of SF through the genre's language distortion and penchant for literalized metaphors.

The meaning of a sentence like "'Ah done been tuh de horizon and back and now Ah kin set heah in mah house and live by comparisons," taken from *Their Eyes,* becomes unmistakably afrofuturist (182). The term *horizon* generates the subjunctive tension of this sentence because it suggests an alternate trajectory for Janie, another world where she finds happiness and acceptance down in the Muck, in a migrant community named Belle Glade. This experience of a utopian reality revises the sense of space-time travel of "been tuh" and "back" while Janie tells her best friend, Pheoby Watson, all about her journeys. Finally, Janie can sit in her house "and live by comparisons" because she can distinguish between the dystopian reality of Eatonville with her utopian perspective of the Muck, and she can now determine her own future trajectory. The final chapter completes the afrofuturist vision of the novel when going back to her frame narrative, when Janie also declares, "It's uh known fact, Pheoby, you got tuh *go* there tuh *know* there'" (183). Janie awakens to the possibility of something better through her intentional storytelling. The afrofuturist mindset is the "the horizon of potentiality" (60) that Edmund Husserl describes, because our daily decisions consciously impact the future in a lifetime process that Janie recognizes and voices by novel's end. She has literally been to and back from the horizon itself. Something afrofuturist happens here when ships, horizons, and "going there" are an integral part of Hurston's much-lauded use of folklore, in which she privileges the speculative over the technological in her depiction of black spaces within the white world.⁹

Afrofuturist Discourse

Although realistic modes of writing may be the best way of expressing the vicissitudes of black experience in America, many black writers have wanted to go beyond the realism of race and racism. A case in point, after being broken by the slave breaker Mr. Covey, Frederick Douglass evokes the supernatural when gazing out at the white sails of ships on Chesapeake Bay. In his yearning for freedom, Douglass proclaims, "Those beautiful vessels, robed in purest white, so delightful to the eye of freemen, were to me so many shrouded ghosts, to terrify and torment me with thoughts of my wretched

---

9. See Deborah Clarke, Laura Dubek, and Rosemary V. Hathaway as recent examples.

condition" (74). Then he declares, "You are freedom's swift-winged angels, that fly round the world; I am confined in bands of iron!" (74). While ghosts and angels connote paranormal desire and spiritual conveyance, the ships themselves denote technology and physical transportation to freedom. Later in this passage, Douglass avows that "there is a better day coming" (75). Such a statement can be easily understood as afrofuturism because Douglass speaks of both near and far future here—freedom for himself and freedom for his race. As Toni Morrison believes, "Black slavery enriched the country's creative possibilities" (*Playing* 38). In fact, the creative and critical possibilities of afrofuturism can be traced back even earlier to Phillis Wheatley's "angelic train" (403). Finding the future in the past should be a core tenet of this critical theory. Intertextual links, however inadvertent, provide a clear impression of the multivalent networked consciousness necessary to sustain and propel black artistry through various oppressions in America.

In any case, afrofuturism is merely the extension of a lengthy process of alternative imaginings for a black-oriented future; for example, early alternative futures include the insurrection novel *Blake, or the Huts of America* and the black separatist utopian *Imperium in Imperio,* as previously discussed in the second chapter. Afrofuturism is, then, a long-standing desire for going beyond racial limitations; it makes black worlds possible through the hope for a better tomorrow, something Fredric Jameson, in speaking more broadly about utopia, calls "Utopian desire and the substance of its hope" (84). In other words, afrofuturism produces a grammar for this desire; it concerns the desire to go beyond the historical and cultural conditions of the African diaspora. At the same time, if "there is an Afro-futurism, it must be sought in unlikely places, constellated from far-flung points" (Dery, "Black to the Future" 738). *Their Eyes Were Watching God* is just such a "far-flung" constellation because it parallels reality: It reflects the crushing, interlocking oppressions of racism and sexism during the Jim Crow era, and yet, significantly, it also offers hope for black Americans—hope for the future and the social changes that could come with it.

Hurston's novel qualifies as a work that can be read as if it were a SF text, if not an afrofuturist one, because of how science-fictional markers such as parallel worlds, psionic powers, and alien encounters repeat themselves here and intertextually resonate with other afrofuturist texts like Schuyler's *Black No More,* Ellison's *Invisible Man,* and Octavia Butler's *Wild Seed* (1980). These texts all have in common an aesthetic resistance to segregation, the literal alienation of a black people historically dislocated by Western ideas of progress, a reclamation of both past and future histories, and black uses for technoscience—all basic tenets of the afrofuturist movement itself. Just a brief comparison between Hurston's novel and Nalo Hopkinson's *Midnight Robber* (2000) reveals that both authors use alienated black women as main characters, and dialectal speech, networked consciousness, folklore, and black world spaces to convey the richness of black cultures in the New World. At its heart, afrofuturism provides "unique analytical frameworks for interpreting black cultural production, as imagery of the near-future" (Nelson, "Introduction" 9). *Their Eyes* is certainly no different, but understanding how Hurston's novel fits into an afrofuturist canon is a different matter entirely.

Throughout the novel, Janie searches for an alternative world other than the one that African Americans were living in at the time. *Their Eyes Were Watching God* has real-life correlatives in the twentieth-century Back to Africa Movement of the Harlem Renaissance and Pan-Africanism, as well as nineteenth-century emigration movements such as the settlement of Liberia by former slaves. Thus, a pseudo-utopian afrofuturist desire was palpable when Hurston was writing the novel, and it infuses her narrative on nearly every level. After all, in her day, Hurston confronted "mythic and historical pasts in order to describe livable futures" (Kilgore, "Beyond the History We Know" 120); thus, Hurston's infusion of folklore with the daily realities of black life makes her novel suitably estranging and ideally suited for an afrofuturist reading. In other words, as an aesthetic register, afrofuturism effectively draws attention to the potential exploration of black cultural memories rooted in thoughts of tomorrow. It allows us to restructure our reading experience of Hurston's novel through the defamiliarization germane to SF in order to explore black cultural spaces.

A good example is the communal bonding and renewal that transpires every time the dozens game is played on the porch of Joe Starks's store. As Trudier Harris maintains, "Porch traditions created a similarity of experience in telling and hearing that became a part of the oral tradition, indeed almost a folk form itself" (*The Power of the Porch* xiii). The big talkers can literally speak things into existence. Matt Bonner's yellow mule becomes a popular subject: Eatonville residents, like Sam, Lige, and Walter, talk about the mule so much that the townsfolk anthropomorphize it as they collaborate and interact. In this world it is perfectly natural for a mule to be counted as an inhabitant. Joe Starks buys the mule and frees it in a grand gesture. For the first time, Janie speaks in public and puts words to thought in complimenting Joe's kindness, creating a visual thought-picture for the town folk to synesthetically hear/see. She states, "Freein' dat mule makes uh mighty big man outa you. Something like George Washington and Lincoln. Abraham Lincoln, he had de whole United States tuh rule so he freed de Negroes.

You got uh town so you freed uh mule'" (*Their Eyes* 54–55). The town even gives the mule a funeral of sorts, with Joe Starks eulogizing this dead honorary citizen out in the swamp while standing on its "distended belly" (57). As Henry Louis Gates Jr. believes, "The myths [Hurston] describes so accurately are in fact 'alternative modes for perceiving reality,' and never just condescending depictions of the quaint" ("Afterword: Zora Neale Hurston" 192). In fact, this alternate mode of knowing becomes possible only by constructing this simulated auditory engagement through afrofuturism.

Networked Consciousness

One of the black cultural spaces under interrogation in *Their Eyes Were Watching God* and afrofuturism more generally is the relationship between mechanization and black bodies. But such a claim requires that we turn our eyes away from more-conventional technologies that appear in the novel (e.g., the lamppost that Joe lights so ceremoniously in Eatonville, and the land-use practices that have converted the swampland of the Muck into sites of agribusiness) and see how a networked consciousness develops. Despite the long tradition of critiques of Hurston as a nostalgic romantic with no interest in modernity,[10] recent work (like Martyn Bone's *American Literature* article, "The (Extended) South of Black Folk," on migrant labor in Hurston's fiction) details the extent to which she maps the *living* circuits that capital carved into the southeast. Discussion of black bodies as these living circuits, in essence, occurs only from an afrofuturistic standpoint, where the black body is a dehumanized "muscle-machine" as Kobena Mercer claims (138). Janie's time in the Everglades with her third husband, Tea Cake, harvesting "cane and string-beans and tomatuhs" for the white man, illustrates the point (122). They "work all day for the money" with "the rich black earth clinging to [their] bodies" (125) while their "house [becomes] a magnet, the unauthorized center of the 'job'" where music, dice, big talk, laughter, and fun bond the black migrant community together (126). This interconnectedness, this metaphorical circuitry, between black folk is necessary for the smooth operation of work in the fields regardless of their exploitation.

More significantly, Hurston produced a social science fiction that engages our emotion to provide a plausible explanation for black behavior in a white world on one level, and to explore the potential and consequences of par-

---

10. For instance, see Stuart Burrows or Leigh Ann Duck.

allel black worlds on a second level. As a way of our experiencing reality, *Their Eyes* concerns the interpersonal relationships of a black society, a "networked consciousness" predating the web, subject to white interference at any time (Nelson, "Introduction" 10). This networked consciousness was winked into existence in the dark, dank holds of slave ships en route to the Americas, as already remarked upon in my introduction. The very future survival of a dislocated race necessitated the development of this consciousness. Black communities became sustainable because mentoring, collaboration, inventiveness, encouragement, motivation, and rapport, among other things, were made available to members plugged into the network which was regulated by afrofuturistic folkways.

Seen through the lens of afrofuturism, Hurston uses segregation to envision the black world spaces of Eatonville and Belle Glade, better known as the Muck. A segregated township is another world all to itself. As early as 1852, nineteenth-century black abolitionist writer Martin R. Delany rightfully claimed:

> That there have in all ages, in almost every nation, existed a nation within a nation—a people who although forming a part and parcel of the population, yet were from force of circumstances, known by the peculiar position they occupied, forming in fact, by the deprivation of political equality with others, no part, and if any, but a restricted part of the body politic of such nations is also true. (*The Condition* 258)

In his 1934 "A Negro Nation within a Nation" speech, Du Bois notes that "this matter of a nation within a nation has already been partially accomplished" (177). Both Delany and Du Bois recognized that few white Americans cared about their black counterparts or their very existence as second-class citizens because people of African descent were typically stereotyped as savage and primitive in all forms of popular culture, vestigial to progress. Embattled, African Americans came together against an incessant white supremacy to foster a sense of communal value, a networked consciousness strong enough to resist white constructions of blackness.

Hurston's Eatonville functions as a parallel black world coexisting with the larger universe that is the United States (or the state of Florida), displaced from the white township of Maitland by the color line. Not truly separate from Maitland since many of Eatonville's inhabitants work for the whites by day, Eatonville is largely left alone by the whites as if it is hidden. With sundown, Hurston describes a fantastic transformation among the townsfolk into a self-sufficient networked consciousness:

> It was the time for sitting on porches beside the road. It was the time to hear things and talk. These sitters had been tongueless, earless, eyeless conveniences all day long. Mules and other brutes had occupied their skins. But now, the sun and the bossman were gone, so the skins felt powerful and human. They became lords of sounds and lesser things. (1)

Their shifted shapes are free of the white oppressive gaze that makes animals of them as they revert back to their black bodies in Hurston's literalized metaphor. They become human in this parallel world as opposed to being alien to themselves in the racist one by linking into the black community. The townsfolk no longer have to wear masks; they no longer have to tread carefully in their own town. Consequently, this separation allows a space where blacks can be together and envision a future of their own. Black folklore, conducive to an operational networked black consciousness, thrives in Eatonville because its inhabitants are translocated nightly beyond the cares of the white world into a world where they are free to speak, act, and love; to enact social privileges and behave as equals to one another; to construct identity absent the terrible white presence. Folklore orders past, present, and future in this black community by generating social cohesion. Transformative cultural retentions are produced by telling stories. Indeed, Eatonville, Florida, is an afrotopia for most of its citizens in that it frees up imaginative energy.

Without the vision of Joe Starks, however, Eatonville might not have become a haven for its residents. He performs a feat of cultural engineering in his community-building by deliberately constructing the town's communal relationships, thereby creating the necessary social cohesion for a networked consciousness. Before setting foot in the community that will become Eatonville, he has plans to run the town as it is being developed, "buying in big" because "De man dat built things oughta boss it. Let colored folks build things too if dey wants to crow over somethin'" (27). On first arriving with Janie, Joe makes his presence immediately felt, organizing the "mensfolk" together to "form a committee" to "get things movin'," and projecting himself as a powerful, big-voiced man capable of getting things done (33). In quick succession, Joe names the town, instantly quadruples its size by purchasing two hundred acres of land with cash, builds a store, procures a post office, personally recruits other black families to move to Eatonville, and incorporates the town "lak every other town" before becoming its mayor (40). Except a black town is not like every other town in this era since it is nearly one of a kind, separate from the white world. Only a few of the town's male inhabitants, like Hicks, are even vaguely disturbed by Joe's rapid success because they are already "used to the world one way and then suddenly have it turn different" (36). This difference creates another world, a black planet with a store as its political and social hub. Indeed, Joe Starks, "as the Mayor—postmaster—landlord—storekeeper," literally builds the networked consciousness of Eatonville's citizens from the ground up (44). Hurston's Eatonville offers a place of racial solidarity, where blacks escape from and resist the constant abuses of the white world; display intelligence, jocularity, and aliveness; and share collective experiences.

Despite the racial restrictions beyond Eatonville, Joe Starks is able to accomplish his vision—to build and govern a black planet. The town's citizens congregate on the steps of his store to pass the time playing checkers, telling tall tales, and courting when they are not buying anything. Joe provides stability through his leadership, creating a town different from its surrounding white environs in that there are no white folks telling them what to do. Eatonville is its own world, one in which vernacular technology encodes a black generational experience—folklore and stories across racial geographies—comprising this networked consciousness. But without a functioning networked consciousness, vernacular technologies would not be perceived as a central component of Hurston's use of folklore which allows for the reworking of past-present-future so vital to afrofuturism.

Vernacular Technology

Hurston produced an unsurpassed vernacular technology[11] by taking folk elements—such as telling tall tales, playing the dozens, speechifying, and sermonizing—and fusing them with depictions of rural Southern society and segregation. As mentioned earlier, Hurston tape-recorded vernacular speech as a part of her folkloric studies and transferred it to her fiction. I define *vernacular technology* as an archive of structures of oral knowledge that have been captured in print, thereby standardizing past cultural practices and preserving them for the future. In reference to African American print culture of the nineteenth century, Grey Gundaker claims, "Vernacular resources offered other possibilities for transforming, improving, or opting out of intolerable situations and for making print a part of African American lives on their own terms" (495). Gundaker's point is that historically, Afri-

---

11. See Houston Baker's *Blues, Ideology, and Afro-American Literature: A Vernacular Theory* (1984) and Henry Louis Gates Jr.'s *The Signifying Monkey: A Theory of Afro-American Literary Criticism* (1988) for examples of scholars who have used the vernacular tradition to theorize about African American literature.

can Americans have turned to print to capture the vernacular—a melding of oral and print cultures. Hurston allows her readers to listen to Janie tell her story with all its folksy black stuff and to experience her social world as a distinctly black Southern aesthetic. Reading and listening fuse as "the preferred mode of knowing" because "the circulation of meanings can be contained within a clearly bounded cultural locale" (Dubey 177). The vernacular technology in *Their Eyes Were Watching God,* among other texts,[12] comprises chronicles of *progress* recuperated from the past and offers direct evidence of afrofuturism. More than simple awareness of dialogue in dialect, the memory and the repetition involved in storytelling function as a native science, outside the bounds of Western notions of science, and exemplify vernacular technology, a triple weaving of the ocular, oral, and aural.

Through vernacular technology, Hurston's folk romance morphs into an afrofuturist text in which afrofuturism encourages readers to reconsider black mythologies of the past that were generated by a white supremacist culture which told blacks who they were. In part, this morphing "requires a voice that can make you see, a voice that celebrates the visible presence of black bodies" (Clarke 600). Thus, Hurston's world-building responds to the challenges of an oppressive society with her prescriptions for the future; her world-building is dependent on vernacular technology as characters' storytelling brings the parallel world to life, particularly during porch scenes. Vernacular technologizing occurs in the lacunae between the written and spoken words of the text. Pregnant with meaning, these blank spaces represent a soundscape, one in which I assume readers wonder about the intonations, inflections, pitch range, dialects, verbal play, improvisation, and performance of the characters. Vernacular technology allows for extrasensory perception (ESP) to exist. ESP is a general label given to describe a range of unsubstantiated, pseudoscientific mental powers that operate beyond the natural senses. ESP (or psi powers) "repackages folkloristic notions of 'second sight' or a 'sixth sense' in scientific jargon" (Clute and Nicholls 390). Such a reframing suits a close reading of Hurston's novel. As a professional folklorist, Hurston, who collected more than a few supernatural stories,[13] saturates her novels with a sense of orality, creating an orature in which knowledge transmission occurs almost without language. Telepathy is one example that can be found in *Their Eyes.*

---

12. Other texts that utilize vernacular technology include Ernest Gaines's *The Autobiography of Miss Jane Pittman* (1971), Toni Morrison's *Beloved* (1987), and Gloria Naylor's *Mama Day* (1988).

13. See Hurston's *Mules and Men* and *Tell My Horse.*

Hurston employs mind reading as a literalized metaphor in Eatonville's parallel world, particularly when its citizens are playing dozens at the store. Hurston writes, "When the people sat around on the porch and passed around the pictures of their thoughts for the others to look at and see, it was nice" (48). As another means of handling segregation, Eatonville's citizens become adept at storytelling. They become so talented at telling stories that it is as if they become telepathic. These "thought pictures" as "crayon enlargements of life" are indicative of direct mind-to-mind communication (48). There is something going on here that speaks to community—a shared vision, a shared perspective, that might come as a result of the oppression they face. At the very least, Hurston applies vernacular technology to project a positive black communal identity, one in which blacks, networked together, can trust reality for themselves.

Vernacular technology comes into play, quite heavily, during porch scenes in *Their Eyes*. Readers can perceive the sonic resonances of these porch sessions with the imagery flying round, dozens being played, and whoppers being told. Again, the hyperbole surrounding Matt Bonner's mule provides a strong example because "everybody indulged in mule talk" to such an extent that the mule "was next to the Mayor in prominence, and made better talking" (48, 50). I believe Hurston's audience instinctively knows and feels that vernacular technology allows the characters' access to a networked consciousness, a subversive black subjectivity, much like the grandfather's in Ellison's *Invisible Man*,[14] that counters the alienation they experience while working for whites during the day. As Philip Joseph states, "The mule draws attention to its value as an abundant source of self renewal and creative expression" (469). I can only assume the reader shares in the imagined declarations of free black people as these stories are told. Hurston is purposefully "adjusting the temporal logics that condemned black subjects to prehistory" (Eshun, "Further" 297).

Like most of Eatonville's citizens, Janie also learns to use telepathy as a coping device. Janie first witnesses the downside of this telepathic power through Joe, who exploits it by "cuffin' folks around in their minds" maintaining his own big-headedness (82). She then learns this psi power through Joe, who, grown old, begins to feel his own mortality. Joe calls Janie "uh ole hen" and insists that she come "off the croquet grounds" because croquet is "somethin' for de young folks" (73). Janie thinks to herself, "If he thought

---

14. From his death-bed, the narrator's grandfather states: "Son, after I'm gone I want you to keep up the good fight. I never told you, but our life is a war and I have been a traitor all my born days, a spy in the enemy's country ever since I give up my gun back in the Reconstruction" (Ellison 16).

to deceive her, he was wrong. For the first time she could see a man's head naked of its skull. Saw the cunning thoughts race in and out through the caves and promontories of his mind" (73). Hurston relies on the suspension of belief here, utilizing telepathy as metaphor to underscore the importance of understanding the psychological ramifications of Joe's mental control over Janie, if not the town itself. Janie's newfound paranormal ability is a means of empowerment and a declaration of freedom. While Joe is on his deathbed, Janie informs him, "You wasn't satisfied wid me de way Ah was. Naw! Maw own mind had tuh be squeezed and crowded out tuh make room for yours in me'" (82). With these words of recognition, Janie cleanses her mind of Joe and frees her heart for love as a consequence of this special skill that has awakened her to a new reality, a world without her second husband and a chance for new adventures over the horizon.

More than simply equating insight to telepathy, Hurston's use of figurative language demonstrates how Janie and other blacks survive as human beings in an uncomfortably raced world. This telepathic power makes it possible for her to endure Joe's mistreatment in the black world as well—to forget the drudgery of her daily existence—and leads to astral projection. She learns to divide her mind and body to cope with disillusionment. The notion of astral projection entails an out-of-body experience in which a person's spirit separates from her corporeal body and travels outside it. The most pertinent example of Janie's second paranormal ability follows her husband's death, when she sends "her face to Joe's funeral, and herself went rollicking with the spring time across the world" (84–85). Hurston highlights the power dynamics of race and gender and questions social hierarchies with this second metaphor where Janie resists victimization. Additionally, these vernacular technologies help explain the struggle to define reality along the primary color line in America.

Alternate Worlds

Using afrofuturism as a mode of reading to interrogate this work of mainstream fiction enables readers to envision how race has alienated black people and has made aliens of them in a science-fictional sense. Janie is the perfect example of what I mean here because of her deep sense of cultural disconnection. Although her future seems less troubled after Joe's passing, she must search inwardly to understand her own alienation. Janie must prepare herself "for her great journey to the horizons in search of *people*," in search of belonging (85). Yet before she can join the networked consciousness, before she can reach the horizon and beyond, readers must first grasp how Janie's estrangement begins.

Her alien existence starts with a group photograph in which the six-year-old Janie, living with her grandmother, Nanny, in the backyard of a white family, is the only black child in the photo, although she is unaware of her color. She does not recognize herself because race was not an issue until the moment she was made aware of her difference by the white children's laughter ringing in her ears. Janie experiences the shame of alienation remarking out loud, "'Aw, aw! Ah'm colored!" instinctively knowing that her blackness is a bad thing (9). As a child seeing that picture at that exact moment, she becomes a being foreign to the environment in which she lives, a black girl in the white world. Houston Baker goes so far as to call Janie "an alien, a 'nigger,' a 'zero' in the white world's structures of perception" (*Blues, Ideology, and Afro-American Literature* 152). Likewise, the black girls at school ostracize Janie by relentlessly teasing her, preventing her from taking part in the ring games, bad-mouthing her beauty, and even mocking her father's absence. These girls reject Janie because they think she acts white, a grave offense in the black community. Janie misses out on connecting to this networked consciousness from an early age.

Feeling responsible for the brunt of her granddaughter's painful alienation, Nanny decides to move away from her white employer's backyard. Nanny's experiences as a former slave—being raped by her master, living a menial existence, and learning of her own daughter's rape—inform her decision because Nanny wants a better life for Janie. However, this move only reinforces Janie's dislocation. Somewhere in the ten-year gap between this move and where the story picks up again, Janie's lived experience produces an alien identity: alien in the sense that she does not know her sixteen-year-old self. Janie's identity remains frozen in terms of race, class, and gender. Locked in her grandmother's past, Janie's sexual awakening under the "pear tree" (10) becomes an important link to her humanity, helping her transform the context of her world, handle the racial complications of her childhood, and open up her future. In afrofuturist terms, "Who we've been and where we've traveled is always an integral component of who we can become" (Nelson, "AfroFuturism" 34).

At this point, the past, present, and future converge during Janie's first kiss with shiftless Johnny Taylor, who suddenly becomes to Janie "a glorious being coming up the road" (11). Reflecting on this moment with Pheoby, Janie determines "that her conscious life had commenced at Nanny's gate" (10). In the framing tale, the older Janie recognizes that her desire to love and be loved arises at that exact moment in her personal history, superseding her grandmother's disastrous experiences with men. This younger Janie wants the romantic adventures that the older Janie will experience. But Nanny marries Janie off to Logan Killicks in an attempt to curtail her granddaughter's passions, although marriage does not "end the cosmic loneliness of the day unmated" (20). Janie soon leaves Logan on her quest for love when she runs off and enters a bigamous marriage with an idealistic Joe Starks, who "spoke for far horizon" (28). His desire for land, the store, a trophy wife, and political power in Eatonville overwhelms Janie, and everyone else for that matter. She ends up doing all the things for Joe that she would not do for Killicks: She works in the store as Joe demands, wraps up her hair, endures his continual insults, and largely remains quiet in the presence of other men on the store's porch because Joe "classed [her] off" from the rest of town (107).

From an afrofuturistic standpoint, Janie has been living "the estrangement that science fiction writers imagine" (Dery "Black to the Future," quoting Tate 768). A denied freedom ensures that Janie lives an alien life because Joe forces his own whitewashed vision on her. Almost as if her body and mind have been colonized by this foreign power, Janie needs twenty years to free herself of Joe. His death completes Janie's self-awakening and allows her to break away from the gravity of Joe's possessions. While Hurston certainly exposes the complexities between men and women, Janie triumphs over her inferior status as a black woman in a patriarchal society. The future now in sight, Janie only awaits the arrival of her third husband, Vergible "Tea Cake" Woods, who will, as I argue, guides her to a second black planet down in the Muck, where she will finally link up with a black network.

As a widow in her prime, Janie's greatest adventures commence with the arrival of Tea Cake, her great love, companion, and guide to the black world. Nomadic and colorful, Tea Cake, a younger man, is a boisterous storytelling gambler who plays guitar. He teaches Janie to play checkers, encourages her to tell stories, and allows her freedom within the restrictions of their relationship beyond anything she has ever known with her previous two husbands. As a bluesman, Tea Cake transports listeners between worlds through his storytelling and with his music. According to Paul Youngquist, "Music becomes a means of materializing new spaces, producing the future, not as some distant never-never land, but in (the) place of today" (339). In this respect, Tea Cake promises and delivers the Muck as an alternate world for Janie, where she momentarily feels her own afrotopia through cultural rootedness in this far-off place.

Unlike in Eatonville, Janie gets involved in the daily life of this seasonal black world and loves Tea Cake all the more for it. For instance, Janie experiences the clang and clamor of all-night jook joints, picks beans right alongside Tea Cake, and even partakes in the banter, whereas Joe barred her from doing any of those things in Eatonville. In fact, Janie "got so she could tell big stories herself" that would make the men "'woof' and 'boogerboo'" themselves (128). As Missy Dehn Kubitschek states, "The storytelling sessions are crucial to community unity and self-definition, since they generate and develop communal tradition" (112). No longer alien, Janie becomes an active member immersed in the Muck. Though these vernacular moments mirror the ones occurring on the porch of Joe's store, the primary difference is that Janie gains agency through direct participation in the community, in turn allowing a redefinition of her own utopian dreams as an everyday black woman. Janie achieves one future, loving freely and being loved, before a hurricane wallops Florida.

A cataclysm strikes the black world when a hurricane devastates the Muck. Disasters, both natural and manmade, are a staple of SF and are also the subject of the work of two of Hurston's peers, Du Bois's "The Comet" (1920) and Schuyler's *Black Empire* (1936–38). Hurston uses the historical 1928 Okeechobee hurricane to illustrate the love between Janie and Tea Cake as they fight for survival against wind, water, a rabid dog, and white people. In the hurricane's aftermath, the social divisions between the races are further crystalized when the black worlds and white worlds collide. In the resulting upheaval, the raced world resets itself, and a diminished population forcibly returns to familiar racial patterns in which whites have the guns, and blacks, Tea Cake among them, are forced "into service to clear the wreckage in public places and bury the dead" (162).[15] The small army of mostly black men find corpses everywhere. Yet, according to the racist logic of the white world, black bodies and white bodies, bloated in the heat and humidity of southern Florida, a pestilential time bomb, cannot be buried together. If by no other means, hair texture becomes the deciding factor in categorizing bodies and where they will be deposited—a mass grave for blacks and cheap pine boxes for whites.

The couple resolves to return to the Muck after Tea Cake escapes from this grisly and involuntary employment and finds Janie in tears. Being known to the white folks governing the Everglades makes their decision easy. As Tea Cake reckons, "It's bad bein' strange niggers wid white folks" (164). Hurston evokes blacks as figurative aliens here because Southern

---

15. Richard Allen, the black founder of the African Methodist Episcopal Church, describes a similar scenario in his autobiography, *The Life, Experience, and Gospel Labours of the Rt. Rev. Richard Allen* (1833). For further information see John Ernest's *Liberation Historiography: African American Writers and the Challenge of History, 1794–1861* (2003).

whites historically fear unknown blacks, which often results in bloodshed. Ida B. Wells-Barnett's *The Red Record: Tabulated Statistics and Alleged Causes of Lynching in the United States* (1895) provides tangible proof for this claim of xenophobia. Certainly, these two types of being alien, foreign and extraterrestrial, are linked to national identity. But combined, they generate a science-fictional blackness powerful enough to resonate transhistorically.

Hurston also literalizes the alien metaphor after Tea Cake contracts rabies during the hurricane. Rabies, the strange alien presence in Tea Cake's body, surfaces about a month after their return to the Muck. Tea Cake's transformation into something alien because of rabies is reminiscent of Octavia Butler's *Clay's Ark* (1984), in which the crashed astronaut, Asa Elias Doyle, exiles himself to a desert community so as to prevent the spread of an extraterrestrial virus that infects him. While waiting for medicine to arrive from Miami, Janie notices "a changing look come in his face" that Tea Cake "was gone" and "something else was looking out of his face" (172). The disease radically changes her Tea Cake into something horribly other, something inhuman, and something that attacks her. In self-defense, Janie must finally shoot her third husband, who still manages to bite her before dying in her arms. The tension of this moment between her gain in knowledge and her loss of love has an emotional resonance that will last well into her future back in Eatonville.

Before returning home, Janie has a final alien encounter when she is on trial for murder with an all-white male jury and judge presiding over her fate. Hurston uses this Jim Crow racial dynamic to generate an alien atmosphere, where "twelve strange men who didn't know a thing about people like Tea Cake and [Janie] were going to sit" in judgment (176). These white men have total power over Janie and represent a threat more real than extraterrestrials ever could. Although "all the Negroes for miles around" come to watch the court case (176), they are all imperiled by whiteness at this moment. Without threat of this crushing power arrayed against the black world, whiteness would have no meaning. The trial progresses quickly, and the jury is only "out five minutes" before rendering a not guilty verdict and setting Janie free (179). Having proved their authority over black people, these seemingly benevolent aliens let Janie go. With tomorrow assured, Janie travels back from the horizon to tell her tale to Pheoby.

Janie can now take comfort in her memories of Tea Cake and move on because he helped her become the woman she wanted to be: free within herself. She gains the cultural connection that she needs to live on her own through the networked black consciousness. As the black heroine of her own planetary romance, Janie's complexity as a lover, dreamer, thinker, warrior, and storyteller becomes visible through her relationships with men. She overcomes the corporeal oppression with which both American and black societies attempted to imprison her by gaining her storytelling voice. Through this voice, Janie helps Pheoby go from a shifted shape, an object of the male gaze, to a shape-shifting subject of black female empowerment, as Pheoby now defines herself. No longer satisfied with the status quo, Pheoby feels "ten feet higher" and will make a new demand of her husband Sam to take her "fishin'" because she has heard Janie's story and wants her very own ventures (182). This transformation of identity through the space-time of Janie's adventures is afrofuturism in action—a liberation of soul, an escape vector from racism and sexism, the future moment of black female bodies in America, another world entirely. She goes there to know there.

Future Blacks

An afrofuturist reading brings into focus how the novel authorizes Janie as a creator of Southern black historical consciousness. She resists the limitations of various oppressions by recovering a trajectory that fully activates a transhistoric feedback loop. With this idea in mind, a critical afrofuturism conceptualizes the past in futuristic ways, offering other means of comprehending the cultural politics of race in America, from David Walker's *Appeal* (1829) to Martin Luther King, Jr.'s "I've Been to the Mountain Top" (1968), among many other black writings.

As an afrofuturist text, *Their Eyes Were Watching God* provides an image of tomorrow with which Zora Neale Hurston's contemporary Richard Wright could not agree. His brutal critique claims that "her novel carries no theme, no message, no thought" ("Between Laughter and Tears" 23). Wright's animosity toward Hurston blinds him from seeing exactly how she penetrates beyond the "narrow orbit in which America likes to see the Negro live: between laughter and tears" (23). His own belief in social protest traps him within the event horizon of racial politics, a black hole from which he could not escape in his own writing. But if we see Hurston's world-building as an achievement of afrofuturism, the black future will be not quite so unjust, and that is the difference between Hurston's and Wright's black worlds, as we shall see in the next chapter.

Janie's journey, literally and figuratively, becomes more than a young girl's dreams and desire for love; the Eatonville and Muck communities become more than black communities weighed down by segregation. Afrofuturism enables agency to desire a better future in spite of that segregation. Afrofuturism enables an unconventional reading of the novel where Hurston challenges the very definition of black reality through her heroine. Readers share in Janie's adventures across space-time on the black planets created by segregation while understanding the forces arrayed against her, namely, white power and black chauvinism. Measured against the backdrop of interlocking oppressions meant to break her spirit, Janie's is a willful existence. Hurston uses literalized metaphors and science-fictional tropes to explore the political and racial truths of black female identity.

Two things are gained by reading *Their Eyes Were Watching God* through a retroactive, rather transhistoric, afrofuturistic lens. First, Janie proves to be a black female character of substance that goes well beyond the tragic mulatta convention—the suicidal mixed-race woman unable to fit in either the black world or the white world—popular in Hurston's day. Inventive and daring, if flawed as well, Janie stands against the oppressions continuously assaulting her. She learns to make her own horizon by remaining open to love despite the overwhelming odds against her finding it. And, second, afrofuturism highlights the future history of an ongoing battle for respect and love from a country that continues to devalue black people in the light of the Trayvon Martin shooting in Florida in 2012, and the University of Alabama forcing its all-white sororities to admit black women in 2013, and the Stephon Clark slaying in Sacramento, California, on March 18, 2018. Segregation still *remains* an issue. Janie willingly fights for such love despite the macrostructures of racial and gender oppression and the internalized microstructures of these same problems evident in her various relationships. For black people this struggle has existed since the Middle Passage. Cultural memory drives this novel, shuttling us between the black planets and white planets of the text and the social and political realities of a segregationist past that haunts us to this day. Readers engage the paradox of future history as we confront these racial attitudes both then and now. As an afrofuturist text, or at the very least as a progenitor of afrofuturism, *Their Eyes* significantly demonstrates Hurston's complex views of racial consciousness, her desire to value and humanize blacks, and her hope for a new and better future.

CHAPTER 5

"METALLICALLY BLACK"

Bigger Thomas and the Black Apocalyptic Vision of Richard Wright's *Native Son*

WITH THE PASSAGE of time, *Native Son* (1940) has increasingly come to be regarded as science fictional, but it has always been afrofuturist. Such an idea regarding Richard Wright's searing classic seems strange at first, but many black people still live with the same oppression seventy-five-plus years after the publication of his novel. Although Wright's contemporary Ralph Ellison had "certain reservations about its [*Native Son*] view of reality," the novel "continues to have a powerful effect" as "one of the major literary events in the history of American literature" (*Collected Essays* 674). That is to say, Wright correctly foresaw a dystopian future for black males in America, considering various encounters and run-ins with law enforcement in the new millennium (Michael Brown in Ferguson, Missouri, and Alton Sterling in Baton Rouge, Louisiana, are salient examples). Ellison digs in a bit here as he reflects on "the circumstances out of which Wright insisted Bigger emerged." He says that "environment is all—and interestingly enough, environment conceived solely in terms of the physical, the non-conscious" (162). Moreover, Ellison reflects on how "in *Native Son* Wright began with the ideological proposition that what whites think of the Negro's reality is more important than what Negroes themselves know it to be. Hence Bigger Thomas was presented as a near-subhuman indictment of white oppression" (162). In fact, Wright uses his own inventiveness to craft such a diabolic character to protest the white power structures necessary to enforce such an oppressive environment—depriving a race of its dignity, intelligence, and strength to this day—that his accomplishment concretizes a science-fictional blackness that Ellison himself ponders with *Invisible Man* twelve years later.

Wright says as much in "How 'Bigger' Was Born," stating that his protagonist, "a Negro Bigger Thomas[,] would loom as a symbolic figure of American life, a figure who would hold within him the prophecy of our future" (447). This prophecy contains the seeds of my afrofuturist reading of the text in which I examine the separate white worlds and black worlds, the emergence of a networked black consciousness, and Bigger's own cyborg/alien/monster existence. Such a neat parallelism, of course, may be difficult to maintain since the United States is much more diverse now than in 1940. We do not live in a world polarized only across black lines and white lines today. Nonetheless, the conflation of black experience in America with a science-fictional paradox suggests how to re-imagine *Native Son* as a hopeful warning about racial oppression and the potential consequences of an all-out race war envisioned by other African American writers such as John A. Williams, who is discussed in the next chapter.

Critical interest in afrofuturism over the past decade provides new directions in SF scholarship, black literary history, and American cultural studies. Yet the ongoing development of afrofuturism as a field depends on our stretching its meaning to reassess the African American cultural canon in an explicit fashion. As Alondra Nelson believes, "Our imaginings of the future are always complicated extensions of the past" ("AfroFutursism" 35). Afrofuturism, therefore, protects black people(s) and black culture(s) and the histories they produced from vanishing in the time ahead (Kilgore, "Afrofuturism" 569). In that respect, I see afrofuturism as a reading protocol for the everyday science-fictional experiences of black people in black texts by black creators (writers, artists, musicians, filmmakers). I must stress that I am looking at a narrow version of afrofuturism because expansiveness dilutes the urgent emphasis on black art.

With these ideas in mind, this chapter begins with the afrofuturist notion that "race itself function[s] as a labor-based technology, whereby black human beings, coded as natural machines [, are] used to generate wealth" (Lavender, "Critical Race Theory" 190). This science-fictional existence symbolizes blacks as cyborgs, part man and part machine, throughout American history. Within such a framework, Wright's *Native Son* could be grasped as afrofuturist because of its portrayals of alienation and dehumanization. Protagonist Bigger Thomas, detached from his humanity, experiences the dystopia of systemic racism. His existence is a stunted one, caught between the American dream and black life. He cannot find a reasonable job, suitable housing, or affectionate relationships. Bigger starts to feel somewhat human only after committing the grisliest of murders: accidentally smothering white heiress Mary Dalton and then cutting her head off and stuffing her body into her parents' furnace; and shortly thereafter raping his black girlfriend, Bessie Mears, bashing her head in with a brick, and throwing her body down an airshaft. After receiving a guilty verdict along with the death penalty, Bigger pronounces, "I didn't know I was really alive in this world until I felt things hard enough to kill for 'em" (429). As Ellison proclaims, "Here lies the source of the basic ambiguity of *Native Son,* wherein in order to translate Bigger's complicated feelings into universal ideas, Wright has to force into Bigger's consciousness concepts and ideas which his intellect could not formulate" (*Collected Essays* 139). The magnitude of Bigger's alienation becomes science fictional. The monstrous nature of white racism and institutionalized oppression create him, an alien to us and an alien to himself. Wright insists on a bleak future for African Americans by perpetuating this black brute stereotype as both a fearful projection of white culture and a felt reality for some blacks.

In effect, Wright uses these three science-fictional metaphors—cyborg, alien, and monster—to demonstrate a dislocated and dysfunctional black existence through Bigger Thomas in an already prevailing dystopian urban landscape. This move to identify and interrogate Bigger Thomas and his cityscape aligns with Darko Suvin's notion of "cognitive estrangement," wherein a sense of unfamiliarity is created from the negative features of Chicago's Black Belt and its de facto segregation (*Metamorphoses of Science Fiction* 4). For the white Daltons *in Native Son,* Wright's dystopia resembles that of Aldous Huxley's *Brave New World* (1932), and we as readers question the lifestyle choices of the celebutante Mary Dalton. However, for the black Thomas family, Wright's portrayal is the straightlaced version of George S. Schuyler's satire on race relations in *Black No More* (1931). Wright cannot imagine a future for his notoriously alienated character trapped by racial oppression. But we can and we must see futures for black people in order for them to have a chance at escaping the black ghettos of white imagination enforced by Wright's "fiction" of reality. Such a move will allow us to problematize default racial assumptions and push toward an afrofuturistic tomorrow, where something better for black people becomes a necessary condition in America: an impulse to dream.

If we do not read *Native Son* through afrofuturism's critical lens, not only do we neglect an interpretation in reading protest fiction, but we also miss the relevance of this novel's relentless if not radical hope. This hidden impulse undermines the structural imbalances of the American dream for black youth who have been made metaphoric aliens—the literalization of white fear, which continually reverberates in US history. Of course, James Baldwin articulates these ideas about Wright's character better than anyone: "We are confronting a monster created by the American republic and we are, through being made to share his experience, to receive illumination as regards the manner of his life to feel both pity and horror at his awful and inevitable doom" ("Many Thousands Gone" 113). It seems so utterly hopeless, but a more equitable world *must* eventually emerge from such a racial dystopia. In pursuit of such a world, critics have interpreted this rich text in a multitude of ways in thousands of published pages contained in books, anthologies, and essays.[1] While all the scholarship adds up to a time-honored critical opinion that regards *Native Son* as an essential work in American literature, the fact that it has never been out of print since its initial publication in 1940 suggests that the novel is also an American classic. In this view of the novel as a classic, the alienation germane to black experiences in the New World deeply concern afrofuturism. Afrofuturism's science-fictional grammar provides the crucial leeway to interpret Wright's novel as an alien encounter in which segregated worlds collide, and this view is what separates my afrofuturist reading from other scholarship. The future exemplified through Bigger represents a black failure. Even though Bigger fails in his cyborg alien monstrousness, the novel itself does not fail in terms of teaching us how to live in a racially mixed world.

Some of Wright's early reading practices suggest that he was at the very least open to genre works. He started selling newspapers after hearing a rebellious classmate recount reading magazine supplements for entertainment, particularly a serialized version of Zane Grey's *Riders of the Purple Sage* (1912), a classic Western with fantastic elements (*Black Boy* 128). He also "read tattered, second-hand copies of *Flynn's Detective Weekly* or the *Argosy All-Story Magazine*" (133). Though SF was not identified as being such in the pulps of the early 1920s, John Clute explains how "Sf stories were a popular and prominent feature of *The Argosy*" (*The Encyclopedia of Science Fiction*). Science fiction was not recognized as a critical term until 1929 when

---

1. Recent analyses of the novel include psychoanalytic, postcolonial, gendered violence, and gothic readings. See Abdul R. JanMohamed's *The Death Bound-Subject: Richard Wright's Archaeology of Death* (2005); Anthony Reed's "Another Map of the South Side": *Native Son* as Postcolonial Novel" (2012); Kadeshia L. Mathews's "Black Boy No More? Violence and the Flight from Blackness in Richard Wright's *Native Son*" (2014); and James Smethurst's "Invented by Horror: The Gothic and African American Literary Ideology in *Native Son*" (2001).

Hugo Gernsback used it in *Amazing Stories*. In this respect, a young Wright was certainly reading SF, or *scientific romance* as it would have been termed. Such reading habits are reflected in his first published story, "The Voodoo of Hell's Half-Acre" (*Black Boy* 165), which "appeared in [the] Jackson [, Mississippi,] black weekly the *Southern Register*" in 1925 and was "modeled on the melodramatic pulp fiction he liked to read" (Rowley 34). Unfortunately, copies of this particular issue of the paper no longer exist according to his biographers Hazel Rowley (*Richard Wright: The Life and Times* [2001]) and Michel Fabre (*The Unfinished Quest of Richard Wright*) [1973]).

Whether *Native Son* should be read as SF or not, a couple of SF critics position Wright and SF together. In "The Necessity of Tomorrow(s)" Samuel R. Delany mentions reading Wright's *Black Boy*; but, growing up "in a world of freedom marches and integration rallies," he thought of it more as "history" (6). Likewise, Greg Tate makes the connection between Wright and speculative fiction explicit by exclaiming in the foundational Dery afrofuturism interviews, "Well, if you look at the black writing that's been done in this century, from Richard Wright on, there's always been huge dollops of fantasy, horror, and science fiction in it" ("Black to the Future" 763). Yet no critics have performed an afrofuturist reading of *Native Son* that views the present future of race relations through the past.

The main question is not whether *Native Son* is an afrofuturist novel or not, but how afrofuturism functions within the novel. Only then can we determine how the novel relates to the future in order to reclaim past historical perceptions of black identity across the nation, because the afrofuturist project primarily aims to build and maintain connections between past, present, and future. Wright creates a hugely devastating image of black male youth through Bigger Thomas, an image that continues to echo in the present and its future and that needs to be repossessed, reclaimed, and reshaped. This revised image of the black brute rapist generated white fear and anger toward black men long before Wright and extends far into future. Obviously, this fear has touched the real world. Otherwise, political ad campaigns, such as George H. W. Bush's controversial 1988 "Revolving Doors" television advertisement, would not be effective in winning the American presidency.[2] To be clear, the character of Bigger Thomas prefigures the actual Willie

---

2. Bush's team put the face of a black convicted criminal, William R. Horton, dubbed Willie Horton, in television ads to win. Playing on racial fears, they continued a seeming apocalyptic drive against black America. The facts that Horton was released from prison on a weekend work furlough, escaped, evaded police for ten months, and raped a white woman before being captured are all secondary to the primary aim of stoking racial animosity to win an election by exploiting the most bitter racial metaphor

Horton and what he did. The pervasive racism that made a story like *Native Son* significant as a social protest novel continues to create the same story in real life over and over again. Wright essentially created a negative pole in the transhistoric feedback loop. As long as racial stereotypes like the black brute remain embedded in the American psyche, generating fear and violence, afrofuturism demands engaging the images Wright made possible for white America to continuously exploit.

If black survival depends on locating the future in the past, then a transhistoric feedback loop becomes important because it helps reboot a networked black consciousness in an urban setting like Chicago, where the development of this network can aid plugged-in members in coping with squalid living conditions and bad social relations with white people which keep them separated in distinct worlds of their own. With black bodies already mechanized, it seems a simple thing to consider the extent to which Wright maps black bodies as living circuits. This interconnectedness, or metaphorical circuitry, between black folk is necessary for the smooth operation of this networked consciousness in an oppressed urban space regardless of their exploitation. But we must never forget the severance of Bigger's connection as the white world forcefully imposes a cyborg/alien/monster identity upon him.

As stated earlier, I call Bigger Thomas a *cyborg,* an *alien,* and a *monster* as I explore the novel's three books: "Fear," "Flight," and "Fate." Such evidence materializes through descriptions of Bigger's skin; through newspaper coverage of his crime, flight, and trial; and through his Communist white lawyer Boris A. Max's long-winded, impassioned but ineffectual defense. Bigger roughly occupies all three science-fictional metaphors simultaneously as he grasps the meaning of his life. Or, perhaps, all three symbols seep into one another as the story advances. Either way, each book tracks a social transformation that the white world must destroy; a world that cannot allow Bigger to live as a "truly modern person" (Gilroy, *Small Acts* 178); a world that requires "a response to predatory Western phenomena" that it created by creating race to justify racial oppression through slavery (Gilroy, *Small Acts* 178). A science-fictional blackness that Bigger cannot escape.

The first book, "Fear," introduces reasons for Bigger's anxiety, namely, white people, racial oppression, and deferred dreams. He is a simple commodity, an organic machine object that generates further wealth for white people. This cyborgized identity grants him access to Mary Dalton. When

---

in America: a black man raping a white woman. Also see pages 238–39 in Adam Z. Newton's *Narrative Ethics* (1997) for a comparison between Bigger and Horton.

he escorts the drunken heiress to her bedroom, he changes from a cyborg into an alien who invades the most sacred space in the white male imagination. After accidentally killing her, Bigger then becomes a monster who decapitates the dead girl in order to cram her body into the furnace to hide his crime.

In the second book, "Flight," Bigger tries to escape from the white world using a fugitive vision to at times outsmart and outrun the white world by employing its writing and reporting technologies. In other words, he writes the kidnap note to extort money from the Daltons, to cast blame on the Reds, and to manipulate racial stereotypes, all to his short-lived advantage. While on the run, he also reads the newspaper to figure out where to hide in the Black Belt as it is cordoned off and searched. Bigger's use of literacy technologies creates the necessary cyborg information feedback loop to reimagine the world that he briefly occupies. But the hunt, as it plays out in the newspapers, depicts him as an alien monster, and his treatment as such is dramatized by his getting blasted off a roof-top water tower in subzero temperatures in the middle of a howling blizzard.[3]

The final book, "Fate," describes the legal process Bigger suffers through on his way to the electric chair. The newspapers, the deputy coroner, and the State's Attorney General Buckley project a monstrous image of Bigger that Max cannot disprove in defending him. Bigger comes to terms with his identity made alien by a racist world and scares Max into believing it too in the closing pages of the novel. As Ellison suggests about Bigger's attempt to express how killing made him feel alive, his incompetence with language represents "the violent gesturing of a man who attempts to express a complicated concept with a limited vocabulary; thwarted ideational energy . . . converted into unsatisfactory pantomime" (*Collected Essays* 139). Although the double murders confirm him as a monster to the white world, these acts begin the process of restoring to him a sense of humanity that has been stripped away by various racial tensions as he discovers the meaning of his own life on his own terms. The afrofuturism elements function in contrast to naturalism here. Whereas naturalism suggests a way to fatalism and maybe even nihilism in *Native Son*, murder and brutality are a way to humanity for a race imagined as being nonhuman in the first place.

---

3. Dan McCall makes an apt comparison between the ape character Kong from the iconic film *King Kong* (1933) and Bigger Thomas: "Climbing buildings is the giant darky we blew up onto the screen, the 'Bigger' black man; he stands roaring on the rooftops until white technology sends him plummeting to the streets below. And *King Kong* ends with the assertion that 'beauty killed the beast' just as *Native Son* shows how the beast—if given a chance—will kill the beauty" (9).

Segregated Worlds

The sociospatial reality of segregation creates a separate white world and a separate black world that engenders the visibly oppressive structures of racism in *Native Son*. The white world is "quiet and spacious . . . [the] houses . . . huge" with soft glowing lights (43). But Bigger and other blacks feel that "this was a cold and distant world; a world of white secrets carefully guarded" (44). The pride, certainty, and confidence emanating from "these streets and houses" cause Bigger to tread warily and to arm himself whenever he crosses the invisible boundaries of the color line, especially when looking for the heart of the white world, the Dalton mansion at 4605 Drexel Boulevard where he is assigned for relief work. He goes armed with his knife and gun because it is not unheard of for "Negroes [to be] molested" (43). Bigger recalls how "bombs had been thrown by whites into houses like these when negroes had first moved into the South Side" (182).[4] In short, whites go to great lengths to maintain this very real cartography, keeping the white world separate from the black world.

Whites have the necessary political power to shape the world as they see fit, to be free themselves, to go anywhere, and to circumscribe others. Thus, an urban Northern city like Chicago proves to be different from the Dixie South in name only; the everyday anxieties of blacks exist in both spaces. As Anthony Reed states, "Though subjects of the law, blacks . . . were not always full citizens before the law, occupying a peculiarly politicized interstitial space, in moments of crisis, their political belonging could be inscribed elsewhere" (608–9). Segregation created extra modes of existence for black people as metaphorical cyborgs, aliens, and monsters because blacks were clear and visible outsiders. If read science fictionally, they are cyborgs because of their labor; aliens because of their skin; and monsters because of racial stereotypes.

Upon arriving at the Dalton's place, Bigger feels alienated by all the evidence of white power surrounding him. The white world bothers him because "he had not thought that this world would be so utterly different from his own that it would intimidate him" (45). In fact, Bigger cannot even understand the English spoken by Mr. and Mrs. Dalton when he overhears them discussing whether they should employ him or not since "the long strange words they used made no sense to him" (1940 edition 48). This defamiliarized moment contains a signpost of afrofuturism in which the language barrier creates an alien identity for Bigger as he attempts but fails to

---

4. See Lorraine Hansberry's play *A Raisin in the Sun* (1959).

comprehend this tongue that he has spoken his whole life. Thought transmission momentarily fails him because of his passage between black worlds and white worlds. To reiterate the point, Bigger feels alien in this strange white world governed by strange white beings. When he is driving Mary and her Communist boyfriend, Jan, around the city, this estrangement arises again. Wright describes Bigger's discomfiture: "His entire mind and body were painfully concentrated into a single sharp point of attention. He was trying desperately to understand" (67). If he did not feel like an alien before interacting with the Dalton family as a domestic laborer, he certainly does now. The social and political forces behind an unthinking white supremacy cause his alienation and result in unfamiliar sensations. Put another way, Bigger "is firmly indoctrinated into a way of thinking that assigns mythic values to the white race . . . and the emblems of white power that ultimately exclude him" (Bodziock 30). By absorbing and internalizing the white racist views of his people, Bigger devalues all of black culture and himself along with it through negative images. He comes to occupy "a shadowy region, a No Man's Land, the ground that separated the white world from the black" because he feels shame regarding his skin color (67). This contact with the Daltons reminds Bigger that he will never have the freedom of whites, the freedom to go anywhere, do anything, and be anyone. In his essay "How 'Bigger' Was Born," Wright himself hammers this point home, declaring that Bigger "was hovering unwanted between two worlds" (*Native Son* 451). Racial anxiety attenuates the transhistoric feedback loop by imbuing the black webbed consciousness with a cautionary vibe, not quite despair.

From an afrofuturist standpoint, the black world exists in a sphere all its own. This second world proves to be a much worse experience for black people who are trapped by housing covenant laws and social customs, forced to stay in terrible living conditions, and hated and feared by white people. Such toxic circumstances are truly apocalyptic. Bigger, his two siblings, and his mother live in a rat-infested, dilapidated, cramped room, where they all eat, sleep, and dress. They rent this tiny one-room apartment in an old, soon-to-be-condemned building for an exorbitant "eight dollars a week" from Mr. Dalton's "SOUTH SIDE REAL ESTATE COMPANY" in a corner of Chicago "tumbling down from rot" (173–74). Blacks are not allowed to cross the line into the white world to find better living conditions because "no white real estate man would rent a flat to a black man other than in the sections where it had been decided that black people might live" (249). This situation is the very definition of *dystopia* wherein they suffer inequality and nobody white cares, just like in earlier iterations of the transhistoric loop. Figuratively speaking, the hope impulse weakens for those with a spotty connection to the networked black consciousness. As a result, Bigger loathes his family and himself because he is ashamed, powerless, and afraid. He cannot help end their suffering because he experiences the same anguish. Bigger knows that "the moment he allowed what his life meant to enter fully into his consciousness, he would either kill himself or someone else" (10). In effect, such a conscious musing on Bigger's part causes Ellison to call Wright "a social determinist" clearly "overcommitted to ideology" (*Collected Essays* 74). Nonetheless, Bigger's stifling of such powerful emotions makes him violent, monstrous, and alien as evinced by the petty crimes always perpetrated by him and his gang, Gus, G. H., and Jack, against other blacks.

Near the end of the opening scene, Bigger's mother relentlessly browbeats him about his behavior, attempting to link him with the networked black consciousness. But he taunts his sister Vera with the dead rat he just killed until she passes out, prompting his mother to go on the offensive. For example, Mrs. Thomas challenges his virility stating, "'We wouldn't have to live in this garbage dump if you had any manhood in you'" (8). Perhaps the reason Mrs. Thomas places too much responsibility on her twenty-year-old son's shoulders is the absence of his father, since Bigger is unsure of taking the relief job with the Dalton family. Yet Mrs. Thomas condemns his self-indulgent ways and insults him further, calling him "the most no-countest man [she has] ever seen" before accurately predicting that "the gallows is at the end of the road you traveling, boy" (9). Instead of building his esteem and securing his future, all her negativity feeds his self-loathing, causing him to despair and to move closer to his apocalyptic end. The negative feedback loop grips him, mind and body, and his network connection becomes even more erratic.

As we already know, Mrs. Thomas's prophesy comes true. But this key moment is important in multiple ways. First, Mrs. Thomas desperately wants to save her son from imminent destruction by the white world. Second, she also wants to restore his sense of humanity, even though she is going about it in the wrong manner with her continual verbal abuse. Bigger confirms such berating with his comment, "'You done told me that a thousand times'" (9). Thus Bigger does not seem to value his own life. Third, she wants to literally plug him into the networked consciousness of black folk to aid his survival by imploring him to come to church, to stop hanging out on street corners with his friends (a large part of the negative feedback loop), and to earn money with an honest job in order to hold his head high. This desire is the reason why Mrs. Thomas wants him to accept the driver position with the Daltons, the cyborg identity it implies, and living with alienation if not being at home with it. However, such "mechanical metaphors" for black people evoke slavery, which is "the original unit of capitalist labor ... the originary form of the post-human" (B. Williams, "Black Secret Technology" 169). As Lawrence Hogue points out, "Bigger's ghetto is a designated site of refuge, exploitation, underdevelopment, and future labor resources" (14). As Eshun notes, compressing the cyborg metaphor with future labor resources produces a sense of the "futures industry that dreams of the prediction and control of tomorrow" to the benefit of whites ("Further" 291). Unmistakably, such tremendous pressure shapes Bigger's science-fictional blackness; his job translates him into a unit of labor, making him a metaphoric cyborg as the organic cog of the Buick he fleetingly drives for the Daltons. This pressure leads to his other science-fictional transformations.

Fourth, Richard Wright offers a radical hope, if not for Bigger, then for his two younger siblings as well as his gang: the hope that they not behave like a cyborg, alien, or monster; and that they endure and live for a better day. This radical hope, basic as it seems, inspires a new racial politics that imagines what is possible—simple communication that will close the gulf between the races. His audacious book is truly monumental in its attempts to overcome reality. This notion prompts Ellison to state, "While I rejected Bigger Thomas as any *final* image of Negro personality, I recognized *Native Son* as an achievement, as on man's essay in defining the human condition as seen from a specific Negro perspective at a given time in a given place" (*Collected Essays* 165). Wright, in weaponizing his words, wants to create a book "so hard and deep" for his audience "that they would have to face it without the consolation of tears" ("How 'Bigger' Was Born" 454). He succeeds. He succeeds so well that renowned critic Irving Howe proclaims, "The day *Native Son* appeared, American culture was changed forever," making "impossible a repetition of the old lies" (355). Only such a radical hope unflinchingly reveals black ghetto life in a white America and zeroes in on segregation and the dystopia it creates.

Outside his decrepit building, street cars noisily pass at regular intervals. A new billboard directly across the street from Bigger's tenement features a poster with the stern white face of State's Attorney General Buckley, who's running for reelection, and tall red letters that proclaim "YOU CAN'T WIN!" (13) In an Orwellian sense, "Big Brother Is Watching" (Orwell 2). Thus, the billboard eerily foreshadows Buckley's successful prosecution of Bigger for murder. This panoptic poster frightens Bigger because its face has a way of uncannily staring back at him whenever he walks past it. It serves as a constant reminder of his downtrodden position, intensifies his pervasive feeling of white surveillance, and demonstrates white authority. "Even if (or precisely because) Bigger is in an open space," as Isabel Soto indicates, "his feeling of being visually controlled 'all the while' coheres with his experience of being trapped by 'white people to either side'" (26). Before even meeting the powerful Buckley, Bigger clearly knows that he endorses a white future without blacks—noncitizens, aliens from some primitive elsewhere. George Orwell's *1984* (1949) again springs to mind with its depiction of social injustice and resistance to totalitarian social practices, much like the white-controlled Chicago described by Wright, where Bigger becomes an "unperson" (38), executed and erased from history. I should say "nearly erased" because Bigger serves well as an afrofuturist example of what not to do—drop out of school; commit petty crimes; drink, smoke, and cuss; degrade women; and hang out on street corners. Such antisocial doings open him up for an afrofuturist critique to aid future generations.

As such, the black world seems entirely oppressed and controlled, if not downright bleak. Few blacks own businesses save for poolrooms, soul food joints, and funeral homes. In fact, Bigger reflects on how "almost all businesses in the Black Belt were owned by Jews, Italians, and Greeks" (249). Likewise, rent costs twice as much for black people who lease the same kind of apartments as whites, and a loaf of bread is sold for more in the black section than anywhere else in the city even though blacks cannot get well-paying jobs. In fact, Wright tells us, "Most houses on the South Side were, ornate, old, stinking; homes once of rich white people, now inhabited by Negroes or standing dark and empty with yawning black windows" (182). The gothic imagery here serves as a precursor of SF. Earlier in the novel a frustrated Bigger expresses his discontent to his friend Gus: "Goddammit, look! We live here and they live there. We black and they white. They got things and we ain't. They do things and we can't" (20).

Briefly, the possibility of a third world (as in a third planet), a Red world, a Communist world, emerges when Bigger drives Mary and Jan around the Black Belt and, under duress, hangs out with them. But the possibility of a third world fades quickly for Bigger because "they made him feel his black skin by just standing there looking at him," and "at that moment he felt toward Mary and Jan a dumb, cold, and inarticulate hate" (67). Just a glimmering of this world proves doubly estranging to Bigger in that it is an alien concept to him while it simultaneously marks him as alien. To be sure, Jan proclaims the beauty of the world to Bigger without realizing that Bigger has no access to it. Then Mary ironically states, "We seem strange to you" and somehow expects Bigger to respond honestly (68). Of course, as white people, they do seem strange to Bigger, alien to what he knows. Bigger *does not* know what Mary means when she talks about seeing how black people live since she has "been to England, France, and Mexico" but could not venture ten blocks down the street from her residence even though "they [blacks] live in our country . . . in the same city with us" (69). How could he know? During the car ride home, Jan remarks how black people "have so much *emo*tion" and Mary asks Bigger if he can sing (77). They clearly have no idea how patronizing their actions are to Bigger and just how much they alienate him in this moment, to the point he chooses to implicate the Communist party in his murder of Mary Dalton. In this instant, this potential Red world disappears beneath the weight of the color line which is fully reasserting itself, even though the Communist lawyer will later defend Bigger because Bigger signs the kidnap note "Red" and draws a hammer and sickle beneath the signature.

Caught between cultural traditions and political ideologies, there does not seem to be much of a future for black people. How can there be if they are not free citizens in such a dystopian environment? How do they survive the present and secure a future? To answer these questions, black people come together and form a networked consciousness, one from which Bigger Thomas is cut loose because he inadvertently chooses a nihilistic pathway to build his brave new world.

Network Disconnection

Ideologically grounding the future in history *is* a fundamental precept of afrofuturism. The very future survival of a dislocated race necessitates the development of this consciousness. Black communities become sustainable because mentoring, collaboration, inventiveness, encouragement, motivation, and rapport, among other things, are made available to members who are plugged into the simultaneously literal and symbolic network. In this respect, black bodies have been metaphorically cyborgized to better represent the black cultural spaces of *Native Son*. The degree to which Wright outlines black bodies as live components of the network arises solely from an afrofuturistic perspective. The best example of this circuitry is Mrs. Thomas, her preacher, and the church. The smooth running of this networked black consciousness greatly depends on communal awareness and its clear sense of a shared cultural and historical heritage, both of which generate the vital interconnectivity to resist racial oppression regardless of what walk of life the black person chooses—religious or secular.

A white liberal reading—perhaps the kind Max offers—suggests that if we change the circumstances and eliminate racism, then black people will no longer have this kind of hopeless future. That is, if we recognize via naturalism how Bigger is determined to follow his narrative, we can fix the things that cause this predestination. However, afrofuturism provides a different response to naturalism, a distinctly black response, where the answers lie not just in fixing the landlord issue or the education issue or redlining or whatever, but also in tapping into the transhistoric feedback loop and linking into this networked consciousness to find hope. Yes, community, but the networked consciousness implies a more complex form of futurity, not a regressive, prescriptively narrow sense of community rather an expansive society across space-time.

A self-sustaining black networked consciousness depends on its combined human filaments to provide the emotional tenacity and gumption to resist white supremacy and to operate in the white world. Information transmitted and received across this raced system provides cultivation and mutual assistance to members associated via the common experience of racism. As Howard Ramsby indicates, words like *network* and *system* are "noteworthy here given the attentiveness in afrofuturist discourse to technological lexicon and concepts" (214). Because "consciousness has been celebrated as the seat of reason, including the ability to engage in symbolic thought and therefore to create language, mathematics, music, and art," a network of millions magnifies the power of racial awareness in understanding the white world in order to endure its hatred and animosity (Hayles 56). For Amiri Imamu Baraka, this "new technology must be spiritually oriented because it must aspire to raise . . . and expand man's consciousness" ("Technology & Ethos" 157). The spiritual orientations of these networked communities remain intangible as relationships based on communication between souls, perhaps expressing the essence of humanity in making other people feel you and your circumstances—realness. Importantly, Wright taps directly into his Jim Crow cultural moment to demonstrate the simultaneous success and failure of this network for Bigger, his family, and his friends in their dystopian existence as he explores the consequences of the colliding worlds.

This networked consciousness functions in a variety of ways for the black community it serves. First, it serves as a coping mechanism for the various troubles that plague the black community. From everyday slights and prejudices to the more extreme displays of racism such as lynching, the networked consciousness helps blacks manage seismic racial pressures. This network also helps with the truly colossal racial events that garner national attention, like the series of sham trials for the Scottsboro Boys[5] between 1931

---

5. Accused of raping two white girls while hoboing on a freight train in Alabama, nine African American teenagers became known as the Scottsboro Boys. In the initial trials, all but one were convicted of rape and sentenced to death or life in prison The

and 1935 and the 1955 murder of fourteen-year-old Emmett Till. Imaginary events like Bigger Thomas's trial and sentencing—death by electric chair—help maintain the relays of this network. Second, it also provides insulation from the anxieties of being black in a white world.

A third network function encompasses the necessity of mentoring for black youth. Whereas Bigger's sister Vera receives wise and influential counseling from her mother and from the Young Women's Christian Association during her sewing lessons, he gets whatever wisdom is to be had from street corners and pool halls. That is to say, the absence of an adult figure hinders his development as a human being. Everything fails for Bigger at home. While Vera learns from her mother, and little brother Buddy learns from Bigger, moments of life in a stable home do not exist for him. Bigger's behavioral issues stem from his parents' abandonment, his taking to the Chicago streets, and the lack of affirmation from a mother who is always at work. He has no desire for hope and what it can offer him. He literally cannot see hope.

Fourth, when linked to a networked consciousness, a subversive black subjectivity, much like that of Uncle Robin in Ishmael Reed's *Flight to Canada* (1976), materializes and counteracts hostilities that blacks feel while they are employed by whites. This subjectivity is subversive in the sense that in order to get ahead, black people learn to mask their feelings when around white employers. A figure like the previous Dalton chauffer, Green, grasps this concept and takes advantage of it by using the Daltons to pay both for his education and for him to live in a nicely appointed room. But Bigger never gets that chance. Just about any room would be nicer than the Thomas's apartment. Disastrously, he kills Mary his first night on the job.

Fifth, a networked consciousness harnesses the power of intentionality by pointing beyond the physical world to the realms of feelings and emotions, spirituality, and the symbolic as a means of transcending the white world. This is why Mrs. Thomas tells Bigger that "God has fixed a meeting place . . . where we can live without fear" and asks him to pray (299). This is what allows Mrs. Thomas to get down on her knees and beg for the Daltons' mercy, in addition to pledging herself in bondage to them the rest of her life to save her eldest child. Regardless, Mrs. Thomas and her remaining children will stay linked by leaning on the network in their time of need. Beyond doubt, this is also why Wright uses the symbolic power of the black brute stereotype to interrogate the complex social forces at work in America

---

convictions were appealed twice, both times to the US Supreme Court, resulting in the 1932 landmark decision *Powell v. Alabama* regarding due process, adequate legal representation, and equal protection.

then and now, thereby providing us with a strange pulsing of hope. There *is* no hope for Bigger, but hope through other characters represents a hope for a black future. Bigger's family, friends, and community will continue to live, to remember, and to learn from his experience. And they will take this knowledge into the indeterminate future still governed by unwritten yet well-known racial codes.

Nonetheless, let me unpack Bigger's termination from the networked consciousness to highlight the value of Wright's novel in afrofuturist terms. At first, Bigger and his gang belong to the network as evinced by Bigger and Gus who decide to participate in an age-old mimicry game in which they "play 'white'" (*Native Son* 17). First Bigger pretends to be a general; then Gus takes a turn as the financier J. P. Morgan; and Bigger ends the game as the president of the United States, who drops everything and calls a cabinet meeting in regard to "niggers . . . raising sand all over the country" despite German aggression in Europe (19). "Playing white" functions as a release valve for the pent-up frustrations of these black urban youth, and it allows them to offer uncompromising critiques of racism by mocking their own deplorable environment. They, too, want to achieve the American Dream of wealth and prosperity but recognize the impossibility of it for themselves. As Farah Jasmine Griffin mentions, "The closest [Bigger] gets to holding the power of the white man is through this game, and yet inherent in the game is a critique of white people" (125). Bigger and Gus, representative of black people in this situation, share a collective belief about white society, and they know what the social consequences will be in acting out of self-interest rather than from cooperation—death. Likewise, Valerie Smith states, "When they 'play white,' for instance, they pretend to be millionaires or public officials, and momentarily forget their own powerlessness" (144). Playing white also demonstrates how the boys participate in the rich black vernacular tradition. The use of such dissident decision-making strategies to challenge whiteness operates within the social norms of the networked black consciousness, even though the game does not have any power in the "real" world to unsettle white supremacy.

Still, the only thing left to them is this make-believe power fantasy. This realization causes Bigger to break the game off because he feels alienated, as if he is "on the outside of the world peeping in through a knot-hole in the fence," to which Gus appropriately responds, "'Aw, nigger, quit thinking about it. You'll go nuts'" (20). Note that playing white is very different from *acting white*, the latter of which suggests disloyalty to black culture and harboring white social beliefs, thus making one a sellout, something of which Bigger cannot be accused.

Concerning Gus's notion, Abdul R. JanMohamed rightly suggests that blacks are "prevented from realizing their full potential as human beings and exclude[d] from full and equal participation in civil and political society" ("Negating the Negation" 286). Bigger's lawyer, Boris Max, says the same thing in his closing argument: "Multiply Bigger Thomas twelve million times . . . . In reality they constitute a separate nation, stunted, stripped, and held captive *within* this nation, devoid of political, social, economic, and property rights" (397). But playing white alleviates the feelings of injustice by temporarily inverting the world, thereby allowing black people to laugh, to relax, and to release ever-present racial tensions. However, as Matthews observes, their final "exchange expresses their sense that, for white Americans, keeping blacks subjugated is more important than any other concern, even world peace" (285). However, playing white also conveys a science-fictional sense of alienation so powerful that these black boys truly cannot imagine a black future all its own. That idea is utterly alien to them. Regardless, playing white demonstrates a network connection, an intermittent one at best, that does provide hope in satirizing white morality.

The faulty linking happens because Bigger and his gang commit crimes against black people. They directly participate in black-on-black violence. Most of their "job[s]" are crimes of convenience in which they "raided newsstands, fruit stands, and apartments" or "always robbed Negroes" (14). They usually plan their illegal activities at innocuous locations like the "South Side Boy's Club" or the corner drugstore and its soda fountain (14, 111), but they use "Doc's poolroom" for this purpose as well. These black boys reckon "that it was much easier and safer to rob their own people, for they knew that white policeman never really searched diligently for Negroes who committed crimes against other Negroes" (14). This banal notion remains prevalent still. Wright aggrandizes this monstrous construct exactly because of how foolish ascribing delinquency to race actually appears. Bigger has no future, and Wright warns future Americans against this construct's social power that drives the nightly appearance of the myth of black-on-black crime on news media.

Even so, Bigger and his gang *do* belong to a small minority of black criminals. He goes even further than his friends by enlisting his girlfriend, Bessie, to help him steal "silver from Mrs. Heard" and to take "Mrs. Macy's radio" (145). He enlists her in his kidnapping note scheme to extort money from the Daltons. Bigger's stealing from white people suggests that the already tenuous connection cannot and will not last. In fact, Gus, G. H., and Jack balk at robbing "Blum's Delicatessen," even though they "had long been planning to do" so (14). They hesitate because of the potentially grave consequences:

They had the feeling that the robbing of Blum's would be a violation of ultimate taboo; it would be a trespassing into territory where the full wrath of an alien white world would be turned loose upon them; in short, it would be a symbolic challenge of the white world's rule over them; a challenge which they yearned to make, but were afraid to. (14)

Fear of white reprisal keeps them within the safety of this linked consciousness when they ultimately decide not to rob Blum because Gus arrives late to the staging area of Doc's poolroom. Bigger masks his own fear by acting tough with Gus. In the tussle Bigger pulls his knife, makes the crying Gus lick the blade, threatens to cut out his belly button, and ends staring down the gun-toting Doc while slashing up a billiard table's green cloth before exiting. As Hogue states, Bigger "covers over his fear of whites and his inferiority complex by acting tough" (17). If we trust the naturalist bent of Wright's novel, the future seemingly becomes even whiter presuming that the cultural myth of black-on-black violence reaches its conclusion with a mass extinction driven by an underlying fear of white supremacy. Bigger even thinks to himself "that white people felt it was good when one Negro killed another" because "it meant that they had one Negro less to contend with" (331)—in other words, one less monster to fear. But the just-mentioned trust requires that the entire gang be cut loose from the networked consciousness, and this action does not happen.

In the interlude between planning the crime in the morning and abandoning it in the afternoon, another moment arises which hints at Bigger's disentanglement. He and Jack leave Doc's and go down to "Forty-seventh Street and South Parkway" to see a movie at "the Regal" (29), where they proceed to see who can climax the quickest while masturbating in the darkened theater. The manager sees them in the act but is afraid to confront them. By authorial design, Bigger sees Mary Dalton for the first time on a newsreel before meeting her in the flesh. At this juncture, Wright gives us this odd scene of carnality as another black male stereotype, odd in the sense of a deviant sexual act performed in a public space. Carnality paired with criminality projects the image of the black rapist in the white imagination, certainly a monstrous alien, and eventually dooms Bigger as the novel progresses to its conclusion.

These minor disturbances to the networked consciousness forewarn of Bigger's permanent disconnection. Bigger's inadvertent killing of Mary Dalton immediately severs his flimsy connection. His deliberate beheading of Mary makes this interruption permanent. His calculated rape and brutal murder of Bessie seem unimportant because she is black, but the coroner hauls out her corpse in front of the pretrial inquest crowd to establish Bigger's brutality and, more important, to imply that Mary had met the same fate. In addition, her implied rape outweighs her murder in a public opinion crafted by the daily newspapers which call him a "sex-slayer" (279). Buckley uses this evidence to good measure in securing the death penalty for Bigger. Still, this double murder "had created a new world for" Bigger not only because it transforms his being but also because he accepts the consequences to come (241). Exactly what has he been transformed into and why? These are questions further explored in the final section of the chapter. For now, Bigger's actions make him feel human even if they ironize him in the sense that he assumes "exactly the role the white world rests upon the Negro in order to justify his oppression" (Margolies 47). As James Baldwin suggests, "Bigger has no discernible relationship to himself, to his own life, to his own people, nor to any other people" ("Many" 113).

In his attempt to elude capture during the manhunt in snowbound Chicago, a symbol of all-pervasive whiteness, Bigger recognizes his separation from the networked consciousness. First, he steals a newspaper and reads that every home and every abandoned building in the Black Belt have been carefully searched by police and vigilante groups; that several hundred black men have been rounded up and detained; and that several hundred other blacks employed by whites have been fired. His use of this freedom technology only makes him feel even more doomed as he inevitably becomes aware that his own end is drawing near. Second, while hiding, he eavesdrops on two black men discussing his situation and realizes that his people would give him over to the enraged 8,000 whites invading the Black Belt. Bigger further realizes that most black people hate him right now. He has no connection to the networked consciousness; he cannot rely on it to save him. He is on his own.

After sleeping in the same derelict apartment, Bigger overhears the spiritual "Steal Away to Jesus" emanating from the church next door. This song "filled his ears; it was complete, self-contained, and it mocked his fear and loneliness, his deep yearning for a sense of wholeness" (254). The song causes him to question: "Would it not have been better for him had he lived in that world the music sang of"; and it evokes "his mother's world" and her absolute connection to the black web (254). Bigger has rejected her world and its spiritual traditions outright because he does not want a life of humility and passivity. That is not to say that passive resistance is the only connection to this network, but only that Bigger has wrongly applied his frustration. He decisively chooses his own alienation and disconnection. Later, after being apprehended, when the Reverend Hammond, his mother's pastor, implores Bigger to let "Gawd's love t' come inter [Bigger's] heart," Bigger rejects the preacher's spiritual attentions, even though the reverend attempts to do the impossible by patching Bigger's broken connection (285). Bigger then tells his mother to "forget me, Ma" (299). He even goes so far as to throw the cross out of his jail cell, the cross that the preacher had given him not once but three times (like Peter rejecting Jesus Christ three times) before the inquest. This Christianized iteration of the networked black consciousness admittedly seems problematic, because the religion has often been used to justify the oppression of black people in the first place. But a carefully censored Christianity was all that slaves were allowed, and they made the best use of it they could to create a viable future for their progeny who continued the practice. Ultimately, Bigger cannot bring himself to accept the version of reality presented to him by the networked black consciousness.

He even becomes alien to Max after his sentencing when Max wearily attempts to convince Bigger of his humanity. Bigger explains in "frenzied anguish" that what he "killed for must've been good" (429). This deep feeling of life—that Bigger killed two women in order for him to fleetingly possess it—forces Max to finally see Bigger's color and to stand still "full of terror," to keep "his face averted," and to say good-bye to Bigger without facing him from the other side of the steel bars (429). The dystopian world Bigger creates for himself may condemn him, it may convince Max of his alien humanity and its monstrosity, but it frees his friends to shape their own futures as they reconnect to the black networked consciousness. That is to say, Bigger's *physical* ending convinces them to go straight and join the community they have rebelled against in their stunted youth. Besieged by white misconstructions of black identity in his own time, Wright demonstrates a political power through his fictional radical black creation that allows us to reclaim the future history of African Americans and to resist erasure. Through the act of writing, and on the basis of whites' lies about black people, Wright shows us truths of a negated future en masse and pleads with us to change it. Yet his casting of a dystopian future has become a harsh present-day reality for many black people caught within the prison–industrial prison complex.[6]

---

6. See Michelle Alexander's explosive *The New Jim Crow: Mass Incarceration in the Age of Colorblindness* (2010).

Cyborg/Alien/Monster

Of all the descriptions of Bigger's skin color throughout the novel, two stand out as greatly supporting my cyborg/alien/monster reading. The first narrative description occurs when Bigger and Gus are about to "play white," inverting the rich vernacular technology of black folklore through their irreverent wordplay. These two boys are holding up a wall, smoking, and watching cars rush by them when Wright states, "Bigger's face was metallically black in the strong sunlight" (17). Why would Wright purposefully evoke SF in describing Bigger's "metallically black" skin? He repeats this depiction a second time 235 pages later: "A wan sun came onto his face, making the black skin shine like dull metal; the sun left and the quiet room filled with deep shadows" (252–53). Such curious phrasings, "metallically black" as well as "black skin shin[ing] like dull metal," deserve further thought because in this novel they project the estrangement for which SF is appropriately famous. But also look at the language more carefully: *wan, dull metal, quiet room,* and *deep shadows*. These words also suggest that Bigger has been depleted of his humanity and is exhausted from it.

At the very least, these dangerous word pairings suggest that Bigger is a nonhuman other with a life devalued by the trappings of skin color. Bigger's degree of marginalization here should astound readers, because Wright transforms Bigger's skin through science, technology, culture, and even myth to generate the fear and excitement of the text itself. Put simply, Wright transposes the alien "other" with the "racial" other. Metal rearranges the element of race—skin color—to create a science-fictional vibe in the text. It is also artificial. In other words, metal combined with black constructs a machine image of Bigger's face, brightly burnished and humanoid as well as suggestive of the constructed nature of race: the face of a robot or a cyborg. This same word combination produces an alien face, too, by suggesting that his skin is scaled and reptilian in texture. As Robert Butler surmises, "Wright was intent on filtering external experience through Bigger's radically alienated consciousness" (105). Bigger certainly comes from another world, the black ghetto, which endows him with a consciousness different from that of white people. In fact, early on in her short relationship with Bigger, Mary Dalton indicates exactly how little-explored this other world is by white people, causing him to momentarily hate her because of the psychological discomfort it stirs in him. She admits to having little contact with black people. Likewise, metallic black skin represents the monstrous from the beginning because it marks Bigger as evil. He may look human, but he serves as an emblem of fear, scaring the white people who fashion him a monster through physical appearance alone, exploit him for wealth, and later victimize him for daring to oppose the white world. Such fear marks him as monstrous and solidifies his science-fictional blackness.

By reading the novel through an afrofuturist lens, we see how Bigger's science-fictional othering continues in the newspapers all throughout his escape, arrest, and prosecution. The press denies Bigger's humanity by incessantly referring to him as a "primitive Negro" (214), "Negro rapist and murderer" (244, 245), and a "black ape" (270, 337), among other things. He becomes a subhuman monster in the eyes of a vengeful public. As McCall notes, "Bigger has nothing to hold him back and nothing to define his responses other than the blackness of his skin" (6). Disorientation of his identity demonstrates the monumental power brought to bear on black people in the twentieth century. Bigger is estranged. Bigger is alienated, collapsed between the science-fictional alien and alienation itself. And Bigger is dislocated in time because white people wield such authority to brand all black people the same—potentially violent lesser beings. He gets trapped in the wrong feedback loop—the white one.

Bigger, being unanchored in time, allows the leading Chicago daily, the *Chicago Tribune*, to successfully define his identity as a "missing link":

"He looks exactly like an ape!" exclaimed a terrified young white girl who watched the black slayer being loaded onto a stretcher after he fainted.

Though the Negro killer's body does not seem compactly built, he gives the impression of possessing abnormal physical strength. He is about five feet, nine inches tall and his skin is exceedingly black. His lower jaw protrudes obnoxiously, reminding one of a jungle beast.

His arms are long, hanging in a dangling fashion to his knees. It is easy to imagine how this man, in the grip of a brain-numbing sex passion, overpowered little Mary Dalton, raped her, murdered her, beheaded her, then stuffed her body into a roaring furnace to destroy the evidence of his crime.

His shoulders are huge, muscular, and he keeps them hunched, as if about to spring upon you at any moment. He looks at the world with a strange, sullen, fixed-from-under stare, as though defying all efforts of compassion.

All in all, he seems a beast utterly untouched by the softening influences of modern civilization. In speech and manner he lacks the charm of the average, harmless, genial, grinning southern darky so beloved by the American people.

The moment the killer made his appearance at the inquest, there were shouts of "Lynch 'im! Kill 'im"!

But the brutish Negro seemed indifferent to his fate, as though inquests, trials, and even the looming certainty of the electric chair held no terror for him. He acted like an earlier missing link in the human species. He seemed out of place in a white man's civilization. (279–80)

"Possessing abnormal physical strength," as evinced by his long dangling arms, and "huge, muscular" shoulders, this image of Bigger evokes the science-fictional. He is something to fear as the "missing link" that evolutionary biologists and anthropologists have long been searching for to connect humans with animals—thereby signaling white humanity's superiority. To achieve such an "internalization—or, better, the epidermalization—of this inferiority," according to Frantz Fanon, a binary relationship must be established (11). The degree of kinship that Bigger has in relation to a humanity defined as white has nothing to do with the happy "darky" of the South and everything to do with being labeled *nonhuman* and *prior to humanity*. Black identity established in such a way becomes a powerful articulation of the alien. In one instance, Bigger is dehumanized as a metallic machine. In a second instance, he is dehumanized as an animal, not unlike "the Beast People" found on Dr. Moreau's Island (Wells 82).[7] Speaking for afrofuturism, such a "totalizing realization" makes "black existence and science fiction . . . one and the same" (Eshun, "Further" 298). Indeed, black experience *is* science fictional, even though the novel is not.

Bigger proves to be helpless against this damaging account of his identity, and it grows worse. As Yaszek posits, "What you tend to see in the mainstream media, again and again and again, is the sense that blackness is a catastrophe. Black spaces are zones of absolute dystopias" ("Race in Science Fiction: The Case of Afrofuturism" 2). Newspaper photographers manage to snap a photo of Bigger with "lips pulled back, showing his white teeth. . . . They had taken his picture showing him with his back against a wall, his teeth bared in a snarl" (336). This feral image and others like it further condemn Bigger as they make a monstrous construction of him and the black world itself. A future projection of this image brings to mind the technologically darkened visage of O. J. Simpson on the June 27, 1994, cover of *Time* magazine to make him appear more menacing to the dominant white American public during his murder trial, a public that adored him for a long time. In other words, "O. J. Simpson was not black enough, so by enrolling computer-related technology to produce the valued racialized image, *Time*'s staff reconstituted his visual representation to meet the dominant Ameri-

---

7. See H. G. Wells's *The Island of Dr. Moreau* (1896).

can culture's perceived expectations of a black felon" (Fouché 648). Clearly, equating blackness to criminality is nothing new in fictional and historical representations of white power. Conflating fiction and history in terms of black experience links Bigger and O. J. through a science-fictional lens to present both of them as stereotypes that were science fictionalized: Bigger through the newspaper, and O. J. through Photoshop. Sci-fying them, for lack of a better term, activates an afrofuturist reading by engaging the transhistoric feedback loop to compare realities, thus helping us recognize the sameness of the experience of being alienated.

This technological mediation of truth rationalizes black identity as a problematic one. Bigger's attorney, Boris Max, even questions himself, pondering how he could possibly help Bigger "when a thousand newspaper and magazine artists have already drawn it [Bigger] in lurid ink upon a million sheets of public print" (384). In short, he cannot. Shaped by the news media, Bigger becomes a black menace akin to the alien creatures commonly featured on the covers of pulp magazines Wright read in his youth. Of course, this victimized and exploited alien emerges from the jungles of white imagination. Recognizing Bigger as a fellow human being becomes impossible because of how the news media misrepresents him in its projection of white reality.

As Max unsuccessfully attempts to save Bigger's life in so many ways, his interminable defense plays right into the hands of the State's Attorney. First, Max works an alien angle by asking the judge "to recognize human life draped in a form and guise alien to ours" (388). Surely, Max chooses his words poorly by pointing out Bigger's immediate racial difference. Second, Max describes Bigger in the same brutish terms as the press: Bigger is an "it" that "has made itself a home in the wild forest of our great cities [, and] it leaps to kill" (392). Max makes a grievous error here by comparing black Chicago to a wild forest and naming Bigger as one of its creatures, ascribing to him a science-fictional blackness. Third, Max claims that Bigger wants to kill white people "every time he comes in contact [as] a physiological and psychological reaction, embedded in his being" (400). This critical mistake alienates Bigger even further because it suggests that murder is a biological response rooted in his soul. Fourth, Max suggests that "another civil war in these states is not impossible" with millions more like him (403). Such a grave miscalculation unquestionably stokes white paranoia to a killing point. Fifth, Max asks the judge to give Bigger a life in prison and bring him "for the first time within the orbit of our civilization" (404). This plea inevitably falls on deaf ears because of Max's unhelpful description of Bigger's humanity. If anything, the context of Bigger's life provided by Max dooms him more quickly because Max reinforces all of the black stereotypes and unwittingly insinuates that Bigger is a black-rage monster who needs to be knocked away from (white) Earth's "orbit," to use Wright's science-fictional language.

Based on the power of stereotype, State's Attorney Buckley effortlessly makes his case against Bigger in the terms constructed in the manner of the day's news media. He further classifies Bigger as being outside of humanity, as "a bestial monstrosity [that] has ravaged and struck down one of the finest and most delicate flowers of our [white] womanhood" (408–9). "This hardened black thing" is the exact mirror image of the news media that Buckley presents in his prosecution (410). Bigger cannot hope to survive against the burden of this nonhuman image. But there *is* an afrofuturist's hope. The title itself offers it: *Native Son*, as in a person who belongs to America, who is a native and therefore should have the same rights that a native son or daughter has. Black people belong here now, then, and into the future United States as interstitial components of American society.

From a critical perspective, *Native Son* starts with naturalism. If naturalism offers us the fatalism of Bigger's (and, by extension, the fatalism of all black men) already determined trajectory to death at the hands of the white supremacist state, then imagining a future would seem to flow out of these white notions of determinism and fatalism. That is why Ellison believed Wright "could not for ideological reasons depict a Negro as intelligent" in this novel (*Collected Essays* 167). So, by way of analogy, the way to fix the problems in a work such as Upton Sinclair's *The Jungle* (1906)[8] is to fix the laws, or, in Bigger's case, to fix redlining and property issues, to fix economics and education, and so on. To work against or even get out of the kind of world naturalism imagines, we must seek to fix the forces that create that determinism in the first place, more or less leaving the subject alone. If the environment changes, then the subject will change. But the afrofuturism portrayed in the novel turns us toward something different from fixing the institutions so that they are less racist, for example. Afrofuturism turns us toward black networked consciousness, metallic skin, a hope principle— toward a different model of consciousness in terms of both group identity (something close to race as an identity or identity category) and individual consciousness, that is, subjectivity. In short, that the "answer" to naturalism is not Marxism or reform, but afrofuturism.

---

8. Upton Sinclair's naturalist work *The Jungle* (1906), which focuses on the meatpacking industry, provides an excellent example of how immigrants lived as working poor in industrialized cities like Chicago.

While there does not seem to be much hope in *Native Son*, Richard Wright offers a prophetic vision with his future history of race relations. Wright scares us with Bigger Thomas because he brings to life the social and cultural forces that create a brutal monster, an id creature that kills dreams of racial harmony. On that account, Wright actually prognosticates in telling a story about a feedback loop that will never stop coming, warning us to break out if we can. And we cannot turn a blind eye to this warning—"the danger signal of a more bitter time to come," as Baldwin suggests ("Many" 117). Yet we did so then, we do so now, and we will continue to do so long into the future. Blacks exist in an alien America with white folks always watching for evidence of this black id monster, always ready to crush it instantaneously, always fearing contamination through blood ties.[9]

From an afrofuturist standpoint, the only way to overcome racial, political, and social oppressions; crippling poverty; and vulnerability—to offer significant resistance to white supremacy, to strip it of authority, to surge toward freedom—is to reshape black identity beyond the enduring stereotypes that kill. Hope pulses throughout a networked black consciousness, creating an afrofuturist vision in which love reinforces this metaphoric technology and expands the network further. Hope impulses engage with American historic racial inequalities by using intelligence, courage, and even humor. If we do not want to share Bigger's fate, or the potential of war between races, we, black and white, must transform the future. For me, that is the reason Wright creates Bigger: to warn future generations. Blacks made alien by alienating white environments need signposts to tomorrow. Indeed, Bigger's fate demands that we stop and find another way. Harsh realities must be faced with a relentless hope. Otherwise, we repeatedly relive the past.

---

9. Muslims are believed to represent a similar threat to American society today.

CHAPTER 6

RACIAL WARFARE, RADICAL AFROFUTURISM, AND JOHN A. WILLIAMS'S *CAPTAIN BLACKMAN*

BECAUSE OF a socially cultivated sense of superiority, white people hate black people or, conversely, black people hate white people because of slavery, as some would have us believe. Both specious and essentialist claims have led authors to supply answers to this lasting racial conflict by suggesting genocidal warfare between the races. In fact, one of the US Founding Fathers, Thomas Jefferson, controversially suggests:

> Deep rooted prejudices entertained by the whites; ten thousand recollections, by the blacks, of the injuries they have sustained; new provocations; the real distinctions which nature has made; and many other circumstances, will divide us into parties, and produce convulsions which will probably never end but in the extermination of the one or the other race. (*Autobiography* 145)

In this respect, a transhistoric feedback loop becomes an important way of reading the relational context between Jefferson's statement and John A. Williams's *Captain Blackman* (1972). In this novel, justice, equality, and freedom simply cannot be achieved without a near-future uprising, because black rage and desperation have only grown stronger with continuing oppression by white people. But such a fictionalized war between blacks and whites certainly unnerves readers who are uncomfortable with the notion of such an enduring racial enmity and who lack an understanding of the unthinking nature of racism. Nonetheless, a particular yet unarticulated ironic hilarity exists here, at least for color-conscious individuals, in imagining blacks kicking white ass. This imagined future relies on a complex combination of black hope, black hatred, and black humor.

At the beginning of the novel, Abraham Blackman, a black officer in the US Army on his second tour of Vietnam, is gravely injured by enemy machine-gun fire. While floating in and out of consciousness during his rescue and subsequent recovery from life-saving surgery, he devises an ultimate plan for defeating the "real" enemy of his people. In this transitory state, drugs and dreams combine with Blackman's admiration for black military history to propel his mind backward in time to the Revolutionary War and each subsequent American military campaign. He witnesses and suffers from racial oppression, prejudice, and violence because of white hatred as he fights for freedom and manhood from 1775 to 1975 and into the next millennium. The novel dilates, if not estranges, our sense of time, space, and action as Blackman lies hurt and largely unconscious for only a few days in the novel's present, but the expansion happens in his drug-induced reveries as he experiences the various wars in which blacks fought. As Williams's biographer Earl A. Cash notes, "The present time of the story covers but a few days, and [Williams] crowds the history of generations into those days," forcing time to merge past, present, and future and creating a transhistoric feedback loop as Williams patches into the black networked consciousness to project an altogether different tomorrow for black people (119–20).

This chapter uses afrofuturism to explore how black militancy manifests in an ongoing war between races, a war ultimately resulting in a black victory as not quite foreseen by Jefferson in *Notes on the State of Virginia* (1785). In doing so, it demonstrates the worth of such cathartic imagining for black people.

Before diving into the novel, I must outline the compendium of existing race war stories to properly situate *Captain Blackman*. Historicizing this miniature subgenre aids in comprehending the importance of Williams's novel, which deftly employs a keen awareness of black military history through classes taught by Captain Blackman. In afrofuturist terms, the novel provides an ideal illustration of the transhistorical feedback loop and a networked black consciousness because of how it plays with time.

Surely many readers have wondered what in the world is this novel doing with time, and more importantly with history itself. They might find all the time-shifting overwhelming if not dizzying. The novel starts in the middle of the Vietnam War; Blackman has been teaching an unsanctioned seminar on black military history to his troops; he goes out on patrol and sustains grievous injuries in a surprise attack while saving his men from it; during his own rescue and hospitalization he experiences drug-induced dreams that closely resemble his own seminar teachings to his troops; these lucid dreams relate to the combat experiences of black men in America's armies from the colonial period to beyond the Vietnam War into the future; in these dreams Blackman gradually moves up the ranks and into the future, paradoxically fighting for freedom on two fronts—for his country and for his race. In other words, his seminar and his dreams blend, creating a transhistoric feedback loop that permits him to move through history—in short, to time-travel. Put another way, Blackman's studying and teaching of history feels like time-travel. Williams deftly intertwines actual historic race events with his character's experiences by creating a transhistoric feedback loop that intensifies the black matrix of relationships existing in the novel.

The cultural context in which Williams himself existed as a member of the Black Arts Movement and as an unacknowledged member of SF's new wave is significant. Consequently, I demonstrate how Blackman in the Vietnam present becomes radicalized. I discuss two key moments from the past, one immediate and one from deep time, where his interaction with so-called yellow and red peoples underpin his hope. With all of this explanatory work finished, I explore Blackman's participation in each war that Williams writes about chronologically through an afrofuturist lens. The temporal complexity of this novel astounds as Captain Blackman frees himself and his troops from a science-fictional blackness by creating a black future.

Revolutions in White

Many white-authored texts and short stories have advocated for race war in the past. The earliest white-authored novel I have found in this vein, Nathaniel Beverly Tucker's *The Partisan Leader: A Tale of the Future* (1836), depicts a future United States of 1849, where most of the South has already seceded to continue the practice of slavery. Hoping to join the Confederacy, Douglas Trevor, the main character, leads secessionist Virginians in a guerrilla war against the federal government and President Martin Van Buren. In fact, Tucker's novel proved so popular that it was later reissued in 1862 as *The Partisan Leader: A Novel, and an Apocalypse of the Origin and Struggles of the Southern Confederacy*, with the author's name truncated to Beverly Tucker. In 1860 Virginian Edmund Ruffin published an epistolary novel in a vein similar to Tucker's, titled *Anticipations of the Future, to Serve as Lessons for the*

Present Time: In the Form of Extracts of Letters From an English Resident in the United States, to the London Times, from 1864 to 1870. Interestingly, both Tucker and Ruffin belonged to an extremist political group known as the Fire-Eaters who desired secession.

At the beginning of the twentieth century, North Carolina minister Thomas Dixon's Klan trilogy—comprising *The Leopard's Spots: A Romance of the White Man's Burden, 1865–1900* (1902); *The Clansman: An Historical Romance of the Ku Klux Klan* (1905); and *The Traitor: A Story of the Fall of the Invisible Empire* (1907)—envisions race war on an epic scale while promoting white supremacy and fear of miscegenation. For instance, the mouthpiece of Dixon in *The Leopard's Spots*, the Reverend John Durham, lectures the protagonist Charles Gaston on racial purity and its necessity to white civilization:

> One drop of Negro blood makes a Negro. It kinks the hair, flattens the nose, thickens the lip, puts out the light of intellect, and lights the fires of brutal passions. The beginning of Negro equality as a vital fact is the beginning of the end of this nation's life. There is enough Negro blood here to make mulatto the whole Republic. (242)

Recognizing how connections between SF, history, and literature demonstrate radical opinions that lay beneath the surface of our country in the past, just as they lie there in the present, helps to sensitize us to such violent imaginings. Only by acknowledging them can we stop them.

But not all speculations on this race war made by white authors imagine genocide if not their own race's victory. In "Way in the Middle of the Air," Ray Bradbury tells the story of how blacks in America, particularly the Deep South, weary of racial oppression, build rocket ships to Mars in order to leave the white world behind (*The Martian Chronicles* [1950]). Other examples include Ward Moore's *Bring the Jubilee* (1953);[1] Mack Reynolds's North African series—*Black Man's Burden* (1961–62), *Border, Breed, nor Birth* (1962), "Black Sheep Astray" (1973), and *The Best Ye Breed* (1978)[2]—and Terry Bisson's *Fire on the Mountain* (1988).[3] Nonetheless, Robert A. Heinlein supplies the most controversial example with *Farnham's Freehold* (1964). Heinlein pres-

---

1. In Moore's alternate history the Confederacy wins at Gettysburg and wins the Civil War, thus irrevocably changing American history.

2. Reynolds's North African series concerns the American black Dr. Homer Crawford who, using the name El Hassan, takes on the mantle of uniting and leading North Africa into the near future with progressive, if tyrannical, ruling.

3. Bisson's counterfactual novel portrays a world where John Brown's 1859 raid on Harpers Ferry succeeds, resulting in the South's becoming a black-majority nation known as *Nova Africa*.

ents a postapocalyptic far-future world where the white middle-aged Hugh Farnham and his family survive in a fallout shelter only to be captured and enslaved by French-speaking Africans with advanced technology. Eventually, Hugh volunteers to test an experimental time machine rather than live as a castrated slave, thus creating an alternate time line when hiding from nuclear war in a different place. While not afrofuturist experiments, these works demonstrate attempts by white authors to imagine colored futures that complicate our whitewashed understanding of speculative fictions.

Revolutions in Black

Williams belongs to a long list of African American writers who have imagined such scenarios. This militant afrofuturist strand begins in the mid-nineteenth century with Delany's serialized *Blake; or the Huts of America* (1859–62) and continues with Griggs's *Imperium in Imperio* (1899). While I talk at greater length about these novels in the second chapter, here I emphasize their significance as precursors to *Captain Blackman*. Biggio stresses how Delany, and perhaps his literary successors, informed their imaginary uprisings with the "belief that the threat of black community was more frightening to whites than the threat of black violence" (440). She makes a relevant point in that this kind of afrofuturist fiction seems to be about black community-building just as much as it is about harming whites. In fact, these writers take that threat and make it feel real through fiction.

Twentieth-century black writers consciously plugged into this networked vision of a radical afrofuture too. The Harlem Renaissance proved itself to be a hotbed of such violent dreams with Walter White's *The Fire in the Flint* (1924),[4] George S. Schuyler's *Black No More* (1931),[5] and Arna Bontemps's *Black Thunder: Gabriel's Revolt: Virginia, 1800* (1936).[6] Schuyler perhaps provides the best example from this period, becoming even more radical in his second novel, *Black Empire,* serialized in weekly installments in the *Pittsburgh Courier* between 1936 and 1938. The evil black genius Dr. Henry Belsidus builds a secret black militant organization, known as the

---

4. White's *The Fire in the Flint* depicts the Ku Klux Klan lynching of black physician Kenneth Harper for daring to attempt to organize African American sharecroppers in his hometown.

5. Schuyler solves the color-line issue when his antagonist, Dr. Junius Crookman, invents a skin-whitening process for black people in the United States, plunging the country into chaos as the black population disappears.

6. In *Black Thunder* Bontemps fictionalizes the historical failure of Gabriel Prosser's conspiracy to capture the Richmond Armory and equip his fellow slaves with weapons.

Black Internationale, inside the United States; establishes an empire within Africa; and conquers the Western world by "cast[ing] down the Caucasians and elevat[ing] colored people" (10).

At the dawn of the civil rights movement, Ralph Ellison's experimental *Invisible Man* (1952) signaled an afrofuturist attitude in its turn away from the social protest tradition best represented by Wright's *Native Son*. Assuredly, my book feels incomplete without a bit more analysis of Ellison's novel, because it is devoted to generating a new canon of afrofuturist classics. By way of explanation, in his own 1981 introduction to the novel Ellison himself claims that he was "well aware that a piece of science fiction was the last thing [he] aspired to write" (xv), and even though he actually did not write SF, he had no other term with which to classify it because afrofuturism as a critical concept did not yet exist and would not for another twelve years. However, his instinct to call it SF was spot-on.

In pondering *Invisible Man*, Ellison ironically describes his nameless narrator in cyborg terminology. During the Golden Day scene of chapter 3, an unnamed mental patient, a shell-shocked World War II veteran, at a brothel/bar engages an emotionally fatigued Mr. Norton in conversation regarding the protagonist. Norton happens to be the rich white benefactor of the unidentified, all-black Southern college modeled on the Tuskegee Institute, founded by Booker T. Washington in Alabama. The narrator has been chauffeuring Norton around the college's surroundings and is seated nearby when the conversation around him unfolds. To be clear, the two characters—the vet and Norton—are talking about the third—the narrator—in his presence. The psychotic war veteran explains the narrator's naïveté to the overwhelmed Norton: The narrator "has eyes and ears and a good distended African nose but he fails to understand the simple facts of life" that "he's invisible, a walking personification of the Negative, the most perfect achievement of your [Norton] dreams . . . the mechanical man!" (94). The vet also calls the nameless protagonist "this automaton . . . made of the very mud of the region" who "cannot see or hear or smell the truth . . . looking for destiny" (95). Trained to think of pleasing white people first, to appease their desires to the detriment of himself and his downtrodden race, the narrator represents the ideal young black man to white people. But the narrator does not recognize his own invisibility; he cannot see his own complexity as an individual because of his skin color even when this veteran mental patient says to his face that he is more or less invisible. Therein lies the problem. The narrator is doubly blind because he cannot see himself or other people and spends the rest of the novel discovering his identity.

Ellison continues the cyborg metaphor later in the novel. While briefly employed at the Liberty Paints factory, a business specializing in making optic white paint "to "KEEP AMERICA PURE" (196), the chief and only boiler-room attendant, Lucius Brockway, describes himself and the nameless protagonist as *"the machines inside the machine"* (emphasis in the original 217), meaning that these black men are literally parts of a white corporate America designed to enrich white people even further while enforcing segregation. The reality described for black Americans here represents a technoculture managed by white people, with blacks mechanized as a form of slave labor that harks all the way back to Thomas Jefferson. In Lisa Yaszek's words, "Ellison strategically deploys the language of science fiction to emphasize the alienation of black subjects from these kinds of whitewashed futures" ("An Afrofuturist" 305). Ellison strongly desires to break with such a reality in which blacks are disposable tools denied their own humanity.

Ellison continues what I call *soul flow,* a metaphoric feedback loop between the black mind and its own body, a perceptual filter of sorts for discerning race and racism, allowing his readers to see, anticipate, and challenge a science-fictional blackness in the real world. I claim an afrofuturistic cyberspace here because we first meet Ellison's nameless protagonist stealing electricity from "Monopolated Light & Power" from his hole beneath Harlem, hacking electricity itself to power his dreams of revolution as he smokes reefer and listens to Louis Armstrong create blues, as I previously indicated in the introduction (5). This stolen "light confirms [his] reality" as a black man stereotyped into invisibility, and he knows it (6). From this viewpoint, Ellison fights against looming black erasure in the future. This battle occurs on two fronts: First, the protagonist creates and colors his own future, and, second, he invites a mixed audience to see the need for liberation from systemic oppression. These two fronts signal how he ended up in the hole in the first place—by running from the Black Nationalist Ras the Destroyer in the middle of a riot in Harlem.

More in line with the intent of this chapter, the race riot in *Invisible Man* symbolizes the self-destructive capacity of a black militancy stirred by lies and racial antagonism. In his function as a speaker for the Brotherhood, a communistlike group led by white men that supposedly wants to better living conditions for all people in Harlem, the narrator provides a rousing eulogy for the fallen and disillusioned black Brotherhood member Tod Clifton, shot to death by the NYPD while resisting arrest. However, the narrator has been lying to the Brotherhood leadership for some time concerning Harlem's pulse or, rather, how the neighborhood feels toward Brotherhood-sponsored programs that lead toward integration with white people. Ras's idea of a black world, preached on the street corners when he was known as the Exhorter, gains traction while the narrator is absent from Harlem, assigned to the woman question earlier in the novel. Ras sparks the race riot with his black power antics, renaming himself Destroyer, and attempts first to spear and then to lynch the narrator whom he sees in the streets while parading "upon a great black horse . . . dressed in the costume of an Abyssinian chieftain" calling for a raid on the Harlem armory to fight white people (556). The narrator evades capture but falls down into the darkness of an uncovered manhole while realizing it was the Brotherhood's plan all along to cause a riot; in this darkness is where we find the narrator at the end and beginning of the novel, "outside of historical time" in his own pocket universe (440). The nameless protagonist has fine-tuned his maladjusted self-perceptual filters to finally understand himself and the world.

Ellison's novel belongs in afrofuturist discussions of a black race war tradition. While squaring with the omission of this tradition in scholarly accounts of SF is difficult, the failure to recognize the tradition as having such early origins is perhaps for good reason: Black people, we might assume, could not possibly want to express disgruntlement with America after landmark civil rights legislation. After all, the Civil Rights Act of 1964 outlaws discrimination in business hiring practices; the Voting Rights Act of 1965 reinforces the African American right to vote, previously guaranteed by the 15th Amendment to the Constitution; the Civil Rights Act of 1968 curtails housing discrimination to create an equitable home-buying market; and the various affirmative action policies of the Kennedy and Johnson presidential administrations attempt to create a perception of equality in the United States during this second Reconstruction.[7] But black-authored novels that appeared after *Invisible Man* was published and after important civil rights legislation was enacted indicate that we would be wrong in this assumption.

Although the Black Arts and Black Power movements were dominated by poetry, a few black writers voiced their frustration with the racial status quo through their race war novels. William Melvin Kelley's *A Different Drummer* (1962),[8] Warren Miller's *The Siege of Harlem* (1964),[9] Ronald L. Fair's

---

7. See the third edition of Manning Marable's classic study *Race, Reform, and Rebellion: The Second Reconstruction and Beyond in Black America, 1945–2006* (2007).

8. Kelley describes a bloodless revolution in which the black Tucker Caliban decides to burn down his house, salt his fields, kill his livestock, and then walk away from his land with his family. His actions cause a black exodus, economically crippling the imaginary Southern state.

9. Miller depicts the first year of Harlem's secession from the United States as a flashback in the memory of an old black man, Lance Huggins.

Many Thousand Gone: An American Fable (1965),[10] and John O. Killens's *'Sippi* (1967)[11] easily come to mind. Regardless, Julian Moreau's (pseudonym for Denis Jackson) *The Black Commandos* (1967) may be the most representative example of the period. Moreau crafts a story in which the "National Secret Police for the Negro People of America—NSPNPA—better known as the black Commandos" kill hundreds of Ku Klux Klan members, the LAPD, and an assortment of racist judges and governors (73). The novel culminates at the battle of Jackson, Mississippi, where "twenty four thousand superbly trained—super athletes" converge on the city because it represents the heart of white supremacy in the South. These black commandos release their toxic pink gas in Jackson; Washington, DC; and many other cities like New York, LA, and Miami, apparently killing millions of white folks and bringing the country to its knees in immediately securing black equal rights (196). Of course, the Black Commandos possess an antidote to the pink mist that revive the white masses within forty-eight hours of equality.

Williams himself wrote two other speculative novels before *Captain Blackman*. *The Man Who Cried I Am* (1967) features an American conspiracy to kill all the black folks in case of civil unrest; the conspiracy was called the King Alfred Plan and was uncovered by the dying black writer Max Reddick. *Sons of Darkness, Sons of Light: A Novel of Some Probability* (1969) depicts the early days of a national race war that began in New York City. The black Eugene Browning of the Institute for Racial Justice hires a hitman to murder a white police officer, Sergeant Carrigan, who has killed an unarmed black boy. These events touch off a race war involving black militants. Sam Greenlee's *The Spook Who Sat by the Door* (1969) stars Dan Freeman, a black man, who uses his CIA training to teach Chicago gang members how to fight a guerilla war against the government while he maintains his cover as a social worker, a job he had at the beginning of this freedom fight.[12] "Promising rupture and new realities," these Black Power–era novels remain a political measure of the racial unrest of the 1960s and the 2010s (Bould, "Come" 221).

---

10. Ronald L. Fair portrays the imaginary town of Jacobsville, Mississippi, where slavery survives in secret into the mid-twentieth century until the black population violently wins its freedom.

11. In Killens's novel the protagonist, Charles Chaney, a college student involved in the voting rights struggle in Mississippi, joins the Elders, a black organization equipped to protect black people and to usher in racial climate change.

12. Greenlee's novel, with its King Cobra gang members sniping cops, hits particularly close to home, reminding me of how Micah Xavier Johnson ambushed Dallas police officers on July 7, 2016, only for this infamous attack to be repeated by Gavin Eugene Long in Baton Rouge ten days later.

The 1970s also featured these militant futures. Blyden Jackson's *Operation Burning Candle* (1973),[13] John Dee's *Stagger Lee* (1973),[14] and Nivi-Kofi A. Easley's *The Militants* (1974)[15] stand out. Undoubtedly, there are other such books depicting violent revolution by black folks, all written by men, which makes Toni Morrison's Seven Days society in *Song of Solomon* (1977) a bit of a novelty. Guitar tells his best friend, the black protagonist Milkman, about the Seven Days:

> There is a society. It's made up of a few men who are willing to take some risks. They don't initiate anything; they don't even choose. They are as indifferent as rain. But when a Negro child, Negro woman, or Negro man is killed by whites and nothing is done about it by *their* law and *their* courts, this society selects a similar victim at random, and they execute him or her in a similar manner if they can. If the Negro was hanged, they hang; if a Negro was burnt, they burn; raped and murdered, they rape and murder. If they can. If they can't do it precisely in the same manner, they do it any way they can, but they do it. (154–55)

Although Morrison's novel probably should not be read in this science-fictional black militant register, her secret society clearly belongs with these other texts because of the planned revenge murders. *Song of Solomon*'s meaning changes as it deals with the complexities of black feeling toward white people and black people. Such meaning implodes when Guitar goes after Milkman because he feels cheated out of Milkman's family's rumored hidden gold, gold that Guitar wants to fund society missions. This suspicion causes Guitar to follow Milkman on an identity quest from Michigan to Shalimar, Virginia, in an attempt to kill Milkman. In Shalimar, Milkman learns that his great-grandfather Solomon escaped slavery by flying back to Africa, abandoning the family in the process. The myth of flight represents the climax of Milkman's quest into his familial past, where his own future is ensured depending on the ambiguous outcome of his leap at the gun-toting Guitar. The future and past come together in a repeating feedback loop.

---

13. Jackson's novel describes how black Vietnam veteran Aaron Rodgers organizes a Harlem underground group of vets like himself to assassinate Southern Democrats who are meeting in New York.

14. Dee's novel features the titular black folk hero leading a black exodus from America to Africa as the world's population declines.

15. In Easley's novel a secret black organization known as COON (Coordinated Organization of Nationalists) dedicates itself "to the overthrow of the government, Capitalism, and Honkyism in general" (53).

Wish fulfillment strongly comes to mind when we think about novels that depict black men triumphing over white men—warring for supremacy in retribution for a life denied. As James Baldwin writes, "The glorification of one race and the consequent debasement of another—or others—always has been and always will be a recipe for murder. There is no way around this" (*The Fire* 82). Surely we can see the effects of black power on each of these writers, even Morrison. They all desire a better future for black people and imagine how it comes about in a variety of ways. The confluence of SF's New Wave and the Black Arts Movement seemingly produced these counterculture moments as revolutionary impulses that can be intensely felt in these largely forgotten writings. The nonviolent practices of the civil rights movement has given way to a more radical expression of a desperate optimism, at least in literature, as the networked black consciousness has metaphorically cycled up to an incandescent speed to achieve a free future, a postrace era that will never come.

B. A. M. and the New Wave

Williams creates an alternate world in a near-future America where such a thing could happen, a race war as Blackman seeks revenge against The Man—the Caucasian honky Mr. Charlie—and in the process a psychological battle physically materializes. Williams's use of elements such as drugs, sex, pessimism, war, inward reflection, and political cynicism analogically resonates with New Wave SF, as do the contraflow of Black Nationalism and its ensuing revolutionary impetus. In fact, the murders of Emmet Till, Medgar Evers, Malcolm X, and Martin Luther King Jr. provide the necessary rage and hurt undergirding a novel like *Captain Blackman*. These feelings carry forward into the so-called postrace-era murders of Trayvon Martin, Michael Brown, Sandra Bland, and many others. Applying afrofuturist theory, I demonstrate how Blackman adopts insurgency measures to kill all the white folks,[16] to borrow Kali Tal's terminology, and also how Williams provides a compelling countercultural critique of white American politics through his

---

16. Kali Tal indicates that a "black militant near-future fiction," rather a "kill-the-white-folks futurist fiction," is "one subgenre of African American science fiction," one in which "African Americans join in violent revolution against the system of white supremacy" (66–67). This subgenre features "secret societies, charismatic leaders, tension between positions of violence and nonviolence, differing status among African Americans (often symbolized by skin color), and marginalization of women characters, whose sole purpose is to further the plot and enhance our understanding of the protagonist" (88–89).

novel's insistence that black people must determine a future for themselves. Williams's art goes beyond mere entertainment in its purpose because the novel offers us a radical vision, fully connected to the looping history of the black networked consciousness. *Captain Blackman* offers us hope in its depiction of a black man with the strength required to be a black man in the white world. This radical departure breaks from the apocalyptic warning Richard Wright offers in *Native Son*. Blackman is a captain, a leader of men, as opposed to a son closely connected with Wright's inner-city environment.

Not known as an SF writer, let alone a member of the American New Wave, Williams navigates the many social upheavals of this turbulent era across the body of his writing: civil rights marches, political assassinations, antiwar protests, cold-war flare-ups like the Cuban Missile Crisis, a massive counterculture movement, hippy-dom, the sexual revolution, the American Indian Movement, second-wave feminism, the gay rights movement, the Stonewall riots in NYC, the rise of the new left, urban unrest, global decolonization, widespread use of drugs like psychedelics and marijuana, music, not to mention the Black Power Movement itself. Such monumental events signify the "generational shake-up," to which noted British SF historian Edward James refers in *Science Fiction in the Twentieth Century* (1994) and which led to the New Wave on both sides of the Atlantic Ocean (167), where younger writers demonstrated an interest in softer sciences like psychology rather than hard sciences like biology. As Roger Luckhurst claims, both British and American groups, best represented by Michael Moorcock[17] and Harlan Ellison,[18] respectively, "regarded Golden Age SF as an exhausted mode of low culture," whereas the New Wave "defined the turn from muscular adventures in outer space to psychological examination of inner space" (141–42). For me, the New Wave in SF expresses formal experimentation within the genre along the lines of racial antagonism, sex, psychological complexity, and exploration of the inner spaces of black rage and frustration, all perfectly captured by any number of twentieth-century black poets such as Claude McKay, Langston Hughes, Nikki Giovanni, Amiri Baraka, and Gwendolyn Brooks—all afrofuturists in the terms widest sense.[19]

---

17. Many scholars date the beginning of SF's New Wave to Michael Moorcock's time as the editor of the British SF magazine *New Worlds* starting in May 1964.

18. Harlan Ellison's anthologies *Dangerous Visions* (1967) and *Again, Dangerous Visions* (1972) best represent the New Wave in America.

19. Claude McKay expresses black courage in "If We Must Die" (1919), stating, "Like men we'll face the murderous, cowardly pack / Pressed to the wall, dying, but fighting back" (lines 11–12). Hughes's well-known "Harlem" (1951) questions what deferred black dreams look like and what their potential for exploding is. And his little-known "Warning" (1967) cautions white people that "Negroes, / Sweet and docile, / Meek,

A link arises between black culture and New Wave SF with afrofuturism as the connection point between the past and the possible future Williams imagines. Yet this connection depends on who is defining afrofuturism, an especially challenging thing to do, which I attempt throughout this book. Afrofuturist tools, such as transhistoric feedback loops, networked black consciousness, and a hope impulse, aid in rethinking and rewriting the prevailing accounts of black culture(s) as they relate to speculative genres, specifically SF. In syncing Black Power and New Wave SF, Williams taps directly into afrofuturism's networked black consciousness through time travel and racial memory in the figure of Captain Blackman.

Radicalizing Blackman

To understand how Abraham Blackman becomes radicalized, we must consider his present military career and the animosity between himself and Major Ishmael Whittman. Obviously, Blackman represents Black America and Whittman represents White America. Not so obvious is that the religious implications of the rivals' first names indicate Ishmael was cast out of Abraham's family, the first great biblical patriarch. Williams mixes Black Arts Movement aesthetics and Nation of Islam theology with these names. According to NOI theology, the white man's enslavement of original man, black man, the seed of Abraham, was foreseen in the Christian Bible, and the domination of the scientifically created white man, who utilizes tricks and lies, would come to an end one day through revolution. His "space blue-eyes" (22) and "flaxen hair" (23) clearly mark Whittman as the "blue-eyed devil"[20] of black power rhetoric, as his Asian origins from various European colonizing efforts in Asia mark him as being of mixed race. Another possible connotation of the name Ishmael Whittman, in which Ishmael echoes the narrator of *Moby-Dick; or the Whale* (1851) and Whittman symbolizes the poet Walt Whitman of *Leaves of Grass* (1855) fame, suggests that Williams is taking

---

humble, and kind: / Beware the day / They change their mind!" (lines 1–5). Giovanni, in "For Saundra" (1968), explains how "i wanted to write / a poem / that rhymes / but revolution doesn't lend / itself to be-bopping" (lines 1–5). In "Black Art" (1969), Amiri Baraka declares, "We want poems that kill. / Assassin poems, Poems that shoot / guns. Poems that wrestle cops into alleys / and take their weapons leaving them dead" (lines 19–22). In "Riot" (1969), Brooks explains how "Negroes were coming down the street" as the white John Cabot gets caught up and killed (line 10).

20. See *The Autobiography of Malcom X*, in which Malcolm X calls the white man a "blue-eyed devil" at least eleven times (169).

on the white canon too by evoking Herman Melville and Walt Whitman of America's Romantic period.

As noted in the beginning of this chapter, we first see Captain Blackman as a forty-year-old black officer in the present of the novel's beginning, late in the Vietnam War sometime in the early 1970s. Ostensibly, Blackman joined the army in 1949 to prove his manliness and to see a bit of the world as a restless eighteen-year-old Harlemite. He scored Grade I on the Army General Classification test—top marks—and was earmarked as officer material. After making corporal and then sergeant, Blackman was assigned to duty in Japan. However, the Cold War heated up in Korea. Pursuant to President Truman's Executive Order 9981, dating back to July 6, 1948, the US Army sent integrated units for the first time to the Pusan region of Korea as part of the United Nations' military forces sometime in July 1950. Blackman and Whittman flew over to Korea on the same plane. All of the black soldiers already knew that Whittman scored in Grade III, got his sergeant stripes earlier than Blackman, and spent his time with the 24th Regiment complaining to headquarters about how he served with Negroes.

The animosity between Blackman and Whittman during their time in Vietnam stems from a map-reading incident near the end of their service in Korea. By that time, Blackman is still a sergeant, and Whittman a master sergeant, Whittman is in charge of both of their squads. Whitman cannot read the map, and Blackman recognizes that Whittman pretends to do so every time Blackman points out an error. Blackman realizes, "This cat don't care. . . . He's so scared of losing face that he's not even worried about getting killed himself" (237–38). At the end of his patience, Blackman reaches for the map, Whittman snatches it away, and "the fight [is] on" as Blackman clubs Whittman "into the ground with his fists and loving it, but at times recoiling from the burning hatred in the blue eyes"; he then attacks Whittman "even more fiercely, until the eyes showed nothing, glazed over like porcelain" (238).

In the Vietnam War present, after learning that Captain Blackman gets hit out on patrol, Major Whittman thinks of Blackman as a "pain in the ass, twenty years of pain, dating from Korea" and from his own "accumulated guilt" over rising in the army while Blackman was passed over (83). Meditating on perceived insults across twenty years, Major Whittman goes to visit Blackman in the hospital "intent on seeing the broken man in the bed . . . . This is what he'd done, finally to the nigger who'd whipped his ass in Korea" and who dared to start a "black military history seminar" (236). Whittman had sent Blackman into the jungle with faulty intelligence, resulting in Blackman's grievous injuries. When protecting his men from an ambush created by drawing the attention of enemy AK-47s, Blackman loses one lung, has his right leg amputated, and nearly has his testicles shot off with "a slug through the bag" (169). As a result of his heroics, Blackman wins the Medal of Honor and gets promoted to major before being honorably discharged. However, not before taunting Whittman, "Well, man, I'm gonna be short in a couple places, but not where it's gonna count. . . . Equal rank. More Pension . . . you turkey motherfucker" (237). He brags about his penis, being more of a man, and finally obtaining equal rank with Whittman. Now done with the army, Blackman disappears into the world.

He vanishes in order to plan revenge for all of the hatred, violence, and vitriol spewed by the white man. His disappearance relates directly to his reasons for starting the black military history seminar in the first place. Blackman recalls a conversation with one of his buddies, Handy, during the Korean War when they overhear a white soldier refer to Korean refugees as "poor fuckin gooks" (239). Handy winks at Blackman and states, "Just like sayin nigger, ain't it, man?" to which Blackman replies, "There's a whole heap of black soldiers callin 'em gooks, too. Even you." . . ."Negroes here out-Whiteying Whitey. Catchin his goddamn disease just hangin out with him in these wars" (239). Blackman uses such contemptuous language to demonstrate his disgust at how easily blacks blindly participate in cruelty, how callously they feel their own power over the weaker brown peoples of the world, complicit with whites in their unthinking hatred and militarism in defense of democracy.

Likewise, Blackman reflects on how "black men became like white men" in Vietnam, because indiscriminately killing Vietnamese allowed blacks "to know what it felt like to kill without fear of punishment, in broad daylight" (247). He wants no part of this science-fictional experience in passing for an automaton, an unfeeling machine obedient to authority, a tool for the government. It is as if the human/machine boundary erodes before his eyes when he sees fellow black soldiers rape, murder, and castrate brown people just like the white men do. He identifies their willingness to perpetrate violence as a sickness and notes how "the whites were relieved that blacks at last had joined them," sacrificing "that essential human quality for which they were well known" (247). No longer empathic or concerned for the other, blacks become much like Philip K. Dick's Nexus-6 androids in *Do Androids Dream of Electric Sheep?* (1968), even though, unlike Bigger Thomas, these soldiers have orders to kill. Blackman decides to investigate black military history to preserve the human distinction of black people from moments just like these, and he goes a step further in teaching it to the men under his command. His research into black military history initiates the transhistoric feedback loop which in turn plugs him into the black webbed consciousness with which to challenge white supremacy.

A fascinating moment arises on this point of complicity with whites when Blackman thinks of a second conversation with his buddy Handy concerning China's use of psychological warfare in Korea. This moment reflects a disentanglement from white thought patterns. The Chinese allies of the North Koreans drop leaflets on the mountainous road toward Pyongyang. Out of curiosity Blackman picks one up and reads:

> Black soldiers of America. You have crossed the 38th Parallel. You are now an Aggressor against the People's Republic of North Korea. You now approach the border of the People's Republic of China. Defensive action to annihilate the Aggressor Armies will commence at once. Our battle is not against the exploited, captive Black Soldiers of America, but against the white imperialist government that threatens the peace of Asia. Lay down your arms. No harm will come to you. We welcome you as Brothers seeking freedom. Bring this with you. (240)

I find this defamiliarized moment poignant because it mirrors the fireside chat that Blackman had with the Native Americans in that there is a strange sense of colored brotherhood expressed in this appeal. Yellow men and black men cooperate with one another for freedom's sake in order to dismantle the construction of racial binaries that uphold white power structures in the political sense. That is a powerful thought and is in line with Vijay Prashad's concept of the "polycultural," which foregrounds "antiracism rather than diversity" in forging "a ferocious engagement with the political world of culture, a painful embrace of the skin and all its contradictions" (xii). In other words, this pan-ethnic connection attempts to distort the identity politics separating blacks from yellows in order to preserve white supremacy. (It recalls W. E. B. Du Bois's earlier attempt to do a similar if not the same thing in *Dark Princess* [1928]).[21] Of course, the leaflet represents a

---

21. In Du Bois's novel the black protagonist, Mathew Townes, gets expelled from medical school because his color bars him from working with white pregnant women. He goes on a self-imposed exile to Berlin, where he meets the Princess Kautilya of India. They fall in love, and she eventually bears him a son, the royal heir of Bwodpur. But in the meantime, Mathew and the princess belong to an international organization of colored people formed to resist white imperialism. This novel also involves assessing black social progress in the United States. The romantic elements of the book firmly distinguish it as an afrofuturist work reflective of Du Bois's desire to improve the world for colored peoples.

blatant psychological ploy to unsettle the invading American troops, to sow further distrust, and to exploit the racial tensions between them.

The propaganda plays upon racial fictions prevalent in the armed forces that blacks were cowards. This unfounded notion persisted even though the largely black 24th Regiment secured "the initial U.N. victory at a time when white units were faltering. . . . White officers prosecuted black soldiers for cowardice as a way of shifting blame for their own leadership failures" (Graham 13). These leaflets function as "militarized technogeometries," defined by Stephen Hong Sohn, in relation to Korean American speculative fiction, as "cultural productions [which] embed the technologies of warfare as a key component to the formation and the development of territorial disputes and conflicts that necessarily involve tactical decisions, mathematical calculations, and biopolitical discourses" (58). In their attempt to win the war, the Chinese make a tactical decision hinged upon biopolitics. In keeping with the Black Arts and Black Power Movements, Williams's historical accuracy heightens the functionality of his revolutionary art in his afrofuturistic portrayal of war as Williams himself attempts to initiate social change in America.

A second and even more captivating moment on this point of complicity with whites occurs during an earlier dream fragment in the text—a flashback to the Plains Wars with Blackman as a Buffalo Soldier approximately eighty years in the past. Originally, the Buffalo Soldiers were an African American regiment of the US Army's 10th Cavalry established by Congress in 1866 to help settlers on the Western frontier of the country after the Civil War through the 1890s.[22] Led by the white Colonel Benjamin Grierson (a historical personage featured as a character in the novel), they rode out of Fort Leavenworth in Kansas. One moment in the story has the feel of an alien encounter in which Williams provides insight on how these black soldiers were named by Native Americans. Blackman makes a mail run through Indian Territory and stops beside a stream for the night. Two Comanche materialize from the night, hold up their right hands in greeting, and proceed to touch Blackman's kinky hair, at which point one of the Indians admiringly states that Blackman's hair "is like the hair of the Buffalo" (74). Blackman experiences a moment of suspicion when reflecting on how his commanding officers insisted "that you couldn't trust Indians," that, in fact, "the only good Indian was a dead Indian," to use their racist logic—a logic that Blackman then reinterprets as "the only good nigger was a dead nig-

---

22. See Shirley A. Leckie and William H. Leckie's *The Buffalo Soldiers: A Narrative of the Black Cavalry in the West* (2007).

ger" (75). This refracted thought describes how easy it becomes to absorb the presuppositions of white racism.

At this realization, and despite his initial misgivings, Blackman decides to relax and share his fire with the two Comanche Man in the Rain and Wolf Heart. A philosophical conversation ensues, with Man in the Rain questioning black participation in Indian removal despite previous friendships between the races. Without rancor, the conversation turns toward the genocide of Native Americans, and Man in the Rain prophetically envisions "the end of the Indian people," seeing "them inside reservations . . . pushed there by missionaries who talk of the love of Christ, but do the work of the Devil" (76). Blackman cannot disagree with this statement of future fact and does not get angry when Man in the Rain gently chides Buffalo Soldiers for their part in it, for believing in Christianity, and for not fighting alongside the natives. Man in the Rain also predicts that the day will come when blacks, exhausted from white racism and its attendant social and physical death, will stand up and fight long after Indians are gone.

I focus on this dialogue because I find it important to comprehend this meeting's significance in the sense that a true alien encounter occurs, not in the sense of little green men but in a meeting of racialized, oppressed human others that are made into aliens by white people. Such alienation symbolizes "the internal conflicts of a humanity marked, or perhaps scarred, by racial experience, our continual state of difference" (Lavender, *Race* 25–26), But this meeting between Blackman and the Comanche entails an often-overlooked iteration of the Du Boisian color line—between black and red. This moment of contact between two alienated groups constitutes a science-fictional alien encounter in which Williams's deft plotting recodes the future of race relations. Blackman realizes that "race always designates a political relationship rather than a biological identity" (Rieder, *Science Fiction and the Mass Cultural Genre System* 141). Such a thought fuels a radical afrofuturism, one in which Blackman's collective black experience of America's martial and social histories both symbolically and literally plugs into his own networked consciousness; loops forward; and continually compounds as a militant, liberatory, and hopeful urgency in the future war envisioned by Man in the Rain. From this point of view, Williams anticipates through Abraham Blackman a divergent future in which blacks gain the upper hand in the race war.

Moments such as these propel not only Blackman but us too through time-space, a black-memory matrix that feeds his will and consciousness, helping him gather the necessary power to unleash a revolutionary black potential in order to escape the soul-crushing effect of white supremacy. Grace Kyungwon Hong views this budding action as a "clear leap" that implies "the ability to believe that a different future might be possible," thereby blasting "a specific era out of the homogenous course of history" (107–8). In this manner, Blackman completes the feedback loop by becoming a living conduit of what Carrington calls "speculative blackness" (3),[23] or what Michelle D. Commander terms "Afro-speculation" (6),[24] to produce a sense of afrotopia. This sense of afrotopia flings hope both forward and backward in time-space, resembling the feedback loop at work throughout afrofuturist literature and directly linking to the networked black consciousness. In Williams's novel, hope, possibility, and future combine to provide a strong example of afrofuturism, an example that demonstrates the power of black art.

Blackman the Teacher

An important part of understanding Williams's novel relates to the black military history seminars that Captain Blackman leads in Vietnam. These seminars reveal exactly how racial friction fueled a seemingly invisible war between black soldiers and white soldiers. As Cash states, "It would not be an exaggeration to say that John A. Williams had been preparing for Captain Blackman since his discharge from the Navy in 1946" because "he had been disappointed and disillusioned by his experiences in the service" (117). Blackman parses together a seminar by reading obscure books secured by his girlfriend Mimosa and by talking to black war veterans "during his travels [where] he'd met old vets from World War I; that old guy with the 369th living near La Rochelle" (245).[25] He attempts to bridge the generational gap between himself and the mainly black soldiers under his command because of the countercultural movement back home in the United States, a move-

---

23. Carrington characterizes "speculative blackness" as "not just a study of how black people are represented in a particular area of popular culture but also an examination of the ways in which black people's heterogeneous interests come to bear on the range of cultural endeavors in which we involve ourselves" (3). He also notes how much black speculative fiction depicts "imaginary settings that rewrite history or positive possible future worlds" (8). We learn what speculative fiction has to say about the meaning of blackness by placing race at the heart of genre discussions.

24. For Commander, Afro-speculation concerns "the artistic reimagining of the function of science and technology in the construction of utopic black futures" (6). Afro-speculation and speculative blackness seem to be similar terms, though they have vastly different nuances, with Carrington focusing on popular culture and Commander interested in ethnography, history, and roots tourism.

25. Think of Toni Morrison's *Sula* (1973) and her World War I veteran Shadrack, who is a shattered potential revolutionary who invents National Suicide Day in the novel.

ment that has produced a "new Afro-American sensibility, informed by the psychological revolution now operative within black America" (Neal 195). Historian Herman Graham III reveals how "black soldiers often congregated informally in their hootches to participate in 'soul sessions' in which they socialized together and discussed racial issues" (100). Williams consciously mirrors such gatherings through Blackman's own soul seminars. In fact, Blackman becomes "a combination ghetto soul brother and militant intellectual" for these young soldiers (195). Blackman helps them cope with a variety of social issues—racism, stereotypes such as cowardice, and black manhood—to awaken their historical consciousness by rejecting their own subordinate status and adopting positive attitudes about their own culture and identity—not radical, but truly fundamental to a healthy black collective consciousness. Blackman begins the process of freeing the soldiers from a science-fictional blackness.

But why teach these seminars? Blackman himself tells us, "'We don't have anything to prove to anybody. . . . We've done it over and over and over again. No heroes. Just do your jobs'" (2). Of course, he refers to all of the black men who have courageously fought in wars for a country that does not respect them. Even more so, Blackman comes to understand the nature of dehumanization by studying black military history, leading to his "active condemnation of black soldiers' . . . adopting and using whites' prejudices" and their becoming "imitation white soldier[s]" in order "to feel good about barbaric acts" (Norman Harris 40–41). He arrives at this point only because of his own studies. Most of all, Blackman unlocks the afrofuture in creating these uncompromising black men who will in turn bring down America by novel's end. Blackman's transhistorical movement relates directly to his experiences of the United States' broken promises to its black soldiers—namely, land, wealth, equality, respect, and freedom, all of which are pieces of the American dream promised in the Declaration of Independence. Consequently, Blackman must revise the historical record of black military service by confronting the racial abuse meted out by white leadership and white common soldiers and by teaching the feedback loop itself—an experiment in time travel.

To make a quick but relevant aside, Blackman's white enemy Whittman and black love interest Mimosa also manifest in most of these periods. Symbolically, Blackman's relationship with Whittman revolves around women and revenge. In fact, it seems rooted in the historical emasculation and criminalization of black manhood wherein white America has a bizarre fetish with containing black sexuality. As Frantz Fanon states, "We know historically that the Negro guilty of lying with a white woman is castrated"

(72). Blackman courts his own doom by participating in these deadly fantasies when he believes he can secure his tormentor's power, represented by white women, in order to escape from "a zone of nonbeing" caused by his skin color (8). An almost alienlike contact with white culture nearly undoes Blackman in the present, which is why Blackman must return and relive racial history in order to destroy a past, present, and future assigned to him from white America. Painful as this history proves, Blackman cannot free himself until he reinvents it and fully understands that power, love, and respect come from within—a lesson Ellison's *Invisible Man* fails to learn by tumbling "outside history" (306). As LeRoi Jones (Amiri Baraka) claims, "The paradox of the Negro experience in America is that it is a separate experience, but inseparable from the complete fabric of American life" (169). Consequently, Blackman must pull back the Du Boisian veil[26] and encounter the physical, economic, and psychological forces immobilizing him.

Blackman has had a keen interest in black military history before he suffers his injuries, and this interest establishes the thought fragments and feelings necessary for him to propel himself into a past he has accumulated by reading histories and by conversing with black veterans. Pinned down against a wet patch of grass, Blackman reflects on his downtime seminar and how he had told his soldiers "with their mushrooming Afros and off-duty dashikis" about other black soldiers in other American wars "going back to the American Revolution to Prince Estabrook, Peter Salem, Crispus Attucks, and all of the unnamed rest" (2). This generational experience aligns itself against the power, terror, and violence historically wielded by white people, thus creating a black future readiness and determination to fight back, to fight for justice, to fight for a black world. There can be no universal humanity until oppression ends with the dismantling of racism. The only way for Blackman to accomplish such a goal: kill all the white folks or, at the very least, make them fear the threat of such a racial genocide! He gains such clarification only by revisiting and confronting the past; he gains a visceral access to this racial memory only through pain.

The mix of pain, fear, and drugs knocks Blackman's consciousness free of his body, and his mind somehow returns to America's first military conflict—the Revolutionary War. (Curiously, this war is the only one where he remembers the future; the past is a dream from which he cannot wake. But

---

26. For W. E. B. Du Bois, the veil represents a visual representation of the color line. It metaphorically separates the black world and the white world; that is, it demonstrates that many black people cannot see beyond the role white America has prescribed for them and, in turn, that white Americans cannot see blacks as truly American. Du Bois talks about the veil in "The Forethought" to *The Souls of Black Folk* (1903).

more on this later.) He fights alongside free blacks and slaves in 1775. He fights with the Freejacks[27] in the battle of New Orleans during the War of 1812. He fights as a Union soldier during the Civil War and survives General Nathan Bedford Forrest's massacre of black troops at Fort Pillow. He fights as a Buffalo Soldier in the 10th Cavalry Regiment during the further pacification of Native American tribes during the Plains Wars and the Manifest Destiny period of the United States. He fights with both the 10th Calvary and the 25th Infantry, segregated units, in Cuba during the Spanish-American War. He fights with the "Harlem Hellfighters" of the 369th Infantry Regiment, formerly known as the New York Fifteenth National Guard,[28] in France during the Great War; with the international mixed Lincoln Brigade for the Spanish Revolution;[29] and again with the segregated 24th Regiment in Italy during World War II. All of these campaigns take place against the racial backdrop of the antebellum and Jim Crow eras—and their inherent white terror campaigns to keep blacks in line—before the present time of the novel and integrated American military forces.

The Secret Unwinnable Race War

Williams achieves his corrective aim through time travel that grants Blackman explicit, firsthand knowledge of various historical moments and figures as he drifts in and out of consciousness after being injured. Solid research on Williams's part heightens the novel's effect because he includes "heavily documented but not much publicized materials . . . to bring to light the unsung heroisms of Black soldiers during the last two centuries" (Cash 117). As previously mentioned, Blackman appears to maintain his memory of military history when first awakening in the days leading up to the American Revolution at the Battle of Lexington and Concord on April 19, 1775. Virginia Smith instructively misidentifies Blackman's original waking "dream" moment in colonial America as witnessing the First "Continental Congress" at Carpenter's Hall in Philadelphia, Pennsylvania, during September and October of 1774 (667). I say "instructively" because I could certainly imagine a clandestine meeting where important white men plotted against the King

---

27. According to ethnographer Darrell A. Posey, "The Fifth Ward Settlement is composed of approximately 2,500 mixed-blood (Black, White and Indian) inhabitants called 'Freejacks'" (177).

28. See Peter Nelson's *A More Unbending Battle: The Harlem Hellfighters' Struggle for Freedom in WWI and Equality at Home* (2009).

29. See Antony Beevor's *The Battle for Spain: The Spanish Civil War 1936–1939* (2006).

of England and planned the future of America while being served by slaves. This moment would have been perfect for Blackman to observe. It would flawlessly initiate the feedback loop, powering his sense of the networked black consciousness over 200 years of racial conflict and generating his hope to bring down The Man. But Williams clearly describes "an inn in Delaware, a colony half way between their homes in Massachusetts, Virginia, North and South Carolina" where conversations about taxing tea, enduring Lord North's incompetence, and expanding slavery take place (2). As the twentieth-century Blackman concludes at this historical moment, "Chuck ain't shit," meaning that the white man had already oppressed black people and planned on continuing such exploitation (4). Of course, enslaved blacks fighting for white freedom represent one of the great ironies of the Revolutionary War.

Blackman cannot escape this historical trap in the future without first learning from history. He walks out of the woods carrying a musket, with a powder horn strapped across his shoulders and a bag of lead balls at his side, exhorting himself to wake up when a white man on horseback tells him to go to the front ranks with the other blacks whether slave or free. Blackman, dressed in his twentieth-century camouflage battle fatigues, immediately notices that the black would-be soldiers are inadequately armed with "stakes, spears, and clubs" while the whites have muskets like him (4). Among others, Blackman meets Prince Estabrook, a slave later emancipated by his master, Benjamin Estabrook, after serving in the Continental Army; and Peter Salem, a black emancipated by his owner, Major Lawson Buckminster, just to fight in the army. Both Estabrook and Salem think Blackman crazy for telling them how the "Redcoats are gonna lay some shit on you dudes . . . that the British are going to win at Lexington" (5). In fact, they mockingly ask Blackman if he's a "voodoo priest" since he provides them with foreknowledge of the battle that they will not believe occurs until he is proven right. Unfortunately, while wrestling over his gun, Blackman gets bashed on the head by what appears to be Major Whittman and forgets the future while retaining his weapon. By the end of the Revolutionary War, the promise of freedom has never materialized.

The novel leaps forward in time forty years, and we next see a young Blackman at the Battle of New Orleans in January of 1815 during the War of 1812. The fluidity of drug-enhanced time grants the novel both a science-fictional effect when we recognize that Blackman has not aged and an afrofuturistic feel in that the impulse to hope propels Blackman forward in the temporal loop. During this loop, he repeats the war experience while he is offered some chance of breaking the white cycle of oppression. However, he remains trapped in this cycle when he, along with other blacks, agrees to fight for General (and future US president due to his heroics in New Orleans) Andrew Jackson, because they have received the incentive of being given "one hundred and sixty acres of land," and money too. Blackman views Jackson as "an exterminator . . . a tough competitor . . . a chilling kind of man" who would not think twice about using "niggers" to win the war since he "already [had] pirates, Choctaws, Creoles and buckskinned Tennesseans" in his army (28, 31). History tells us that Jackson made the right choice because he won the war at New Orleans. Blackman gets his promised land as a Freejack, "a tough, isolated, proud clan, asking the white man for nothing and giving nothing in return" (36); he is free, but still black. Ethnographer Posey indicates how Freejack is now a "derogatory" term "because of its connotations of racial mixture," because Freejacks claim to be white while "vehemently deny[ing] racial mixture" (177). Thus, their freedom is tainted by continuing and worsening racial oppression as part of the other invisible war between races.

The novel time-shifts again to the second half of the Civil War, in which Blackman fights as a free man with the Union Army. The war within the war heats up as all-black regiments face Confederate soldiers. Williams astutely mentions key battles of this secret war within the Civil War, jump-starting his time loop and injecting it with even more history and black pride. First, Williams mentions the June 7, 1863, Battle of Milliken's Bend[30] in northeastern Louisiana along the Mississippi River, where Confederate troops attempted to cut Union supply lines for the Vicksburg campaign. In a minor, if pivotal, battle, freed black slaves with little military training and inferior weaponry managed to rebuff Texas Confederates. From this minor battle, a doubtful Northern public learned that freed blacks could indeed fight. Of course, Blackman recognizes how "hateful killings that had little to do with war but everything to do with color . . . these constant murders of black soldiers . . . made other black soldiers better fighters" (42). Blackman continues: "Behind their line of march the traded atrocities became legend: prisoners shredded by bayonets; prisoners decapitated; prisoners castrated; prisoners pulled asunder by horses. Still they marched on across the southland, ever fearful that worse could happen" (43). This hot moment in the quiet race war symbolizes an operational networked black conscious-

---

30. In *Milliken's Bend: A Civil War Battle in History and Memory* (2013), archivist Linda Barnickel chronicles "the mistreatment and possible murder of black Union soldiers at Milliken's Bend" and examines "the murder of Union prisoners at Confederate hands" (144, 169).

ness, one in which both free and enslaved black people become freedom fighters to end their oppression. Backed by collective action, they struggle for true freedom.

The second battle mentioned by Williams, Fort Pillow on April 12, 1864, becomes infamous because General Nathan Bedford Forrest[31] massacres approximately 300 black soldiers after surrendering at the fort in Henning, Tennessee, in his desire to maintain white supremacy in the South. Blackman and his regiment later hear of this atrocity and of how "the Mississippi, which flows fast and deep past Memphis, ran red with blood for two days, and that the black civilians fished out heads, arms, legs, and torsos" (44).[32] The third battle to which Williams refers occurred six days later on April 18, 1864, in Ouachita County, Arkansas, and came to be known as the Battle of Poison Spring. At Poison Spring, Confederate soldiers butchered nearly half of the 1st Kanas Colored Infantry. Williams provides a horrifyingly vivid description: "Three black soldiers were left like hunks of buffalo meat on an Arkansas landscape" (44). Blackman's only reflection on this battle reveals that he and his black colleagues "gave up trying to stay human," vowing by their "ancestors, and by the Mother whose name is Africa, to kill with a swift, sure arm, without hesitation" white soldiers "in revenge" (44–45). Monstrosity and contained madness end up being the only hope for black soldiers during the Civil War and the not-so-secret race war that Williams brings to light through the transhistoric feedback loop.

Blackman actually participates in the fourth race battle that Williams names—the Battle of the Crater, July 30, 1864—a battle in which the Union Army attempts to sap under Confederate fortifications around Petersburg. The Union Army blew up the mine about 4:45 a.m., creating a crater 170 feet long, 125 feet wide, and 30 feet deep. After charging through the smoke, Blackman enters the crater; is immediately surrounded by "rebels firing at point-blank range"; is shot twice in the leg; and is nearly trampled to death (54). In fact, Williams quotes Captain Kilmer of the New York 14th Heavy Artillery here:

---

31. See Brian Steel Wills's *A Battle from the Start: The Life of Nathan Bedford Forrest* (1992). Forrest himself was an early member of the original Ku Klux Klan formed in 1866, although "there is some question as to whether he actually was the Grand Wizard" (336).

32. See Richard Fuchs's *An Unerring Fire: The Massacre at Fort Pillow* (2002), in which Fuchs reckons that "the affair at Fort Pillow was simply an orgy of death, a mass lynching to satisfy the basest of conduct—intentional murder—for the vilest of reasons—racism" (14).

> When the colored assault halted, broke, and streamed back, the bravest lost heart and the men who distrusted the Negroes vented their feelings freely. Some colored men came into the Crater, and there they found a fate worse than death. It had been positively asserted that white men bayoneted blacks who fell back into the Crater. This was in order to preserve the whites from Confederate vengeance. Men boasted in my presence that blacks had thus been disposed of, particularly when the Confederates came up. (55)

What this quote means *is* that black soldiers were killed by white men on both sides of the war because white Union soldiers feared a Confederate retaliation.[33] While Civil War Blackman survives the Battle of the Crater, Vietnam Blackman knows he is hit badly. His knowing translates as traumatic knowledge of this ongoing invisible race war; having a sense of disjointed temporality, he is surrounded by his men, whom he has just saved, as they await the medical evacuation helicopter that Whittman sends at three-quarter power. I say "disjointed temporality" because Blackman relives three wars in only a minute between getting hit, passing out, and regaining consciousness in the presence of his men, who knock him out again with a morphine syrette. His re-memory of the past could be interpreted as post-traumatic stress, but an afrofuturist framework is a better interpretation here because a future-bent perspective demonstrates how Blackman learns a little bit more about the white enemy on each of his loops through time.

The secret race war changes when Blackman is put under again by a morphine injection. He awakens in a Civil War hospital and spots the Whittman from his past, now a Union officer, riding in a wagon with a Confederate widow driven by an old black servant named Tom Flood. Earlier in the war, Whittman and a friend manage to get the jump on Blackman, knock him out, and rape the first iteration of Mimosa as a slave. Revenge *is* the utmost thought in Blackman's mind. In short, Blackman devises a new battlefield—the blond widow's body—a diabolic plan to continue the war. He learns that she lives by herself on the Green Pines Plantation with only the old house slave for company, although Yankee Whittman does frequent the location. Blackman recovers from his injury, locates the plantation one evening, and with the help of Tom Flood makes his way to her bedroom. He pistol-whips the sleeping Whittman, ties him up in a chair to watch, and proceeds with his revenge:

---

33. In *No Quarter: The Battle of the Crater, 1864* (2009), Richard Slotkin reports how Confederate Major General William Mahone's men needed no incentive "to make them give 'no quarter,' as it is understood amongst us that we take no negro prisoners" (117).

to plant black seed in her so that what she hated would always be next to her, it's heart beating time with hers for three quarters of a year, and if she tried to rip it out and succeeded, she would still have the memory; it would start her on nights like this for her entire life; she would sleep behind barred doors, flinch at the sound of every black voice, and weep at the site of every black face. She would not have her officer to console her; he would despise her (yet in some strange way, perhaps, desire her all the more, outside the bonds of marriage). More, he, too, would think of nights like this and grow uneasy about his women, uneasy about himself, and would nightmarishly over and over again imagine the sheer audacious horror of it, a black man barreling through centuries of monumental and ritualized taboo to avenge himself. (60–61)

This terrible action brings to life the predominant white fear of the black rapist. Katherine Kinney makes an important point: "By enacting this psychodrama, Blackman only demonstrates his own position within that nightmare rather than escaping from it" (92). History will not change from his action. Blackman gains nothing by it, certainly not self-autonomy. In outlining this stereotype, Tal calls Blackman, and other black literary characters like him, a "'superspade,' the all-powerful black man [whose] potency in the bedroom underlines his effectiveness as a leader" (78).[34] However, Williams carefully humanizes Blackman in later wars, particularly the Spanish Civil War, where a terrified Blackman survives an air raid with bombs falling everywhere and feeling "his bladder go, his sphincter suddenly relax. . . . The smell of his urine, his feces, and his sweat merged into one ugly miasma" (165).

Despite this delayed humanizing, Blackman's pent-up rage and desperation defeat him in this Civil War time loop. His violent sexual assault on the blond widow does not help him win freedom and equality for all black

---

34. Tal makes a strong point about women characters being marginalized in these novels, noting that Williams plays up "the hyper-masculinist attitudes[,] and self-presentation of the black power movement reinforce[s] the already extremely sexist biases of the genre" (69). Regarding World War I, Blackman states, "The last thing the French were worried about was black men getting French pussy" (125). During World War II Blackman thinks to himself, "Pussy, who's getting it, sure worries the white man to death" (203). In Korea, Blackman reflects on how "the battle for women was far more intense and murderous than the battles against the North Koreans and the Chinese" (241). Make no mistake: Williams objectifies the female body in this novel. Clearly, this brand of fiction does not advocate a woman-centered afrofuturism. As Tal says, "These are not the books to read if one is searching for black women's perspectives on revolution and struggle" (69).

people; it only exacerbates the dangerous stereotype for which other black military men pay the price later during the Spanish-American War iteration loop and the 1906 Brownsville Affair in Texas. President Theodore Roosevelt reflected on how after he and his Rough Riders were saved by the Buffalo Soldiers, they all shared canteens on El Caney; yet he had to dishonorably discharge 167 Buffalo Soldiers from the 25th Regiment because they had been involved in a racial incident. Blackman learns that it "was the crackers did the shooting. Claimed a soldier'd tried to assault her, a woman named Evans ran a boarding house there. You go in the South that's all you got to do is holler rape and they can't find trees fast enough" (98). Not only were these soldiers dishonorably discharged, even though they never left the barracks on the night in question, but they also lost their pensions after being dismissed without a trial.[35]

Further flare-ups in this centuries-long race war occur. For instance, Blackman goes to officer training school in Des Moines, Iowa, in 1917 against the backdrop of the Houston Riot,[36] in which approximately 150 black troops of the 24th Regiment rioted one night in the deeply segregated city. Blackman feels pride in the 24th, but his lead instructor, First Lieutenant John Gahagan, thinks to himself, "That sonofabitch is a mistake" (109), including in his thoughts not just Blackman but all of the other black officer candidates. Later, Blackman accidentally knocks Gahagan down on the sidewalk in the middle of a rainstorm. Gahagan does his best to get Blackman out of officer training, but Blackman's unblemished record saves him.

Blackman gets shipped to the frontlines in France during World War I as a part of the Harlem Hellfighters to ostensibly fight against the Germans. Instead, General John J. Pershing wants the colored regiment to clean, dig, and count supplies as a labor detail. But the French command have no time "to continue playing that stupid black-and-white game" and are willing to "let the blacks cover themselves with glory" by fighting (121). And they do so, only to return home to the Red Summer,[37] a series of race riots in dozens of cities across the United States stemming from heightened racial tensions between discharged blacks and whites competing for jobs, homes, and respect. Nothing changed for the black men who had fought against autocratic oppression in Europe: They still continued to experience Jim Crow segregation at home, all the while desiring the rights promised them in the passing of the Thirteenth, Fourteenth, and Fifteenth amendments to the US

---

35. See John D. Weaver's *The Brownsville Raid* (1970).
36. See Robert V. Haynes's *A Night of Violence: The Houston Riot of 1917* (1976).
37. See Cameron McWhirter's *Red Summer: The Summer of 1919 and the Awakening of Black America* (2011).

Constitution. As Alexs D. Pate claims, this novel "drives home the passionate and the sincere desire of African American men to put themselves in harm's way, if need be, to prove their humanity and their loyalty to the United States, their hope for a better future" (vi). Realism and factuality combine with time and dream to produce the afrofuture that ends the novel with the charismatic Blackman besting the white world.

But that future does not come yet. Blackman's science-fictional progress through American military history makes two more stops before the Korean War and the start of Blackman's present. During the Spanish Civil War (1936–39), Blackman fights in an integrated, international volunteer unit from the United States which is known as the Abraham Lincoln Brigade and is led by African Americans Oliver Law and Walter Garland. He experiences equality and brotherhood for the first time in the fight against General Franco's authoritarian regime (Carroll 136–37). "There wasn't a white in the Lincolns who had a prejudiced bone in his body, not even the Southerners" according to Blackman's Jewish buddy, Robert Doctorow (156). Blackman feels "a personal power he'd not been aware of before" because oppressive conditions back home would not allow him to feel like a man (154). This new experiential moment encodes itself into the feedback loop and becomes part of the black networked consciousness Blackman creates with his seminars. Such a small difference in treatment, respect, and pride will become apparent in the future when Blackman wins the race war. Of course, this treatment by whites does not last into World War II.

Endemic racial problems throughout the Mediterranean theater of World War II come to the forefront of this short section in the novel. Williams describes, or perhaps contrives, an incident in Tombolo, Italy, where 200 African American soldiers desert their posts, take their European "girls, food, and guns" into the swamps, and make a last stand against the US Army (204). Naturally, all of these deserters are intentionally killed, along with their women and several German deserters. Gilbert Muller indicates how "Blackman is witness to this hidden dimension of history, one that has never been substantiated as fact, but which emerged as rumor and inference during the author's research for the novel" (114). Williams himself speaks of it as fact in an October 25, 1971, interview with Earl A. Cash, stating that he "uses a lot of documentary material" before each section in the novel he was revising and that chapter 20 "is about the murder of two hundred black soldiers during World War II by the American army" (153). Williams wanted to tell the story as a nonfiction book, but he had difficulty in getting clearance from the Pentagon to visit and interview active officers in Vietnam, hence making the decision "to do it as a novel just to show that what I wanted to say, I wanted to say badly enough to do it in one form or another" (Cash 154).

I can only speculate on the Tombolo incident, if it even occurred, but Williams seems to think that it did and embeds clues in the novel as to who took part in the attack: for example, the US Fourth Corps; a nameless two-star general, perhaps Willis D. Crittenberger or Geoffrey T. Keyes; the American Fifth Army; the German sixteenth SS Division; the Gothic Line; the 92nd Infantry Division Buffalo Soldiers; and the Tombolo swamp killings near Pisa. It all seems to fit, and Williams provides an unerring account of other race moments in military history. That it occurred seems likely, but I cannot find any proof of it myself.[38] I know that Major Ray Farran of the British Special Air Service led Operation Tombola in late March through April 1945 in that vicinity, providing arms to resistance fighters behind enemy lines. I also learned that his guerrilla tactics were briefly suspended because the American Fifth Army launched an operation in Tombolo that was later canceled. Who knows? Maybe the canceled operation was the Tombolo incident? But there is no verifiable record of its ever having occurred. C. Lynn Munro identifies the Tombolo incident as "the most unsettling scene" of the novel with its "depiction of the Tombolo Massacre . . . The humiliations and discrimination which prompt the blacks to desert rather than endure extant conditions serve not to vindicate the reprisal, but rather to demonstrate the tragic web spawned by years of abuse" (93).

Tombolo does not seem *too* far-fetched in light of all the other historical documentation of racism in the military that Williams provides of the other American wars. In order to carefully document his novel, he utilizes the "Drumtaps" and "Cadences"—interchapters and epigraphs taken from historical figures and papers: memoirs, congressional hearings, newspaper articles, and military orders. Blackman, now a lieutenant and morale officer to the incomplete regiment of black soldiers, explains to the general that blacks have gone into the swamps to fight for themselves and their women because of all the racial abuse. The general thinks to himself, "I can't change history. But they have deserted; the regs are clear. They won't come out with their hands up; it'll be a war between black and white, and a real one. Imagine it. In an Italian swamp" (207). Out loud, the general, with his full

---

38. Recently, Michael Cooney wrote a novella, titled *In the Forest of Tombolo* (2015), motivated by the real experiences of an American deserter, John Squillace, in the last days of World War II. Squillace took up residence in the renegade camp in Tombolo; the camp consisted of Italian women; black deserters tired of prejudice; and German deserters. American forces eventually stormed the camp, and the story made many headlines in Italian newspapers.

staff assembled, states, "We're in the middle of a war. There is no doubt that Jerry is on the run. But we're also in the middle of another, older war, and we're going to have to fight that one, too" (207). He verbally acknowledges the impending operation as a hot moment in the ongoing race war. Under emotional duress, Lieutenant Blackman understands why the general allows him to attend the battle-planning session and to witness its aftermath. Blackman sullenly concedes that "no battle order would ever be discovered that would read: Commenced attack against two hundred niggers holed up in Tombolo" (208).

The general assigns Whittman to guard Blackman as they enter the swamps after four days of battle. Blackman reflects on "a kind of integration in the swamp [between black and German deserters] that wouldn't be believed back home" (209). This science-fictional reflection indicates how truly strange the situation is in that a group of deserters from both sides could come together for themselves regardless of the color line in a near-utopian arrangement. The American Army simply cannot fathom or allow such a future in the present, the Jim Crow era back home, in the middle of the deadliest war ever fought, so they destroy it. Blackman and Whittman see the devastation everywhere as they tour the swamp, and Blackman angrily declares, "'I don't know when. I don't know how, but Whittman, I swear before God, man, before God, you motherfuckers'll pay for this'" (210). Such a repressed memory, real or constructed, creates the dream of seizing freedom and control in the future. It revolutionizes Blackman in the Vietnam present as he relives these horrible events while he is unconscious in his hospital bed, discovering hidden knowledge about this old race war: hidden to allow this cycle of history to continuously repeat, hidden to prevent an inevitable black uprising.

When It Changed

Including my prior discussions of the Plains, Korean, and Vietnam wars, Blackman, again representative of all black soldiers, exists in the double bind of an alien existence. On the one hand, he fights America's enemies, and on the other, he fights against his own "epidermilization" in American culture which results in racism (Fanon 11). While laid up in the hospital, Blackman devises a thirty-year strategy to win the race war, beginning with a map of Africa that he asks Mimosa to acquire for him. The plan itself is simple. First, Blackman withdraws from the world by getting lost on the African continent. Second, he gains control of twenty-five African cities. Third, he recruits light-skinned blacks—mulattoes, octoroons, quadroons—to pass for white, *"an American Trojan horse"* of sorts, seen but not perceived (emphasis in the text 259) by further intensifying race pride with black power propaganda back in America. To Blackman's way of thinking, his agents will be embedded at NORAD, the Pentagon, and various tracking stations *"sit there lookin white, but be as black as a mothafucker"* (emphasis in the text 261). These revolutionaries slowly infiltrate America's nuclear forces over the course of thirty years, a quiet revolution meticulously designed to overthrow the white world through subversion and espionage. Now seventy, Blackman emerges from hiding to announce black liberation in a phone call to Whittman, now a general in charge of the nuclear arsenal, declaring, "'It's over, man,'" and further elaborating that "'nothing will work, Ishmael' . . . 'It's ours. All of it. I've kicked your ass again'" (262). Blackman achieves a flawless victory, a bloodless revolution.

Even if marginalized as a character, Mimosa has a crucial role in winning the race war. She pops up during the Civil War, the Great War, World War II, and Vietnam, and perhaps elsewhere. Mimosa has meaning for Blackman and grows in influence throughout the novel, evolving from a slave to a student to a Foreign Service Officer capable of procuring things like the obscure texts for Blackman's seminar—she goes from being illiterate to being a multilingual diplomat. That is something in its own right. Likewise, she inspires Blackman's loyalty, even though she considers leaving him, injured as he is, because "he's too proud of a black man to want to have me around doing things for him that he can no longer do himself" (229). When Blackman tells the light-skinned medic Woodcock, "'If you didn't have nappy hair, you could pass for white; be like Doctorow, know that?'" (251), Mimosa challenges him: "'Abe, why'd you say that to that boy? You hurt him. Did you see his face?'" and she compels him to apologize (252). Woodcock later becomes Blackman's top infiltrator in his plan to bring down The Man, and Mimosa has a direct hand in the plan's construction.

Fittingly, the novel ends with Major Woodcock, onboard Whittman's plane, outing himself as Blackman's chief insurgency operative. Woodcock sings the chorus to the minstrel song "Sewanee River" written by Stephen Foster in 1851. Through Woodcock, Williams ironizes the sense of nostalgia for home that whites intuited blacks must have felt, even if the song captures a feeling of despair at being sold to another plantation: "All de world am sad and dreary, / eb-rywhere I roam; / oh, darkeys, how my heart grobes weary / Far from de old folks at home!" (264). His singing serves as a powerful reminder of how spirituals functioned according to Frederick Douglass, as previously discussed in chapter 1, in that slaves sang most when they were most troubled. Now, the whites will know the hidden meaning of these sorrow songs even if they were written by a white man. Likewise, Woodcock is re-appropriating the minstrel tradition itself, public entertainment that made caricatures of black people, shaped racial assumptions, and lasted well into the mid-twentieth century. For black people, the future *is* now; black hearts are happy; and nearly 400 years of American history has been reversed.

With *Captain Blackman,* John A. Williams provides a dark version of afrofuturism, one in which bitterness, determination, and a focused rage support black people's hope for a different, if not better, future. Williams's purpose with this novel goes way beyond entertainment. He demonstrates how black men find the strength to be black in the white world. Without ever exploring this new world itself, he provides a meaningful vision of how a black world emerges. He offers hope, whereas in *Native Son* Wright offers a warning.

I mentioned hilarity in the second paragraph of this chapter in imagining such a far-flung revenge scenario. And some may not see the humor, and some might not recognize the incongruities, present in Blackman's victory. It seems much too serious a novel with its forecast of a dark future ... for *white people.* That is the great irony here. Like Tal, I, too, fancy "readers" who take "a certain pleasure in imagining white people getting their comeuppance at the hands of a black genius and his army" (79). Such impossible scenarios must be read as a critique of the historical treatment of black people by white people. Imagining an afrofuture, developed by ingeniously splicing various historical timelines together; hacking the created feedback loop that resonates on the same frequency of a networked black consciousness; daring to hope for a better future—seems like fun to me. Ultimately, *Captain Blackman* provides catharsis.

CONCLUSION

INTO THE BLACK-O-SPHERE

IT SEEMS NATURAL to ponder whether afrofuturism is merely a "colored wave" within SF history, analogous to aesthetic movements such as the New Wave or cyberpunk. However, by symbolically thinking of afrofuturism as its own pocket universe—a color-shifted black-o-sphere—we see and read the wavelengths radiating from this distant universe as its gravity expands. Constellated as it is by black SF stars such as Samuel R. Delany, Octavia Butler, and Nalo Hopkinson, among many others, it also feels natural, if not logical, to pull in canonical black writers such as Zora Neale Hurston, Richard Wright, and John A. Williams since they also grappled with a science-fictional blackness in different eras. This philosophic force, this afrofuturism, bends the curvature of racial history with its energy and momentum and radiates the universal light of hope that merges with separate black literary traditions (as well as other aesthetic genres). *Things Fall Apart* (1958), by the celebrated Nigerian author Chinua Achebe, strongly resonates with these other powerful novels—*Their Eyes Were Watching God, Native Son,* and *Captain Blackman*—because of the friction generated by white supremacy; but many people would contend the annexation of these titles to SF, even though afrofuturism makes it possible. It may feel out of context because of my US literary framework, but *Things Fall Apart* certainly fits the time period as a mid-twentieth-century global classic and opens the entirety of the African continent to afrofuturist speculation. In this conclusion, while magnifying afrofuturist space, I also expand afrofuturist time into the twenty-first century, briefly considering Colson Whitehead's contemporary classic *The Underground Railroad* (2016) by building on (and perhaps complicating) my study in further analyzing representations of slavery through the speculative. Concluding the book with these two key writers, Whitehead and Achebe, indicates the ways afrofuturism has proliferated through time-space.

Expanding Afrofuturist Space

Reaching deeper into the black-o-sphere, a robust debate exists on whether or not to include African-authored texts within afrofuturism as opposed to SF in general. As Jessica Langer proclaims, "Science fiction has always been, in some way, about colonialism, about the imposition of power, about the encounter with the other" (quoted in Higgins 382). The "Dark Continent" has proven fruitful to Europe's proto-SF writers such as H. Rider Haggard, in *King Solomon's Mines* (1885) or *She* (1887), or Joseph Conrad, in *Heart of Darkness* (1899), not to mention the lone African American entry to this point in history made by Pauline Hopkins as well, *Of One Blood: Or, the Hidden Self* (1903), as previously discussed in the second chapter.[1] Having this conversation at length makes a great deal of sense, but such a discussion *is* very clearly the subject of another book that other scholars are working feverishly to complete.

Nonetheless, Kodwo Eshun sparks the conversation by stating:

> Afrofuturism's first priority is to recognize that Africa increasingly exists as the object of futurist projection. African social reality is overdetermined by intimidating global scenarios, doomsday economic projections, weather predictions, medical reports on AIDS, and life expectancy forecasts, all of which predict decades of immiserization. ("Further" 291–92)

And Mark Bould guides this dialogue further with his special issue of *Paradoxa* titled *Africa SF*, in which his impressive collection of scholarly voices carefully positions African SF in three ways: Africa in the genre's imaginary itself, SF produced across the African Diaspora, and the historical development of the SF genre in relation to European colonization of Africa

---

1. See John Rieder's *Colonialism and the Emergence of Science Fiction* (2008).

and its concomitant problems in the postcolonial global era. Bould reveals that this special issue "is intended to complement and add to the growing literature on afrofuturism [and] Afrodiasporic SF" (Introduction 7). Bould justly questions whether African-produced narratives should even be located "in a literary tradition that has hitherto been largely the product of colonial and neo-colonial powers . . . without misunderstanding or misrepresenting them" as another kind of "colonial appropriation" ("From Anti-Colonial" 17). Adam Levin frames this concern another way, revealing how "the supremacy of Western cultures over the centuries has undoubtedly played a key role in distorting, and even retarding, the evolution and progress of Africa's innumerable cultures," where "the most tragic irony of any romantic afrofuturist vision lies in just how brutally social and economic hardships have realised notions of 'alien' Africans" ("Africa's space oddities"). However, Francophone scholar Justin Izzo shows the way forward with his notion of an "ethnographic Afrofuturism" that creates a "historical reversibility" capable of performing a "critical diagnostics on the extratextual cultural present" in his analysis of Djiboutian writer Abdourahman A. Waberi's 2006 satiric novel *In the United States of Africa* (164–65).[2] Basically, Izzo means switching roles by reimagining past colonial encounters in racial and political contexts to create a counterfactual viewpoint with which to examine the effects. This historical reversibility makes it possible to see the moments of colonial encounter between Europeans and Africans from a science-fictional Afrocentric perspective as it figuratively loops inside and outside history at afrofuturism's endpoint, weaving a global connected black consciousness together with hope.

Chinua Achebe's *Things Fall Apart*—the most canonical of African texts—represents the true starting point of an African afrofuturism. Achebe wrote *Things Fall Apart* in 1958, near the end of the British colonial project in Nigeria, with occupation ending in 1960. Under pressure as an economic and political entity after World War II, Britain relinquished control of Nigeria because it self-evidently could not hold on to the most populous nation in Africa in response to the upsurge of Nigerian nationalism and the effects of continental independence. Achebe vehemently counters racist European distortions of the African continent (like Conrad's *Heart of Darkness*) as a place "peopled by savage cannibals with guttural languages who belong to human prehistory, a science fiction itself driven by imperialism" (Lavender, "Reframing" 32).

---

2. This alternate history features the united African continent as a stable superpower and flips the global south to a global north where the poor (Europeans and Americans) come to Africa's shores to seek their fortunes.

A familiar reading of *Things Fall Apart* considers the life and times of Okonkwo, a warrior and clan leader in Umuofia; depicts the fullness of Nigerian culture in a positive light; and then describes the colonization of the Ibo by the British Empire and its missionaries. But an afrofuturist reading might change our perception of the text as it defamiliarizes the colonial project, namely, revisiting it as a story about contact with an alien race of white humans who wish to terraform Umuofia and its surrounding territories with advanced technologies by condemning the indigenous scientific practices and spiritual traditions of the natives. Achebe responds to European distortions of the African continent (like Conrad in *Heart of Darkness*) by first portraying a precontact, precolonial Nigerian society.

Precontact, Umuofia symbolizes a primordial ideal, not a utopia, in the sense that everyone—men, women, and children—knows their place within the customs and laws structuring the culture. A patriarchal power structure is tempered by the supernatural realm, where womanly energy has value as evinced by the celebration of an earth goddess as well as the decrees of the always-female "Oracle of the Hills and the Caves" (12). In the day-to-day workings of the culture, the men primarily farm yams, build and expand their homes, and make war when called upon as dictated by the ancestral spirits and deities they worship while the women largely raise children, cook, clean, and take care of their men. The children perform chores, listen to stories, and grow in the ways of their people. Some of these traditions might seem harsh to foreign eyes, such as the tradition of abandoning people with incurable illnesses in "the Evil Forest . . . to die" (18); discarding newborn twins, who are "put in earthenware pots and thrown away in the forest" (62); or mutilating the corpses of dead children who are thought to be "*ogbanje*, . . . wicked children who, when they died, entered their mother's wombs to be born again" (77). Nonetheless, the people of Umuofia have harvests, weddings, and funerals while honoring their beliefs like other human cultures, which is, of course, Achebe's point. Yet first contact inevitably generates an apocalyptic vibe, where Okonkwo's own epic fall transforms and hastens the cultural demolition of his society when the races collide.

Another way of looking at the novel involves its three-part structure. In the first part, Okonkwo accidentally kills the son of a respected village elder during this great man's funeral when his archaic gun explodes. This unprecedented and accidental death at an important funeral results in Okonkwo's seven-year banishment as well as the destruction of his compound while fleeing to his motherland in Mbanta. He has inadvertently committed "a crime against the earth goddess," thus paving the way to colonialism's cultural apocalypse (124). During Okonkwo's exile in the second part of the novel, the British missionaries arrive with Umuofia's "proud and imperious emissary of war" absent (12). The village's "racial destiny" unfolds in the manner "that formed the Official Story of colonialism," an alien invasion in which SF participates (Rieder, "Science Fiction, Colonialism, and the Plot of Invasion" 373–74). These visitors from another world will force submission from the entire African continent through a religion that is backed by advanced technologies. As Sofia Samatar remarks, Achebe "portrays the dissolution of a society from within, instigated by sudden exposure to an alien way of thinking represented by the Christian religion" (63). Because Okonkwo misses this alien encounter at this exact instant, Umuofia's greatest hero is not there to prevent the alien worldview from taking hold and destroying all that he loves, even if he could have done anything to prevent it.

In the third part, when Okonkwo returns home with a plan to resume clan life at its pinnacle, he has become out of sync with Umuofia's altered reality. His village has changed because of the influence of the missionary, Mr. Brown, who has quickly realized "that a frontal attack on the clan's beliefs" would fail (181). Instead, he uses education and medicine in addition to religion to advance his truth while a colonial government, laws, and commerce are administered by the nameless white District Commissioner. Both of these white men are protected by the shadow of the British Army at Umuru and the memory of the Abame clan's destruction. Somewhat delusional, Okonkwo perceives that his opportunity to save the clan arrives with Mr. Smith, the ailing Mr. Brown's replacement, who saw things only in black and white. Because of Mr. Smith's draconian outlook, tensions between the clan, the church, and the colonial government boil over when a fanatical convert named Enoch dares "to unmask an *egwugwu* in public," thus shaming and killing the ancestral spirit in the communal mind (186). In précis, the clan burns down the church, and the District Commissioner imprisons and orders the beating of the village's leaders, Okonkwo among them. The day after the leaders' release, the clan gathers at the marketplace again to discuss going to war; Okonkwo slays the head messenger, who had whipped him during his brief capture; walks away in disgust with his brethren; and hangs himself. On the one hand, Okonkwo does not recognize Umuofia any longer. It has become strange/foreign/other/alien to him, and that is another possible reason for his suicide. On the other hand, he is now an alien to his former fatherland, disconnected, and that alienation is perhaps what kills him.

In his subaltern presentation of colonization, Achebe inverts this African estrangement by casting the white European missionary invaders as aliens who bring alien ways of thinking with them, such as Christianity. Okonkwo recognizes the coming death of his clan, Umuofia, and his own way of life. "The world seemed to stand still" just before Okonkwo decapitates the white District Commissioner's court messenger, hoping but failing to spark his people to war in a futile attempt to repel the outsiders (204). Okonkwo chooses suicide rather than witness the fall of his civilization resulting from this ongoing "alien" invasion, and Achebe identifies and interiorizes this doom for us through Okonkwo's suicide. "For such peoples," as Lisa Yaszek states, "apocalypse is not a divine or natural phenomenon, but the result of very human contact between Eurowestern and indigenous cultures ("Rethinking Apocalypse in African SF" 50). A clear science-fictional moment of white appropriation occurs when the District Commissioner resolves to write his official version of Okonkwo's story in "a reasonable paragraph" of an envisaged book titled *The Pacification of the Primitive Tribes of the Lower Niger* (209). Achebe chooses to close the novel in this fashion to demonstrate how Nigerian culture became alien and unrecognizable to Western eyes, thereby forcing his readers to reconcile the cultural dissonance with something akin to afrofuturism.

To focus on two specific moments of colonial encounter within *Things Fall Apart,* the novel further refines the cultural dissonance necessary to discuss the flexile nature of historical reversibility in relation to afrofuturism. The first moment concerns the initial alien encounter in which the Abame clan kill a Christian missionary. They kill the white man for three reasons. First, *white* is a polite way of saying *leprosy*; second, white *egwugwu* masks inspire awe and fear; and third, the Abame cannot communicate with him. Seeing a truly white person, in the sense of light skin pigmentation, terrifies the Abame, particularly since the stranger rode a bicycle, something the Abame have never seen before. The missionary appears entirely alien and uses an advanced technology that seems amazing. His slaying directly results in the clan's annihilation on a market day by three other whites and a band of men who surround the market and gun down almost everyone. In talking about this village massacre, Obierika, Okonkwo's best friend, muses, "'Who knows what may happen tomorrow? Perhaps green men will come to our clan and shoot us'" (142). Significantly, Achebe's choice of green men here reveals how the black men do not truly believe in the white man's existence until the annihilation of the Abame clan—after which they must face the reality of its existence and the possible existence of other alien races. Obierika, voicing Achebe here, uses this well-worn SF cliché to indicate the strangeness of the entire encounter which results in the destruction of an entire clan. The Ibo worldview shifts, becoming racially charged for the first time because of this violent interaction as it relates to skin color.

The second science-fictional moment involves Christian terraforming. The missionaries deliberately alter the Ibo environment to make it safe and conducive for an alien religion to take root and thrive among the native population, not unlike the spreading red weeds in the H. G. Wells novel *The War of the Worlds* (1898). With economic, technological, and military support from the queen, the practicality of creating this habitable zone benefits colonizing efforts. The missionaries start by asking the local leadership for land to establish a church, and the Ibo give away the Evil Forest, a place "alive with sinister forces and powers of darkness" (148). The evangelists terraform this ominous plot of land by building a church on it and disrupting native rituals as a means of damaging the Ibo belief system. The simultaneous conquests of the physical and supernatural spaces represent an irrevocable reshaping of the indigenous environment that quickly wins Christian converts. Many of Okonkwo's people abandon their cultural roots, further disintegrating the community and destroying their values. In fact, Okonkwo loses his oldest son, Nwoye, to the white man's religion, causing Okonkwo to reflect on exactly how his son's abandonment of the gods "was the very depth of abomination" that clearly revealed "the prospect of annihilation" facing his world (153). Outside and unethical interference by the church paves the way for routine destruction of indigenous lifeways on the African continent as Europeans build their empires to support the racist fallacy of their moral and cultural superiority.

Things Fall Apart provides an alternate narrative that challenges accepted African stereotypes. In this respect, Achebe triumphs over British colonialism in its own language, collapsing its prejudicial rationales by rehumanizing Africans and making aliens of whites. He describes a world transformed by this profound alien encounter between races in terms of language, identity, and culture—a simultaneous definition of afrofuturism and colonialism.

In Achebe's novel we move through an African transhistorical feedback loop, hoping for a better future that is plugged into a networked black consciousness. Afrofuturism's historical reversibility is signaled as we engage with this painful past, a past that has been recontextualized to serve the future present as a cautionary tale against the race and racism inherent in colonialism.

Expanding Afrofuturist Time

In terms of contemporary literature, mainstream African American writer Colson Whitehead has long dabbled with speculative themes bordering on afrofuturism in his fiction.[3] That is to say, he represents the edge between the

---

3. See Whitehead's use of elevator technology in *The Intuitionist* (1999); the folklore-imbued *John Henry Days* (2001); the black geek fest *Sag Harbor* (2009); and, finally, his zombie apocalypse effort *Zone One* (2011), all proof of his afrofuturist tendencies.

marginalized and the mainstream in his fiction—a marginalized voice, writing in a speculative genre-mode, garnering a deep conventional respect from the literary establishment. His latest novel, *The Underground Railroad* (2016), winner of the Arthur C. Clarke Award for best SF novel in 2017, also won the Pulitzer Prize, not to mention the National Book Award. These three honors mean significantly different things. We are talking about the eroding and imagined difference between high-brow and popular cultures, where literature conveys a sense of universal interest connected to lasting ideas such as love or politics, among others, in written form. Science fiction has long been considered the literary ghetto, but Whitehead won this prestigious British Award for his speculative take on American slavery. The Pulitzer Prize has honored excellence in journalism and the arts since 1917, and the committee chose his novel because it fuses myth and realism in its interrogation of slavery, thus creating a text that resonates with America today. Likewise, the National Book Award for Fiction represents the year's best novel in America while emphasizing the cultural importance of good writing, and Whitehead won because of his hallucinatory take on American slavery's horrors. For good measure, his book was also selected by Oprah Winfrey for her book club which helped launch its reception into the stratosphere because of a female slave's heroic escape from the peculiar institution. Let us not forget her global cultural influence as a black woman from rural Mississippi and her televisual empire forty-plus years in the making. That's afrofuturism too. While Whitehead might not be a SF writer in the classic sense, he is an afrofuturist.

In Whitehead's novel, the Underground Railroad is an actual underground train system. Starting from the cotton fields of Georgia with the escaping slave protagonist Cora onboard, its first stop is a progressive, near-utopian, South Carolina city. However, the surreal quality of Cora's (renamed Bessie) experience working as an actor in the Museum of Natural Wonders' slavery exhibit while slavery is yet ongoing represents the estrangement created by afrofuturism's critique of the past—the haunting reality of brutality against black people across time into the present. Likewise, the new hospital, ostensibly built to better black lives, operates as a front for clandestine medical experiments related to population control, sterilization, and syphilis research reminiscent of the notorious Tuskegee experiment.[4] The use of black bodies for scientific and social experimentation for white mankind's betterment likewise strangely resonates across time.

Whitehead forthrightly and darkly taps into science-fictional black objectification to demonstrate afrofuturism's entanglement with all sorts of cul-

---

4. See James H. Jones's *Bad Blood: The Tuskegee Syphilis Experiment* (1993).

tural advancement. To clarify, afrofuturism's increasing entanglement with global culture demonstrates how the past influences the future in black letters as technological innovation drives macroculture, further revealing an ongoing sinister treatment of colored people, particularly black. Whitehead indicates that the skin trade has always been the foundation of America. As the slave catcher Ridgeway pontificates on "Manifest Destiny," he defines it as "taking what is yours, your property, whatever you deem it to be. And everyone else taking their assigned places to allow you to take it. Whether it's red men or Africans, giving up themselves, giving of themselves, so that we can have what's rightfully ours . . . the American spirit" (221). Afrofuturism contextualizes this bloody chapter in racial history in order to bear witness and to provide alternative meanings to blackness in the popular imagination by *properly* "blacking up" a white legacy of abuse and genocide sadly overlooked.

With afrofuturism as a critical framework, Whitehead takes his readership through the toxic legacy of slavery and its stamp on the future as Cora's escape, capture, and rescue take her to North Carolina, Tennessee, Indiana, and, finally, North and West. For example, North Carolina's state government decides to sell all its slaves further south to end the race problem before it can manifest in a slave uprising. To make the state white-only, they also capitalize on the heavy wave of European migration by advertising overseas. In this respect, the North Carolina leadership recruit Irish immigrants, once considered another black race,[5] by offering to pay moving expenses in return for seven-year indentured-servitude agreements. Finally, any blacks, slave and free alike, or their white sympathizers caught within state borders by the Nightriders get lynched and hang along the Freedom Trail[6] like the "Strange Fruit" of Billie Holiday's famous 1939 song.[7]

Similar to Harriet Jacobs's "loophole of retreat" (*Incidents* 95) discussed in chapter 3, Cora enters a pocket universe, hiding in an attic crawl space before ultimately being captured by Ridgeway. This artificial space exists within the North Carolina town, where Cora witnesses an awful weekly

---

5. See Ignatiev's *How the Irish Became White* (1995) and David R. Roediger's *Working toward Whiteness: How America's Immigrants Became White: The Strange Journey from Ellis Island to the Suburbs* (2005).

6. Whitehead both ironizes the city of Boston's 2.5-mile-long Freedom Trail, which honors sixteen historical locations important to US history, and terrifyingly amplifies The Trail of Tears, where President Andrew Jackson's forced removal of Native American nations from the Southeast United States to Indian Territory west of the Mississippi River began in 1831.

7. For more information on this evocative song's history, consult David Margolick's *Strange Fruit: The Biography of a Song* (2001).

ritual every Friday night for months on end: the townsfolk gather to watch and celebrate the lynching of a black person while she is safe and isolated in her micro-universe. Such stasis allows Cora to painstakingly refine her mind by improving her reading using the little light she has. She redirects her own future even when caught and taken by Ridgeway through a Tennessee blighted by fire and fever on the way west to deliver another captured slave. With a mere look at a free black man in a nameless Tennessee town, Cora sets in motion her own deliverance from Ridgeway and slavery itself.

Royal, the free black man at whom Cora glances, happens to be a conductor on the Underground Railroad. He ambushes Ridgeway and his men and absconds with Cora to the Valentine Farm in Indiana, owned by the free black John Valentine, who is passing for white. For a while Cora experiences true freedom, frequently visiting the library, gaining more proficiency with words, and acquiring further knowledge of the world while being gently courted by Royal. She prepares for her future in Indiana because it feels safe, far enough away from slavery without actually being so. But Indiana is an impermanent stay. Royal offers her the best gift in revealing the final station on the Underground Railroad just in case of an emergency. However, this peace of mind in freedom does not last, as rival black factions—blacks born free versus those who escaped, more or less—fight over the fate of the farm. This fight allows jealous whites to stage a raid on the property, burn it to the ground (including the library), kill Royal and other blacks, and take the land. Among the whites, Ridgeway captures Cora a final time and forces her to reveal to him the last Underground Railroad station beneath the abandoned house. As they descend the rock stairway, she grabs him and they fall into the darkness. Cora makes her escape by handcar, pumping away to propel herself North as a physically broken Ridgeway dictates his final hunt to his free black assistant, Homer. Days later Cora emerges somewhere North and hitches a ride West with a colored wagon driver at the novel's closing.

From an afrofuturist perspective, the novel's Indiana section represents an imperiled black future in which divided loyalties, petty rivalries, and white jealousy mirror our present state. It is as much a warning about as it is a meditation on an entwined racial history in the United States, where racial resentments, deliberately cultivated, preserve white power. Whitehead also offers a still-unfulfilled promise, as long as we do not forget our troubled past—freedom somewhere over the horizon, just like the freedom Cora seeks in heading West.

Applying afrofuturism to Whitehead's novel reflects the temporality—past, present, and future—necessary for saturating history, literature, and the future with colored imaginings. The ebb and flow of black hope resides in this novel as Whitehead seeks to reclaim and hold the future for an entire race, acknowledging a painful past while being a change agent as he brings it forward. The metaphoric power of Whitehead's novel brings this painful past to life as we travel through the transhistoric feedback loop fully connected to the black networked consciousness. *The Underground Railroad* helps us transcend space-time to better understand this black utopian impulse, to create counternarratives, to illustrate the many challenges we face once we understand that slavery is still with us in one form or another. In popular black parlance, we call this WOKE.

That the afrofuturism movement embodies many forms, from music, art, and dance to film, graphic narratives, and social activism, is a given.[8] My brief exegesis of afrofuturism's literary dimension hopefully demonstrates how it can be useful to black mainstream texts. Writ large, all black creativity in the Western world expresses afrofuturism. Slavery's black descendants are interpreted as alien humans, captured, transported, and domesticated; or they are reinscribed with technologized flesh as natural machines, where race functions as a labor technology, going through repetitive motions to improve agribusiness as cyborgs, automatons, or clones. But that reasoning goes beyond my point. What concerns me most is that afrofuturism offers hope to a downtrodden race, hope for a variety of tomorrows, some good and some bad, to rephrase Samuel R. Delany's thoughts on the usefulness of science fiction for black people mentioned in the first chapter. Prolific black writer Walter Mosley agrees with Delany when he writes "Science fiction allows history to be rewritten or ignored. Science fiction promises a future full of possibility, alternative lives, and even regret" ("Black" 405). These black writers dare to ask "what if," science fiction's most basic question, and this question changes reality and its perception. This sentiment concerns how imagination powers future visions for black people, and that is exactly afrofuturism. It takes us further into the black-o-sphere—unconfined, if not actualized, emancipatory mindscapes—by using intelligent resistance to negate harmful appropriation by an encroaching culture that desires to further rewrite an already whitewashed history.

---

8. In terms of afrofuturist activism, see *Mothership: Tales of Afrofuturism and Beyond* (2013), edited by Bill Campbell and Edward A. Hall; and *Octavia's Brood: Science Fiction Stories from Social Justice Movements* (2015), edited by Adrienne M. Brown and Walidah Imarisha.

WORKS CITED

Abraham, William E. "The Life and Times of Anton Wilhelm Amo, the First African (Black) Philosopher in Europe." *African Intellectual Heritage: A Book of Sources,* edited by Abu S. Abarry amd Molef Kete Asante, Temple UP, 1996, pp. 424–40.

Achebe, Chinua. *Things Fall Apart.* 1958. Anchor, 1994.

Africans in America, 1998, www.pbs.org/wgbh/aia/part4/4h3106t.html.

Alexander, Michelle. *The New Jim Crow: Mass Incarceration in the Age of Colorblindness.* The New Press, 2010.

Allen, Richard. *The Life, Experience, and Gospel Labours of the Rt. Rev. Richard Allen.* Philadelphia, 1833.

Anderson, Jeffery E. *Conjure in African American Society.* Louisiana State UP, 2005.

Anderson, Reynaldo, and Charles E. Jones, editors. *Afrofuturism 2.0: The Rise of Astro-Blackness.* Lexington Books, 2016.

Andreeva, Nellie, and Denise Petski. "N. K. Jemisin's 'The Fifth Season' Book To Be Developed as TV Series at TNT." *Deadline Hollywood,* 16 Aug. 2017, https://deadline.com/2017/08/nk-jemisin-the-fifth-season-book-developed-tv-series-tnt-1202150542/.

Aptheker, Herbert. *American Negro Slave Revolts.* Columbia UP, 1943.

———. *Nat Turner's Slave Rebellion: Including the 1831 "Confessions."* 1966. Dover, 2006.

Baker, Houston A. Jr. "The Black Bottom Line: Reflections on Ferguson, Black Lives Matter, and White Male Violence in America." *American Literary History,* vol. 28, no. 4, 2016, pp. 845–53.

———. *Blues, Ideology, and Afro-American Literature: A Vernacular Theory.* U of Chicago P, 1984.

Baker, Kyle. *Nat Turner.* Abrams, 2008.

Baldwin, James. *Another Country.* 1963. Vintage, 1993.

———. *The Fire Next Time*. 1962. Vintage International, 1993.

———. "Many Thousands Gone." 1951. *Critical Essays on Richard Wright*, edited by Yoshinobu Hakutani, G. K. Hall, 1982, pp. 107–19.

———. *The Price of the Ticket: Collected Nonfiction, 1948–1985*. St. Martin's, 1985.

Banks, Adam J. *Race, Rhetoric, and Technology: Searching for Higher Ground*. Routledge, 2005.

Banneker, Benjamin. "Letter to Thomas Jefferson." 1791. *Black Writers of America; A Comprehensive Anthology*, edited by Richard Barksdale and Keneth Kinnamon, Macmillan, 1972, pp. 50–52.

Baraka, Amiri. "Black Art." 1969. *Transbluesency: The Selected Poems of Amiri Baraka/LeRoi Jones (1961–1995)*, edited by Paul Vangelisti, Marsilio, 1995, pp. 142–43.

Baraka, Imamu Amiri. "Technology & Ethos." *Raise Race Rays Raze: Essays since 1965*. Random House, 1969, pp. 155–57.

Barber, Janet E., and Asamoah Nkwanta. "Benjamin Banneker's Original Handwritten Document: Observations and Study of the Cicada." *Journal of Humanistic Mathematics*, vol. 4, no. 1, 2014, pp. 112–22.

Barker, Thomas P. "Spatial Dialectics: Intimations of Freedom in Antebellum Slave Song." *Journal of Black Studies*, vol. 46, no. 4, 2015, pp. 363–83.

Barnes, Steven. *Lion's Blood*. Warner, 2002.

———. *Zulu Heart*. Warner, 2003.

Barnickel, Linda. *Milliken's Bend: A Civil War Battle in History and Memory*. Louisiana State UP, 2013.

Baudrillard, Jean. *Simulacra and Simulation*. 1981. Translated by Sheila F. Glaser, U of Michigan P, 1994.

Beevor, Antony. *The Battle for Spain: The Spanish Civil War 1936–1939*. Penguin, 2006.

Bennett, Lerone Jr. "Pioneers in Protest: Benjamin Banneker." *Ebony*, Mar. 1964, pp 48–58.

Bibb, Henry. *Narrative of the Life and Adventures of Henry Bibb*. 1849. U of North Carolina at Chapel Hill, 2000, http://docsouth.unc.edu/neh/bibb/menu.html. Documenting the American South.

Biggio, Rebecca Skidmore. "The Specter of Conspiracy in Martin Delany's *Blake*." *African American Review*, vol. 42, nos. 3–4, 2008, pp. 439–54.

Bisson, Terry. *Fire on the Mountain*. Arbor House, 1988.

Bloch, Ernst. *The Principle of Hope*. 1955. Translated by Neville Plaice, et al., MIT Press, 1986. 3 vols.

Bloom, Harold. *Bigger Thomas*. Chelsea House, 1990.

———, editor. *Major Literary Characters: Bigger Thomas*. Chelsea House, 1990.

———. *Richard Wright's* Native Son. Chelsea House, 1988, pp. 5–22.

Bodziock, Joseph. "Richard Wright and Afro-American Gothic." *Richard Wright: Myths and Realities*, edited by C. James Trotman, Garland, 1988, pp. 27–42.

Bone, Martyn. "The (Extended) South of Black Folk: Intraregional and Transnational Migrant Labor in *Jonah's Gourd Vine* and *Their Eyes Were Watching God*." *American Literature*, vol. 79, no. 4, 2007, pp. 753–79.

Bontemps, Arna. *Black Thunder: Gabriel's Revolt: Virginia, 1800*. 1936. Beacon, 1992.

Bould, Mark. "Come Alive By Saying No: An Introduction to Black Power SF." *Afrofuturism*, special issue of *Science Fiction Studies*, vol. 34, no. 2, 2007, pp. 220–40.

———. "From Anti-Colonial Struggle to Neoliberal Immiseration: Mohammed Dib's *Who Remembers the Sea*, Sony Labou Tansi's *Life and a Half*, and Ahmed Khaled Towfik's *Utopia*." *Africa SF*, special issue of *Paradoxa*, vol. 25, 2013, pp. 17–46.

———. Introduction. *Africa SF*, special issue of *Paradoxa*, vol. 25, 2013, pp. 1–16.

———. "Revolutionary African-American Sf before Black Power Sf." *Extrapolation*, vol. 51, no. 1, 2010, pp. 53–81.

Brackman, Barbara. *Facts & Fabrications—Unraveling the History of Quilts and Slavery: 8 Projects, 20 Blocks—First-Person Accounts*. C &T Publishing, 2006.

Bradbury, Ray. *The Martian Chronicles*. Bantam, 1950, pp. 89–102.

———. "Way in the Middle of the Air." *The Martian Chronicles*, Bantam, 1950, pp. 89–102.

Brooks, Daphne. *Bodies in Dissent: Spectacular Performances of Race and Freedom, 1850–1910*. Duke UP, 2006.

Brooks, Gwendolyn. "Riot." 1969. *Norton Anthology*, edited by Gates and Smith, vols. 1 and 2, 3rd ed., Norton, 2014, pp. 339–40.

Brown, Adrienne M., and Walidah Imarisha, editors. *Octavia's Brood: Science Fiction Stories from Social Justice Movements*. AK Press, 2015.

Brown, Lois. *Pauline Elizabeth Hopkins: Black Daughter of the Revolution*. U of North Carolina P, 2008.

Brown, William W. *Clotel; or the President's Daughter*. 1853. Edited by M. Giulia Fabi, Penguin Classics, 2004.

———. *Narrative of William W. Brown, A Fugitive Slave*. 1847. U of North Carolina at Chapel Hill, 2001, http://docsouth.unc.edu/neh/brown47/brown47.html. Documenting the American South.

Buckell, Tobias S. *Crystal Rain*. Tor, 2006.

Burroughs, Edgar R. *A Princess of Mars*. 1917. Modern Library, 2003.

Burrows, Stuart. "'You heard her, you ain't blind': Seeing What's Said in *Their Eyes Were Watching God*." *Novel*, vol. 34, no. 3, 2001, pp. 434–52.

Butler, Octavia E. *Clay's Ark*. Warner, 1984.

———. *Kindred*. Beacon, 1979.

———. *Parable of the Talents*. Warner, 1998.

———. *Wild Seed*. Warner, 1980.

Butler, Robert. "Farrell's Ethnic Neighborhood and Wright's Urban Ghetto: Two Visions of Chicago's South Side." *MELUS*, vol. 18, no. 1, 1993, pp. 103–11.

Campbell, Bill, and Edward A. Hall, editors. *Mothership: Tales of Afrofuturism and Beyond*. Rosarium, 2013.

Campbell, Jane. *Mythic Black Fiction: The Transformation of History*. U of Tennessee P, 1986.

Campbell, Stanley W. *The Slave Catchers: Enforcement of the Fugitive Slave Law, 1850–1860*. U of North Carolina P, 1972.

Canavan, Gerry. *Octavia E. Butler.* U of Illinois P, 2016.

Carrington, André M. *Speculative Blackness: The Future of Race in Science Fiction.* U of Minnesota P, 2016.

Carroll, Peter N. *The Odyssey of the Abraham Lincoln Brigade: Americans in the Spanish Civil War.* Stanford UP, 1994.

Cartwright, Samuel A. "Diseases and Peculiarities of the Negro Race." 1851. *Africans in America,* 1998, www.pbs.org/wgbh/aia/part4/4h3106t.html.

Cash, Earl A. *John A. Williams: The Evolution of a Black Writer.* Third Press, 1975.

Cerami, Charles A. *Benjamin Banneker: Surveyor, Astronomer, Publisher, Patriot.* Wiley, 2002.

Chang, Justin. "Film Review: 'The Birth of a Nation.'" *Variety,* 26 Jan. 2016, variety.com/2016/film/festivals/the-birth-of-a-nation-review-sundance-nate-parker-1201688498/.

Chesnutt, Charles W. *The Conjure Woman.* 1899. U of Michigan P, 1993.

———. "The Goophered Grapevine." 1877. *Norton Anthology,* edited by Gates and McKay, Norton, 2007, pp. 604–12.

Child, Lydia M. "The Quadroons." 1842. *The Norton Anthology of American Literature, Volume B: 1820–1865.* 8th ed., edited by Nina Baym, Norton, 2012, pp. 183–90.

Clark, Ashley. "Alien abductions: 12 Years a Slave and the past as science fiction." *BFI: Film Forever,* 14 Apr. 2015, www.bfi.org.uk/news-opinion/sight-sound-magazine/features/alien-abductions-12-years-slave-past-science-fiction.

Clarke, Deborah. "'The porch couldn't talk for looking': Voice and Vision in *Their Eyes Were Watching God.*" *African American Review,* vol. 35, no. 4, 2001, pp. 599–613.

Clarke, John Henrik, editor. *The Second Crucifixion of Nat Turner.* 1968. Black Classic, 1998.

Clute, John. "SF Magazines." *The Encyclopedia of Science Fiction,* www.sf-encyclopedia.com/entry/sf_magazines.

Clute, John, and Peter Nicholls, editors. *The Encyclopedia of Science Fiction,* St. Martin's Griffin, 1995.

Coleman, Finnie D. *Sutton E. Griggs and the Struggle against White Supremacy.* U of Tennessee P, 2007.

Commander, Michelle D. *Afro-Atlantic Flight: Speculative Returns and the Black Fantastic.* Duke UP, 2017.

Condé, Maryse. *I, Tituba Black Witch of Salem.* 1982. Translated by Richard Philcox, UP of Virginia, 1992.

Conrad, Joseph. *Heart of Darkness.* 1899. Dover, 1990.

Coogler, Ryan, director. *Black Panther.* Marvel Studios, 2018.

Cooney, Michael. *In the Forest of Tombolo.* Wilderness Hill, 2015.

Cooper, Merian C., and Ernest B. Schoedsack, directors. *King Kong.* Radio Pictures, 1933.

Craft, Ellen, and William Craft. *Running a Thousand Miles for Freedom; Or, the Escape of William and Ellen Craft.* 1860. Dover, 2014.

Crafts, Hannah. *The Bondwoman's Narrative: A Novel.* Edited by Henry Louis Gates Jr., Warner, 2002.

Crawley, Laura K., and Joseph C. Hikerson. "Zora Neale Hurston: Recordings, Manuscripts, Photographs, and Ephemera." *The Archive of Folk Culture and Other Divisions of the Library of Congress*, Feb. 2014, www.loc.gov/folklife/guides/Hurston.html.

Curry, Eric. "'The Power of Combinations': Sutton Griggs' *Imperium in Imperio* and the Science of Collective Efficiency." *American Literary Realism*, vol. 43, no. 1, 2010, pp. 23–40.

Cutter, Martha J. "Will the Real Henry 'Box' Brown Please Stand Up?" *Common-place: the journal of early American life*, vol. 16, no. 1, 2015, http://common-place.org/book/will-the-real-henry-box-brown-please-stand-up/.

Daniels, Melissa A. "The Limits of Literary Realism: *Of One Blood*'s Post-Racial Fantasy by Pauline Hopkins." *Callaloo*, vol. 36, no. 1, 2013, pp. 158–77.

Davis, David B. *Inhuman Bondage: The Rise and Fall of Slavery in the New World.* Oxford UP, 2006.

Davis, Patty. "Man shipped from New York to Texas in crate." *CNN*, 10 Sept. 2003, www.cnn.com/2003/US/Southwest/09/09/plane.stowaway/.

Davis, Thadious M. *Southscapes: Geographies of Race, Region, and Literature.* U of North Carolina P, 2011.

Davis, Thulani. "The Future May Be Bleak, but It's Not Black." *The Village Voice*, vol. 28, no. 5, 1 Feb. 1983, pp. 17–19.

Dee, John. *Stagger Lee*. 1973. Manor, 1974.

Delany, Martin R. *Blake; or, the Huts of America.* 1859–62. Beacon, 1970.

———. *The Condition, Elevation, Emigration and Destiny of the Colored People of the United States.* 1852. *Norton Anthology*, edited by Gates and McKay, Norton, 2007, pp. 258–78.

Delany, Samuel R. *Babel-17.* Ace, 1966.

———. *The Ballad of Beta-2.* Ace, 1965.

———. *The Jewels of Aptor.* Ace, 1962.

———. *The Jewel-Hinged Jaw: Notes on the Language of Science Fiction.* 1977. Revised ed., Wesleyan UP, 2009.

———. "The Necessity of Tomorrow(s)." *Starboard Wine: More Notes on the Language of Science Fiction,* by Samuel R. Delaney, Dragon Press, 1984.

———. "Racism and Science Fiction." 1998. *Dark Matter,* edited by Thomas, Warner, 2000, pp. 383–97.

———. *Tales of Nevèrÿon.* 1979. Wesleyan UP, 1993.

Delgado, Richard, and Jean Stefancic. *Critical Race Theory: An Introduction.* 2nd ed., New York UP, 2012.

Dery, Mark. "Afrofuturism Reloaded: 15 Theses in 15 Minutes." *Fabrikzeitung Magizin*, 1 Feb. 2016, www.fabrikzeitung.ch/afrofuturism-reloaded-15-theses-in-15-minutes.

———. "*Black to the Future*: Interviews with Samuel R. Delany, Greg Tate, and Tricia Rose." *Flame Wars: The Discourse of Cyberculture,* special issue of *South Atlantic Quarterly*, vol. 92, no. 4, 1993, pp. 735–78.

Desta, Yohana. "Octavia Butler Is Finally Heading to TV, Thanks to Ava DuVernay." *Vanity Fair*, 9 Aug. 2017, www.vanityfair.com/hollywood/2017/08/ava-duvernay-octavia-butler-tv.

Dick, Philip K. *Do Androids Dream of Electric Sheep?* 1968. Del Rey, 1996.

Dillon, Grace L. "Imagining Indigenous Futurisms." *Walking in the Clouds: An Anthology of Indigenous Science Fiction,* edited by Grace L. Dillon, U of Arizona P, 2012, pp. 1–12.

Dixon, Thomas. *The Clansman: An Historical Romance of the Ku Klux Klan.* Doubleday, 1905.

———. *The Leopard's Spots: A Romance of the White Man's Burden, 1865–1900.* Doubleday, 1902.

———. *The Traitor: A Story of the Fall of the Invisible Empire.* Doubleday, 1907.

Dobard, Raymond G., and Jacqueline L. Tobin. *Hidden in Plain View: A Secret Story of Quilts and the Underground Railroad.* Anchor Books, 2000.

Doolen, Andy. "'Be Cautious of the Word 'Rebel'": Race, Revolution, and Transnational History in Martin Delany's *Blake; or, The Huts of America.*" *American Literature,* vol. 81, no. 1, 2009, pp. 153–79.

Douglass, Frederick. *Life and Times of Frederick Douglass.* 1881. Boston: De Wolfe & Fiske, 1892. U of North Carolina at Chapel Hill, 2001, http://docsouth.unc.edu/neh/douglasslife/douglass.html. Documenting the American South.

———. *My Bondage and My Freedom.* 1855. Penguin Classics, 2003. Print.

———. *Narrative of the Life of Frederick Douglass.* 1845. Signet Classic, 1997.

Dubek, Laura. "'[J]us' listenin' tuh you': Zora Neale Hurston's *Their Eyes Were Watching God* and the Gospel Impulse." *Southern Literary Journal,* vol. 41, no. 1, 2008, pp. 109–30.

Dubey, Madhu. *Signs and Cities: Black Literary Postmodernism.* U of Chicago P, 2003.

Du Bois, W. E. B. "The Comet." 1920. *Dark Matter,* edited by Thomas, Warner, 2004, pp. 5–18.

———. "The Forethought." *The Souls of Black Folk.* 1903. Signet Classic, 1995.

———. *Dark Princess: A Romance.* 1928. UP of Mississippi, 1995.

———. "A Negro Nation within a Nation: June 26, 1934." *Ripples of Hope: Great American Civil Rights Speeches,* edited by Josh Gottheimer, Basic Civitas, 2003, pp. 174–77.

———. *The Quest of the Silver Fleece.* 1911. Oxford UP, 2007.

———. *The Souls of Black Folk.* 1903. Signet Classic, 1995.

duCille, Ann. "The Intricate Fabric of Feeling: Romance and Resistance in *Their Eyes Were Watching God.*" *Forum,* vol. 4, no. 2, 1990, pp. 1–16.

Duck, Leigh Anne. "'Go there tuh know there': Zora Neale Hurston and the Chronotope of the Folk." *American Literary History,* vol. 13, no. 2, 2001, pp. 265–94.

Due, Tananarive. *The Good House.* Atria, 2003.

———. *My Soul to Keep.* HarperCollins, 1997.

Dunbar, Paul L. "Ode to Ethiopia." 1893. *Norton Anthology,* edited by Gates and McKay, Norton, 2007, pp. 907–8.

Easley, Nivi-Kofi A. *The Militants.* Carlton, 1974.

Ellison, Harlan. *Dangerous Visions.* Doubleday, 1967.

———. *Again, Dangerous Visions.* Doubleday, 1972.

Ellison, Ralph. *The Collected Essays of Ralph Ellison.* Edited by John F. Callahan, Modern Library, 2003.

———. *Invisible Man.* 1952. Vintage, 1990.

Engels, Jeremy. "Friend or Foe? Naming the Enemy." *Rhetoric & Public Affairs,* vol. 12, no. 1, 2009, pp. 37–64.

Equiano, Olaudah. *The Interesting Narrative of the Life of Olaudah Equiano, or Gustavas Vassa, the African, Written by Himself.* 1789. *The Classic Slave Narratives,* edited by Henry Louis Gates Jr., Signet, 2002, pp. 1–182.

Ernest, John. *Liberation Historiography: African American Writers and the Challenge of History, 1794–1861.* U of North Carolina P, 2003.

Eshun, Kodwo. "*Further* Considerations of Afrofuturism." *CR: The New Centennial Review,* vol. 3, no. 2, 2003, pp. 287–302.

———. *More Brilliant than the Sun: Adventures in Sonic Fiction.* Quartet, 1998.

Everett, Anna. "The Revolution Will Be Digitized: Afrocentricity and the Digital Public Sphere." *Afrofuturism,* special issue of *Social Text,* vol. 20, no. 2, 2002, pp. 125–46.

Fabre, Michel. *The Unfinished Quest of Richard Wright.* Morrow, 1973.

Fair, Ronald L. *Many Thousand Gone: An American Fable.* Harcourt, Brace, 1965.

Fanon, Frantz. *Black Skin, White Masks.* Translated by Charles Lam Markmann, Grove, 1967.

Faulkner, William. *Requiem for a Nun.* 1951. Vintage International, 2011.

Fernandez, Manny, and Christine Hauser. "Texas Mother Teaches Textbook Company a Lesson on Accuracy." *The New York Times,* 5 Oct. 2015, www.nytimes.com/2015/10/06/us/publisher-promises-revisions-after-textbook-refers-to-african-slaves-as-workers.html.

Ferreira, Rachel H. *The Emergence of Latin American Science Fiction.* Wesleyan UP, 2011.

Fett, Sharla M. *Working Cures: Healing, Health, and Power on Southern Slave Plantations.* U of North Carolina P, 2002.

Fouché, Rayvon. "Say It Loud, I'm Black and I'm Proud: African Americans, American Artifactual Culture, and Black Vernacular Creativity." *American Quarterly,* vol. 58, no. 3, 2006, pp. 639–61.

Freedgood, Elaine, and Michael Sanders. "Strategic Presentism or Partisan Knowledges." *Victorian Studies,* vol. 59, no. 1, 2016, pp. 117–21.

Fuchs, Richard. *An Unerring Fire: The Massacre at Fort Pillow.* Stackpole, 2002.

Gaines, Ernest J. *The Autobiography of Miss Jane Pittman.* 1971. Bantam, 1982.

Gates, Henry L. Jr. "Afterword: Zora Neale Hurston: A Negro Way of Seeing." *Their Eyes Were Watching God,* by Zora Neale Hurston, Perennial Library, 1990, pp. 185–95.

———, editor. "Criticism in *The Jungle.*" *Black Literature and Literary Theory,* edited by Henry L. Gates Jr., Methuen, 1984, pp. 1–27.

———. *Figures in Black: Words, Signs, and the "Racial" Self.* Oxford UP, 1987.

———. *The Signifying Monkey: A Theory of Afro-American Literary Criticism.* Oxford UP, 1988.

———. *The Trials of Phillis Wheatley: America's First Black Poet and Her Encounters with the Founding Fathers.* Basic, 2003.

———. "What Were the Earliest Rebellions by African Americans?" *The Root,* 22 April 2013, www.theroot.com/what-were-the-earliest-rebellions-by-african-americans-1790896118.

Gates, Henry L. Jr., and Nellie Y. McKay, editors. *The Norton Anthology of African American Literature.* 2nd ed., Norton, 2007.

Gates, Henry L. Jr., and Valerie A. Smith, editors. *The Norton Anthology of African American Literature.* vols. 1 and 2, 3rd ed., Norton, 2014.

Gibson, Christine. "Nat Turner, Lightning Rod." *American Heritage.com,* 11 Nov. 2005, www.americanheritage.com/articles/web/20051111-nat-turner-slavery-rebellion-virginia-civil-war-thomas-r-gray-abolitionist.shtml.

Gillman, Susan. "Pauline Hopkins and the Occult: African-American Revisions of Nineteenth-Century Sciences." *American Literary History,* vol. 8, no. 1, 1996, pp. 57–82.

Gilroy, Paul. *The Black Atlantic: Modernity and Double Consciousness.* Harvard UP, 1993.

———. *Small Acts: Thoughts on the Politics of Black Cultures.* Serpent's Tail, 1993.

Giovanni, Nikki. "For Saundra." 1968. *Norton Anthology,* edited by Gates and Smith, vols. 1 and 2, 3rd ed., Norton, 2014, pp. 880–81.

Goyal, Yogita. *Romance, Diaspora, and Black Atlantic Literature.* Cambridge UP, 2010.

Graham, Herman III. *The Brothers' Vietnam War: Black Power, Manhood, and the Military Experience.* UP of Florida, 2003.

Gray, Thomas R. *The Confessions of Nat Turner, The Leader of the Late Insurrection in Southampton, VA.* Baltimore, 1831.

Green-Barteet, Miranda A. "'The Loophole of Retreat': Interstitial Spaces in Harriet Jacobs's *Incidents in the Life of a Slave Girl.*" *South Central Review,* vol. 30, no. 2, 2013, pp. 53–72.

Greenlee, Sam. *The Spook Who Sat by the Door.* Bantam, 1969.

Grey, Zane. *Riders of the Purple Sage.* 1912. Dover, 2002.

Griffin, Farah Jasmine. *Who's Set You Flowin': The African-American Migration Narrative.* Oxford UP, 1995.

Griffith, Cyril E. *The African Dream: Martin R. Delany and the Emergence of Pan-African Thought.* Pennsylvania State UP, 1975.

Griffith, D. W., director. *The Birth of a Nation.* David W. Griffith Corporation, 1915.

Griggs, Sutton E. *Imperium in Imperio.* 1899. Modern Library, 2003.

Gundaker, Grey. "Give Me a Sign: African Americans, Print, and Practice." *A History of the Book in America,* vol. 2, edited by Robert A. Gross and Mary Kelley, U of North Carolina P, 2010, pp. 483–95.

Haggard, H. R. *King Solomon's Mines.* 1885. Modern Library, 1957.

———. *She.* 1887. Modern Library, 1957.

Hammon, Jupiter. "An Address to Miss Phillis Wheatly." 1778. *Norton Anthology,* edited by Gates and McKay, Norton, 2007, pp. 165–68.

Hansberry, Lorraine. *A Raisin in the Sun.* 1959. Vintage, 1994.

Haraway, Donna. "A Cyborg Manifesto: Science, Technology and Socialist-Feminism in the Late Twentieth Century." *The Cybercultures Reader*, edited by David Bell and Barbara M. Kennedy, Routledge, 2000, pp. 291–324.

Harris, Norman. *Connecting Times: The Sixties in Afro-American Fiction*. UP of Mississippi, 1988.

Harris, Trudier. *The Power of the Porch: The Storyteller's Craft in Zora Neale Hurston, Gloria Naylor, and Randall Kenan*. U of Georgia P, 1996.

———. "The Trickster in African American Literature." *Freedom's Story, TeacherServe©*. National Humanities Center, http://nationalhumanitiescenter.org/tserve/freedom/1865-1917/essays/trickster.htm.

Hathaway, Rosemary V. "The Unbearable Weight of Authenticity: Zora Neale Hurston's *Their Eyes Were Watching God* and a Theory of 'Touristic Reading.'" *Journal of American Folklore*, vol. 117, no. 464, 2004, pp. 168–90.

Havard, John C. "Mary Peabody Mann's *Juanita* and Martin R. Delany's *Blake*: Cuba, Slavery, and the Construction of Nation." *College English*, vol. 43, no. 3, 2016, pp. 509–40.

Hayles, N. Katherine. "Greg Egan's *Quarantine* and *Teranesia*: Contributions to the Millennial Reassessment of Consciousness and the Cognitive Nonconscious." *Science Fiction Studies*, vol. 42, no. 1, 2015, pp. 56–77.

Haynes, Robert V. *A Night of Violence: The Houston Riot of 1917*. Louisiana State UP, 1976.

Heinlein, Robert A. *Farnham's Freehold*. 1964. Baen, 1994.

Higgins, David, editor. "Symposium on Science Fiction and Globalization." *Science Fiction Studies*, vol. 39, no. 3, 2012, pp. 374–84.

Hinks, Peter P. *To Awaken My Afflicted Brethren: David Walker and the Problem of Antebellum Slave Resistance*. Pennsylvania State UP, 1996.

Hobbs, Allyson. *A Chosen Exile: A History of Racial Passing in American Life*. Harvard UP, 2014.

Hochschild, Adam. *King Leopold's Ghost: A Story of Greed, Terror, and Heroism in Colonial Africa*. Houghton Mifflin, 1998.

Hogue, W. Lawrence. "Can the Subaltern Speak? A Postcolonial, Existential Reading of Richard Wright's *Native Son*." *Southern Quarterly*, vol. 46, no. 2, 2009, pp. 9–39.

Hong, Grace Kyungwon. "'The Future of Our Worlds': Black Feminism and the Politics of Knowledge in the University under Globalization." *Meridians*, vol. 8, no. 2, 2008, pp. 95–115.

Hopkins, Pauline. *Of One Blood: Or, The Hidden Self*. 1903. Washington Square, 2004.

Hopkinson, Nalo. *Brown Girl in the Ring*. Warner, 1998.

———. *Midnight Robber*. Warner, 2000.

———. *The Salt Roads*. Warner, 2003.

Howe, Irving. "Black Boys and Native Sons." *Dissent*, vol. 10, 1963, pp. 353–68.

Hughes, Langston. "Harlem." 1951. *Norton Anthology*, edited by Gates and Smith, vols. 1 and 2, 3rd ed., Norton, 2014, p. 1319.

———. "I, Too." 1925. *Norton Anthology*, edited by Gates and McKay, Norton, 2007, p. 1295.

———. "Warning." 1967. *The Black Poets*, edited by Dudley Randall, Bantam, 1971, p. 91.

Hume, David. *Essays, Moral, Political, and Literary.* 1742. *Online Library of Liberty*, 2012, oll.libertyfund.org/titles/hume-essays-moral-political-literary-lf-ed.

Hurston, Zora N. *Mules and Men.* 1935. Harper Perennial Modern Classics, 2008.

———. *Tell My Horse: Voodoo and Life in Haiti and Jamaica.* 1938. Harper Perennial Modern Classics, 2008.

———. *Their Eyes Were Watching God.* 1937. Perennial Library, 1990.

Husserl, Edmund. *Cartesian Meditations: An Introduction to Phenomenology.* Translated by Dorion Cairns, Kluwer, 1988.

Huxley, Aldous. *Brave New World.* 1932. Perennial Classics, 1998.

Hyde, Carrie. "Novelistic Evidence: The Denmark Vesey Conspiracy and Possibilistic History." *American Literary History*, vol. 27, no. 1, 2015, pp. 26–55.

Hynek, Joseph A. *The UFO Experience: A Scientific Inquiry.* Henry Regnery, 1972.

Ignatiev, Noel. *How the Irish Became White.* Routledge, 1995.

Izzo, Justin. "Historical Reversibility as Ethnographic Afrofuturism: Abdourahman Waberi's Alternative Africa." *The Futures Industry,* special issue of *Paradoxa*, vol. 27, 2015, pp. 161–82.

Jackson, Blyden. *Operation Burning Candle.* Third Press, 1973.

Jacobs, Harriet. *Incidents in the Life of a Slave Girl.* 1861. Dover, 2001.

Jacobson, Mathew F. *Whiteness of a Different Color: European Immigrants and the Alchemy of Race.* Harvard UP, 1998.

James, C. L. R. *The Black Jacobins: Toussaint L'Ouverture and the San Domingo Revolution.* 1938. 2nd ed., Vintage, 1989.

James, Donald. "Explanation of 'Follow the Drinking Gourd.'" NASA Quest, n.d., quest.nasa.gov/ltc/special/mlk/gourd2.html.

———. "History of 'Follow the Drinking Gourd.'" quest.nasa.gov/ltc/special/mlk/gourd2.html.

James, Edward. *Science Fiction in the Twentieth Century.* Oxford UP, 1994.

Jameson, Fredric. *Archaeologies of the Future: The Desire Called Utopia and Other Science Fictions.* Verso, 2005.

JanMohamed, Abdul R. *The Death-Bound-Subject: Richard Wright's Archaeology of Death.* Duke UP, 2005.

———. "Negating the Negation: The Construction of Richard Wright." *Richard Wright: Critical Perspectives Past and Present*, edited by Henry Louis Gates Jr. and K. A. Appiah, Amistad, 1993, pp. 285–301.

Japtok, Martin. "Pauline Hopkins's *Of One Blood*, Africa, and the 'Darwinist Trap.'" *African American Review*, vol. 36, no. 3, 2002, pp. 403–15.

Jefferson, Thomas. *The Autobiography of Thomas Jefferson.* 1821. *The Norton Anthology of American Literature, Volume A: Beginnings to 1820.* 9th ed., edited by Robert S. Levine, Norton, 2017, pp. 704–10.

———. *Notes on the State of Virginia.* 1785. Penguin Classics, 1998.

Jemisin, N. K. *The Fifth Season.* Orbit, 2015.

Jirousek, Lori. "Ethnics and Ethnographers: Zora Neale Hurston and Anzia Yezierska." *Journal of Modern Literature*, vol. 29, no. 2, 2006, pp. 19–32.

Johnson, James W. *The Autobiography of an Ex-Colored Man*. 1912. Dover, 1995.

Jones, James H. *Bad Blood: The Tuskegee Syphilis Experiment*. Revised ed., Free Press, 1993.

Jones, LeRoi (Amiri Baraka). "The Myth of a 'Negro Literature.'" 1966. *Within the Circle: An Anthology of African American Literary Criticism from the Harlem Renaissance to the Present*, edited by Angelyn Mitchell, Duke UP, 1994, pp. 165–71.

Joseph, Philip. "The Verdict from the Porch: Zorah Neale Hurston and Reparative Justice." *American Literature*, vol. 74, no. 3, 2002, pp. 455–83.

Kant, Immanuel. "Observations on the Feeling of the Beautiful and Sublime." 1764. *Observations on the Feeling of the Beautiful and Sublime and Other Writings*, edited by Patrick Frierson and Paul Guyer, Cambridge UP, 2011, pp. 11–64.

Kaplan, Carla. "The Erotics of Talk: 'The Oldest Human Longing' in *Their Eyes Were Watching God*." *American Literature*, vol. 67, no. 1, 1995, pp. 115–42.

Kawash, Samira. *Dislocating the Color Line: Identity, Hybridity, and Singularity in African-American Literature*. Stanford UP, 1997.

Kearney, Douglas. *The Black Automaton*. Fence, 2009.

Kelley, James B. "Song, Story, or History: Resisting Claims of a Coded Message in the African American Spiritual '"Follow the Drinking Gourd."'" *Journal of Popular Culture*, vol. 41, no. 2, 2008, pp. 262–80.

Kelley, William M. *A Different Drummer*. 1962. Anchor, 1990.

Kilgore, De Witt D. "Afrofuturism." *The Oxford Handbook of Science Fiction*, edited by Rob Latham, Oxford UP, 2014, pp. 561–72.

———. "Beyond the History We Know: Nnedi Okorafor-Mbachu, Nisi Shawl, and Jarla Tang Rethink Science Fiction Tradition." *Afro-Future Females: Black Writers Chart Science Fiction's Newest New-Wave Trajectory*, edited by Marleen S. Barr, Ohio State UP, 2008, pp. 119–29.

Killens, John O. *Great Gittin' Up Morning: A Biography of Denmark Vesey*. Doubleday, 1972.

———. *'Sippi*. 1967. Thunder's Mouth, 1988.

Kim, Hyejin. "Gothic Storytelling and Resistance in Charles W. Chesnutt's *The Conjure Woman*." *Orbis Litterarum*, vol. 69, no. 5, 2014, pp. 411–38.

King, Martin L. Jr. "I've Been to the Mountaintop." 1968. *Norton Anthology*, edited by Gates and McKay, Norton, 2007, pp. 110–16.

———. "I Have a Dream." 1963. *Norton Anthology*, edited by Gates and McKay, Norton, 2007, pp. 107–9.

Kinney, Katherine. *Friendly Fire: American Images of the Vietnam War*. Oxford UP, 2000.

Kubitschek, Missy D. "'Tuh De Horizon and Back': The Female Quest in *Their Eyes Were Watching God*." *Black American Literature Forum*, vol. 17, no. 3, 1983, pp. 109–15.

Larsen, Nella. *Passing*. 1929. Penguin Classics, 2003.

Lavender, Isiah III. "Critical Race Theory." *The Routledge Companion to Science Fiction*, edited by Mark Bould, et al., Routledge, 2009, pp. 185–93.

———, editor. *Dis-Orienting Planets: Racial Representations of Asia in Science Fiction*, edited by Isiah Lavender III, UP of Mississippi, 2017.

———. *Race in American Science Fiction*. Indiana UP, 2011.

———. "Reframing *Heart of Darkness* as Science Fiction." *Extrapolation*, vol. 56, no. 1, 2015, pp. 15–39.

Leckie, Shirley A., and William H. Leckie. *The Buffalo Soldiers: A Narrative of the Black Cavalry in the West*. Revised ed., U of Oklahoma P, 2007.

Levin, Adam. "Africa's space oddities are transformed into fetishes." *Mail & Guardian*, 12 Dec. 2014, https://mg.co.za/article/2014-12-12-africas-space-oddities-are-transformed-into-fetishes.

Luckhurst, Roger. *Science Fiction*. Polity, 2005.

Marable, Manning. *Race, Reform, and Rebellion: The Second Reconstruction and Beyond in Black America, 1945–2006*. 3rd ed., UP of Mississippi, 2007.

Margolick, David. *Strange Fruit: The Biography of a Song*. Ecco Press, 2001.

Margolies, Edward. "Native Son and Three Kinds of Revolution." *Major Literary Characters*, edited by Bloom, 1990, pp. 43–53.

Martin, Kameelah L. *Conjuring Moments in African American Literature: Women, Spirit Work, and Other Such Hoodoo*. Palgrave Macmillan, 2013.

Mathews, Kadeshia L. "Black Boy No More? Violence and the Flight from Blackness in Richard Wright's *Native Son*." *Modern Fiction Studies*, vol. 60, no. 2, 2014, pp. 276–97.

Matthews, Donald H. *Honoring the Ancestors: An African Cultural Interpretation of Black Religion and Literature*. Oxford UP, 1998.

Mbembe, Achille. *On the Postcolony*. 2000. U of California P, 2001.

McCall, Dan. "The Bad Nigger." *Richard Wright's* Native Son, edited by Bloom, 1988, pp. 5–22.

McKay, Claude. "If We Must Die." 1919. *Norton Anthology*, edited by Gates and Smith, vols. 1 and 2, 3rd ed., Norton, 2014, p. 1005.

McKittrick, Katherine. *Demonic Grounds: Black Women and the Cartographies of Struggle*. U of Minnesota P, 2006.

McWhirter, Cameron. *Red Summer: The Summer of 1919 and the Awakening of Black America*. Henry Holt, 2011.

Melfi, Theodore, director. *Hidden Figures*. 20th Century Fox, 2016.

Melville, Herman. 1851. *Moby-Dick; or, the Whale*. Simon & Brown, 2013.

Mercer, Kobena. *Welcome to the Jungle: New Positions in Black Cultural Studies*. Routledge, 1994.

Miller, Warren. *The Siege of Harlem*. Fawcett Crest, 1964.

Mitchell, Margaret. *Gone with the Wind*. 1936. Warner Books, 1999.

Moore, Ward. *Bring the Jubilee*. 1953. Avon, 1972.

Moreau, Julian. *The Black Commandos*. Cultural Institute Press, 1967.

Morley, David, and Kevin Robins. "Techno-Orientalism: Japan Panic." *Global Media, Electronic Landscapes, and Cultural Boundaries,* edited by David Morley and Kevin Robins, Routledge, 1995, pp. 147–73.

Morrison, Toni. *Beloved.* 1987. Plume, 1998.

———. *Playing in the Dark: Whiteness and the Literary Imagination.* Harvard UP, 1992.

———. *Song of Solomon.* 1977. Vintage, 2004.

———. *Sula.* Knopf, 1973.

Moses, Wilson J. *Afrotopia: The Roots of African American Popular History.* Cambridge UP, 1998.

Mosley, Walter. "Black to the Future." *Dark Matter,* edited by Thomas, Warner, 2000, pp. 405–7.

Moylan, Tom. *Demand the Impossible: Science Fiction and the Utopian Imagination.* 1986. Peter Lang Press, 2014.

———. *Scraps of the Untainted Sky: Science Fiction, Utopia, Dystopia.* Westview Press, 2000.

Muller, Gilbert H. *John A. Williams.* Twayne, 1984.

Munro, C. Lynn. "Culture and Quest in the Fiction of John A. Williams." *CLA Journal,* vol. 22, no. 2, 1978, pp. 71–100.

Naylor, Gloria. *Mama Day.* 1988. Vintage, 1993.

Neal, Larry. "The Black Arts Movement." *Within the Circle: An Anthology of African American Literary Criticism from the Harlem Renaissance to the Present,* edited by Angelyn Mitchell, Duke UP, 1994, pp. 184–98.

Nelson, Alondra. "AfroFuturism: Past-Future Visions." *Color Lines,* Spring 2000, pp. 34–37.

———. "Introduction: Future Texts." *Afrofuturism,* special issue of *Social Text,* vol. 20, no. 2, 2002, pp. 1–15.

Nelson, Peter. *A More Unbending Battle: The Harlem Hellfighters' Struggle for Freedom in WWI and Equality at Home.* Basic Civitas, 2009.

Nesbitt, Nick. *Universal Emancipation: The Haitian Revolution and the Radical Enlightenment.* U of Virginia P, 2008.

"Network to Freedom." National Park Service, n.d., www.nps.gov/subjects/ugrr/index.htm. Newton, Adam Z. *Narrative Ethics.* Harvard UP, 1995.

@Nnedi Okorafor, PhD. "I am an Africanfuturist. BEFORE you start asking for or debating it's meaning, please call me the name first." *Twitter,* 4 Nov. 2018, 11:10 a.m., https://twitter.com/Nnedi/status/1059130871360368640.

Northup, Solomon. *Twelve Years a Slave.* 1853. Dover, 1970.

Obama, Barack. "A More Perfect Union." 2008. *We Are the Change We Seek: The Speeches of Barack Obama,* edited by E. J. Dionne Jr. and Joy-Ann Reid, Bloomsbury, 2017, pp. 237–51.

O'Dell, Wesley. "'Slightly too late, or far too soon:' The Stono Rebellion and the Abolitionist Movement." *Southern Studies,* vol. 19, no. 1, 2012, pp. 40–64.

Okorafor, Nnedi. *Lagoon.* Saga Press, 2014.

———. *Who Fears Death.* DAW Books, 2010.

Orwell, George. *1984*. 1949. Signet Classics, 1950.

Parker, Nate, director. *The Birth of a Nation*. Fox Searchlight Pictures, 2016.

Pate, Alexs D. Introduction. *Captain Blackman*, by John A. Williams, Coffee House, 2000, pp. i–ix.

Peele, Jordan, director. *Get Out*. Universal Pictures, 2017.

Pelletier, Kevin. "David Walker, Harriet Beecher Stowe, and the Logic of Sentimental Terror." *African American Review*, vol. 46, nos. 2–3, 2013, pp. 255–69.

Petry, Ann. *Tituba of Salem Village*. 1964. HarperCollins, 1991.

Posey, Darrell A. "Origin, Development and Maintenance of a Louisiana Mixed-Blood Community: The Ethnohistory of the Freejacks of the First Ward Settlement." *Ethnohistory*, vol. 26, no. 2, 1979, pp. 177–92.

Prashad, Vijay. *Everybody Was Kung Fu Fighting: Afro-Asian Connections and the Myth of Cultural Purity*. Beacon, 2002.

Public Enemy. "Prophets of Rage." *It Takes a Nation of Millions to Hold Us Back*, Def Jam/Columbia, 1988.

Pulliam-Moore, Charles. "HBO and George R. R. Martin Set to Produce Nnedi Okorafor's *Who Fears Death* TV Series." *io9*, 10 July 2017, https://io9.gizmodo.com/hbo-and-george-r-r-martin-set-to-produce-nnedi-okorafo-1796778796.

Raboteau, Emily. *The Professor's Daughter: A Novel*. Henry Holt, 2005.

Ramsby, Howard Jr. "Beyond Keeping It Real: OutKast, The Funk Connection, and Afrofuturism." *American Studies*, vol. 52, no. 4, 2013, pp. 205–16.

Randle, Gloria T. "Between the Rock and the Hard Place: Mediating Space in Harriet Jacobs's *Incidents in the Life of a Slave Girl*." *African American Review*, vol. 33, no. 1, 1999, pp. 43–56.

Rasmussen, Daniel. *American Uprising: The Untold Story of America's Largest Slave Revolt*. HarperCollins, 2011.

Ray, Angela G. "'In My Own Hand Writing': Benjamin Banneker Addresses the Slaveholder of Monticello." *Rhetoric & Public Affairs*, vol. 1, no. 3, 1998, pp. 387–405.

Reed, Anthony. "Another Map of the South Side": *Native Son* as Postcolonial Novel." *African American Review*, vol. 45, no. 4, 2012, pp. 603–15.

Reed, Ishmael. *Flight to Canada*. 1976. Scribner, 1998.

Reynolds, Mack. *The Best Ye Breed*. 1978. Ace, 1978.

———. *Black Man's Burden*. 1961–62. Ace, 1972.

———. "Black Sheep Astray." *Astounding: John W. Campbell Memorial Anthology*, edited by Harry Harrison, Random House, 1973, pp. 201–30.

———. *Border, Breed, nor Birth*. 1962. Ace, 1972.

Rhodes, Jewell Parker. *Vodoo Dreams: A Novel of Marie Laveau*. St. Martin's, 1993.

Rieder, John. *Colonialism and the Emergence of Science Fiction*. Wesleyan UP, 2008.

———. "Science Fiction, Colonialism, and the Plot of Invasion." *Extrapolation*, vol. 46, no. 3, 2005, pp. 373–94.

———. *Science Fiction and the Mass Cultural Genre System*. Wesleyan UP, 2017.

Roach, Marilynne K. *The Salem Witch Trials: A Day-by-Day Chronicle of a Community under Siege.* Cooper Square, 2002.

Robertson. David. *Denmark Vesey: The Buried Story of America's Largest Slave Rebellion and the Man Who Led It.* Knopf, 1999.

Roediger, David R. *Working toward Whiteness: How America's Immigrants Became White: The Strange Journey from Ellis Island to the Suburbs.* Basic, 2005.

Robbins, Hollis. "Fugitive Mail: The Deliverance of Henry 'Box' Brown and Antebellum Postal Politics." *American Studies*, vol. 50, nos. 1/2, 2009, pp. 5–25.

The Roots. "Somebody's Gotta Do It." *The Tipping Point*, Geffen/Interscope, 2004.

Rose, Mark. *Alien Encounters: Anatomy of Science Fiction.* Harvard UP, 1981.

Rowley, Hazel. *Richard Wright: The Life and Times.* U of Chicago P, 2001.

Ruffin, Edmund. *Anticipations of the Future, to Serve as Lessons for the Present Time: In the Form of Extracts of Letters From an English Resident in the United States, to the London Times, from 1864 to 1870.* 1860. HardPress, 2017. J. W. Randolph, 1860.

Rusert, Britt. "Delany's Comet: Fugitive Science and the Speculative Imaginary of Emancipation." *American Quarterly*, vol. 65, no. 4, 2013, pp. 799–829.

Samatar, Sofia. "Charting the Constellation: Past and Present in *Things Fall Apart*." *Research in African Literatures*, vol. 42, no. 2, 2011, pp. 60–71.

Schalk, Sami. *Bodyminds Reimagined: (Dis)ability, Race, and Gender in Black Women's Speculative Fiction.* Duke UP, 2018.

Schuyler, George S. *Black Empire: George S. Schuyler Writing as Samuel I. Brooks. 1936–38.* Edited by Robert A. Hill and R. K. Rasmussen, Northeastern UP, 1991.

———. *Black No More.* 1931. Northeastern UP, 1989.

Scott, Colin. "Science for the West, Myth for the Rest? The Case of James Bay Cree Knowledge Construction." *The Postcolonial Science and Technology Studies Reader*, edited by Sandra Harding, Duke UP, 2011, pp. 175–97.

Shawl, Nisi. *Everfair.* Tor, 2016.

Sidbury, James. *Ploughshares into Swords: Race, Rebellion, and Identity in Gabriel's Virginia, 1730–1810.* Cambridge UP, 1997.

Siegel, Don, director. *Invasion of the Body Snatchers.* Allied Artists Pictures, 1956.

Sinclair, Upton. *The Jungle.* 1906. Dover, 2001.

Skloot, Rebecca. *The Immortal Life of Henrietta Lacks.* Crown, 2010.

"Slave Quilts." National Cryptologic Museum Past Exhibits Image Gallery. National Security Agency, 3 May 2016. www.nsa.gov/resources/everyone/digital-media-center/image-galleries/cryptologic-museum/past-exhibits/.

Slotkin, Richard. *No Quarter: The Battle of the Crater, 1864.* Random House, 2009.

Smethurst, James. "Invented by Horror: The Gothic and African American Literary Ideology in *Native Son*." *African American Review*, vol. 35, no. 1, 2001, pp. 29–40.

Smith, Valerie. "Alienation and Creativity in *Native Son*." *Bigger Thomas*, by Harold Bloom, Chelsea House, 1990, pp. 143–50.

———. "Black Life in the Balance: *12 Years a Slave*." *American Literary History*, vol. 26, no. 2, 2014, pp. 362–66.

———. "'Loopholes of Retreat': Architecture and Ideology in Harriet Jacobs's *Incidents in the Life of a Slave Girl.*" *Reading Black, Reading Feminist: A Critical Anthology*, edited by Henry Louis Gates Jr., Meridian, 1990, pp. 212–26.

Smith, Venture. *A Narrative of the Life and Adventures of Venture Smith, A Native of Africa: But Resident Above Sixty Years in the United States of America. Related by Himself.* 1798. *Norton Anthology*, edited by Gates and McKay, Norton, 2007, pp. 170–85.

Smith, Virginia W. "Sorcery, Double-Consciousness, and Warring Souls: An Intertextual Reading of *Middle Passage* and *Captain Blackman.*" *African American Review*, vol. 30, no. 4, 1996, pp. 659–74.

Sohn, Stephen Hong. "'Perpetual War': Korean American Speculative Fiction, Militarized Technogeometries, and Yoon Ha Lee's 'Wine.'" *Dis-Orienting Planets*, edited by Lavender III, 2017, pp. 56–70.

Soto, Isabel. "'White People to Either Side': *Native Son* and the Poetics of Space." *The Black Scholar*, vol. 39, nos. 1–2, 2009, pp. 23–26.

Stearns, Charles. *Narrative of Henry Box Brown, Who Escaped from Slavery Enclosed in a Box 3 Feet Long and 2 Wide. Written from a Statement of Facts Made by Himself. With Remarks Upon the Remedy for Slavery.* Brown and Stearns, 1849. U of North Carolina at Chapel Hill, 2001, http://docsouth.unc.edu/neh/boxbrown/boxbrown.html. Documenting the American South.

Stivers, Richard. *Technology as Magic: The Triumph of the Irrational.* Continuum, 1999.

Stowe, Harriet B. *Uncle Tom's Cabin.* 1852. Bantam Classics, 2003.

Stringer, Dorothy. "Slavery & the Afrofuture in Samuel R. Delany's *Stars in My Pocket like Grains of Sand.*" *Speculating Futures: Black Imagination & the Arts*, special issue of *Obsidian*, vol. 42, nos. 1/2, 2016, pp. 204–17.

Styron, William. *The Confessions of Nat Turner.* 1967. Vintage, 1992.

Sundquist, Eric J. *To Wake the Nations: Race in the Making of American Literature.* Belknap Press of Harvard UP, 1993.

Suvin, Darko. *Defined by a Hollow: Essays on Utopia, Science Fiction and Political Epistemology.* Peter Lang Press, 2010.

———. *Metamorphoses of Science Fiction: On the Poetics and History of a Literary Genre.* Yale UP, 1979.

Tal, Kali. "'That Just Kills Me': Black Militant Near-Future Fiction." *Social Text*, vol. 20, no. 2, 2002, pp. 65–91.

Thomas, Sheree R., editor. *Dark Matter: A Century of Speculative Fiction from the African Diaspora.* Warner, 2000.

Thomas, Sheree R. "And So Shaped the World." *Speculating Futures: Black Imagination & the Arts*, special issue of *Obsidian*, vol. 42, no. 1/2, 2016, pp. 3–10.

Thompson, George A. Jr. *A Documentary History of the African Theater.* Northwestern UP, 1998.

Thompson, Tade. *Rosewater.* Apex, 2016.

Thoreau, Henry David. *Walden.* 1854. *The Norton Anthology of American Literature: Volume B: 1820–1865*, 9th ed., edited by Robert S. Levine, Norton, 2017, pp. 970–1144.

Thornton, John K. "African Dimensions of the Stono Rebellion." *American Historical Review*, vol. 96, no. 4, 1991, pp. 1101–13.

Thrasher, Albert. *"On to New Orleans!": Louisiana's Heroic 1811 Slave Revolt*. Cypress, 1995.

Tucker, Beverly. *The Partisan Leader: A Novel, and an Apocalypse of the Origin and Struggles of the Southern Confederacy*. 1862. Nabu Press, 2010.

Tucker, Nathaniel Beverly. *The Partisan Leader: A Tale of the Future*. 1836. U of North Carolina P, 1971.

Turner, James. "David Walker and the Appeal: An Introduction." *David Walker's Appeal, in Four Articles; Together with a Preamble, to the Coloured Citizens of the World, But in Particular, and Very Expressly, to Those of the United States of America*, by David Walker, 1829, Black Classic, 1993, pp. 9–19.

Tyson, Timothy B. *The Blood of Emmett Till*. Simon & Schuster, 2017.

Vallee, Jacques. "Physical Analysis in Ten Cases of Unexplained Aerial Objects with Material Samples." *Journal of Scientific Exploration*, vol. 12, no. 3, 1998, pp. 359–75.

Veslá, Pavla. "Neither Black nor White: The Critical Utopias of Sutton E. Griggs and George S. Schuyler." *Science Fiction Studies*, vol. 38, no. 2, 2011, pp. 270–87.

Vizenor, Gerald. *Manifest Manners: Narratives on Postindian Survivance*. U of Nebraska P, 1999.

Waberi, Abdourahman A. *In the United States of Africa*. 2006. Translated by David Ball and Nicole Ball, U of Nebraska P, 2009.

Walker, David. *David Walker's Appeal, in Four Articles; Together with a Preamble, to the Coloured Citizens of the World, But in Particular, and Very Expressly, to Those of the United States of America*. 1829. Black Classic, 1993.

Walker, Margaret. "For My People." 1937. *Norton Anthology*, edited by Gates and McKay, Norton, 2007, pp. 319–20.

Walters, Kerry. *American Slave Revolts and Conspiracies: A Reference Guide*. ABC-CLIO, 2015.

Warren, Kenneth W. *What Was African American Literature?* Harvard UP, 2011.

Washington, Harriet A. *Medical Apartheid: The Dark History of Medical Experimentation on Black Americans from Colonial Times to the Present*. Doubleday, 2006.

Weaver, John D. *The Brownsville Raid*. 1970. Texas A&M UP, 1992.

Webb, Frank J. *The Garies and Their Friends*. 1857. Johns Hopkins UP, 1997.

Weheliye, Alexander G. *Habeas Viscus: Racializing Assemblages, Biopolitics, and Black Feminist Theories of the Human*. Duke UP, 2014.

Wells-Barnett, Ida B. *The Red Record: Tabulated Statistics and Alleged Causes of Lynching in the United States*. 1895. *Project Gutenberg*, 8 Feb. 2005, www.gutenberg.org/files/14977/14977-h/14977-h.htm.

Wells, H. G. *The Island of Dr. Moreau*. 1896. Dover, 1996.

———. *The War of the Worlds*. 1898. Dover, 1997.

Welter, Barbara. "The Cult of True Womanhood: 1820–1860." *American Quarterly*, vol. 18, no. 2, 1966, pp. 151–74.

Wheatley, Phillis. "On Being Brought from Africa to America." 1773. *Norton Anthology*, edited by Gates and McKay, Norton, 2007, pp. 219–20.

———. *Poems on Various Subjects, Religious and Moral*. London, 1773.

White, Walter. *The Fire in the Flint*. 1924. U of Georgia P, 1996.

Whitehead, Colson. *The Intuitionist*. Anchor, 1999.

———. *John Henry Days*. Doubleday, 2001.

———. *Sag Harbor*. Doubleday 2009.

———. *The Underground Railroad*. Doubleday, 2016.

———. *Zone One*. Doubleday, 2011.

Whitman, Walt. "I Hear America Singing." 1860. *The Complete Poems*, edited by Francis Murphy, Penguin Classics, 2004, p. 47.

———. *Leaves of Grass*. 1855. Penguin Classics, 1981.

Widdicombe, Toby, et al. *Historical Dictionary of Utopianism*. 2nd ed., Roman & Littlefield, 2017.

Wideman, John E. *Philadelphia Fire*. Henry Holt & Co., 1990.

Williams, Ben. "Black Secret Technology: Detroit Techno and the Information Age." *Technicolor: Race, Technology, and Everyday Life*, edited by Alicia H. Hines, et al., New York UP, 2001, pp. 154–76.

Williams, Eric. *Capitalism & Slavery*. 1944. U of North Carolina P, 1994.

Williams, John A. *Captain Blackman*. 1972. Coffee House, 2000.

———. *The Man Who Cried I Am*. Little, Brown, 1967.

———. *Sons of Darkness, Sons of Light: A Novel of Some Probability*. 1969. Northeastern UP, 1999.

Wills, Brian S. *A Battle from the Start: The Life of Nathan Bedford Forrest*. HarperCollins, 1992.

Winters, Ben H. *Underground Airlines*. Mulholland Books, 2016.

Womack, Ytasha L. *Afrofuturism: The World of Black Sci-Fi and Fantasy Culture*. Lawrence Hill, 2013.

Woodard, Vincent. *The Delectable Negro: Human Consumption and Homoeroticism within U.S. Slave Culture*. New York UP, 2014.

Wright, Richard. "Between Laughter and Tears." Reviews of *Their Eyes Were Watching God*, by Zora Neale Hurston, and *These Low Grounds*, by Waters Turpins, *New Masses*, vol. 25, no. 5, 5 Oct. 1937, p. 22+.

———. *Black Boy*. 1945. Harper Perennial, 2006.

———. "How 'Bigger' Was Born." 1940. *Native Son*. Harper Perennial, 2005, pp. 431–62.

———. *Native Son*. Harper Perennial, 2005.

———. *Native Son*. Harper and Row, 1940.

Wu-Tang Clan. "The City." *Wu-Tang Forever*, Loud/RCA/BMG, 1997.

X, Malcolm. *The Autobiography of Malcolm X as Told to Alex Haley*. 1965. Ballentine, 1992.

———. "The Ballot or the Bullet." 1964. *Norton Anthology*, edited by Gates and McKay, Norton, 2007, pp. 116–28.

Yaszek, Lisa. "An Afrofuturist Reading of Ralph Ellison's *Invisible Man*." *Rethinking History*, vol. 9, nos. 2/3, 2005, pp. 297–313.

———. "The Bannekerade: Genius, Madness, and Magic in Black Science Fiction." *Black and Brown Planets*, edited by Isiah Lavender III, UP of Mississippi, 2014, pp. 15–30.

———. "Race in Science Fiction: The Case of Afrofuturism." *A Virtual Introduction to Science Fiction: Online Toolkit for Teaching SF*, edited by Lars Schmeink, virtual-sf.com/?page_id=372.

———. "Rethinking Apocalypse in African SF." *Africa SF*, special issue of *Paradoxa*, vol. 25, 2013, pp. 47–64.

Youngquist, Paul. "The Space Machine: Baraka and Science Fiction." *African American Review*, vol. 37, nos. 2/3, 2003, pp. 333–43.

Zafar, Rafia. *We Wear the Mask: African Americans Write American Literature, 1760–1870*. Columbia UP, 1997.

INDEX

abolitionists/abolitionist movement, 28, 52, 62, 64, 209

Abraham Lincoln Brigade, 174, 174n29, 181, 200

Achebe, Chinua, 20, 186–92, 197, 211

acting white, 142. *See also* playing white

Africa, 5n7, 20, 51, 60, 65–66, 71–76, 75n27, 81, 102, 157, 162, 183–84, 187–88: Angola, 52; Congo

Africa, John, 13

African American history, 5, 16, 36, 39, 49, 51, 65–104, 123n15, 155, 167–85, 209

African American vernacular, 117–20, 142

African diaspora, 6, 20, 29, 36, 39–40, 82, 112, 115, 187–88, 204, 212

Afro-alienation, 84. *See also* alienation and Daphne Brooks

Afrofuturism: The World of Black Sci-Fi and Fantasy Culture (Womack), 36, 102, 214

afrotopia, 5, 116, 122, 171, 209

Afrotopia: The Roots of African American Popular History (Moses), 5, 209

Alabama, 140–41n5, 193, 193n4: Birmingham, 13

Alexander, Michelle, 25n1, 82, 146n6, 197

aliens, 19–20, 120–25, 128–29

alien abduction narratives, 77, 79–104, 84n8, 200

Alien Encounters: Anatomy of Science Fiction (Rose), 110n8, 211

alien encounters/interactions, 19, 82, 86, 112, 124, 130, 169–70, 190–92: alien encounters scale, 86, 86n8; alien first contact, 20, 20n29, 20n30, 43, 189–91

alienation, 1, 9, 15, 19, 26, 44, 67, 71, 98, 112, 119–22, 128–30, 135–36, 143, 145, 147–48, 159, 170, 190, 193, 211. *See also* Afro-alienation

alternative future, 71, 79–80, 109–12

alternative history, 75n27, 153–85, 156n1, 156n3, 188n2

American chattel slavery, 2–4, 6, 8–9, 11, 16–18, 25–26, 28–76, 66, 75n27, 77n2, 79–104, 111, 137, 153, 155, 159, 161n10, 162, 175, 187, 193–94, 205: apologists for, 25, 28, 57–58. 78; in colonial America, 82, 175

American Civil War, 28, 53, 60, 63–65, 78n3, 156n1, 169, 174, 176–79, 176n30, 181, 184, 198, 200

American dream, the, 86, 129–30, 142, 172

American history, 2–3, 26–29, 39, 62–76, 79 103, 123n15 155: American racial history, 18, 27, 62–104, 153–86, 192–94; sanitation of, 28–29, 75, 82, 203

217

American Negro Slave Revolts (Aptheker), 50–51, 56, 197
American Revolutionary War, 20, 52, 154, 173–75
American Slave Revolts and Conspiracies: A Reference Guide (Walters), 50, 213
American Uprising: The Untold Story of America's Largest Slave Revolt (Rasmussen), 56n10, 57, 210
Another Country (Baldwin), 16, 197
Antebellum America, 11, 18, 26–104, 174: gender norms, 91, 91n12
antebellum literature, 3, 8, 26–104
anti-literacy laws. *See* literacy, anti-literacy laws
Aptheker, Herbert, 50–51, 56, 62, 197
Archaeologies of the Future: The Desire Called Utopia and Other Science Fictions (Jameson), 4, 4n6, 112, 206
Armstrong, Louis, 10, 159
astronomy, 37, 44, 47, 68–69
@Nnedi Okorafor, 209
Autobiography, 8, 11–12, 26–27, 33, 36–38, 43, 49, 63, 97n15, 153, 165, 203, 206, 214
Autobiography of Malcolm X, as Told to Alex Haley (Malcolm X), 165, 214
Autobiography of Thomas Jefferson (Jefferson), 49, 153, 206

Babel-17 (Delany), 109n6, 201
Back to Africa Movement, 113
"Bad Nigger, The" (McCall), 133n3, 148, 208
Bailey, Frederick, 94. *See also* Douglass, Frederick
Baker, Houston A., 14n25, 82, 117n11, 121, 197
Baker, Kyle, 61–62, 197
Baldwin, James, 16, 16n27, 103, 130, 145, 152, 163, 197–98
Ballad of Beta-2, The (Delany), 109n6, 201
"Ballot or the Bullet, The" (Malcolm X), 51n3, 214
Banks, Adam J., 38, 198
Banneker, Benjamin, 18, 25, 39–40, 44–47, 44n14, 51, 63, 68, 198
Baraka, Amiri, 3, 3n4, 140, 164, 164–65n16, 173, 198, 207, 215

Barnes, Steven, 75, 75n27, 77, 77n2, 198
Baudrillard, Jean, 11–12, 198
Beloved (Morrison), 118n12, 209
"Between Laughter and Tears" (Wright), 125, 214
Bibb, Henry, 18, 33–34, 79, 97–99, 101–2, 198
biopolitics/biopolitical knowledge, 94, 96, 100, 169, 213
Bisson, Terry, 77, 78n3, 156, 156n3, 198
"Black Art" (Baraka), 164, 164–65n19, 198
Black Arts Movement, 16, 155, 160, 163, 165, 169, 172, 209
Black Atlantic: Modernity and Double Consciousness, The (Gilroy), 7, 204
Black Automaton, The (Kearney), 40, 40n11, 207
Black Boy (Wright), 27–28, 46, 214
Black Commandos, The (Moreau), 161, 208
Black Empire: George S. Schuyler Writing as Samuel I. Brooks. 1936–38 (Schuyler), 123, 157, 211
black history. *See* African American history and American history
black humanity, 35–36, 38, 41, 48, 53–61, 64, 81–84, 115–16, 121, 26, 133, 140, 146–47, 150, 167, 181
Black Jacobins: Toussaint L'Ouverture and the San Domingo Revolution, The (James), 53, 206
Black Lives Matter, 14n18, 57, 82, 197
black militancy, 19–20, 152–85
black music, 6, 36–38, 46, 62, 122, 145, 159, 164, 184–85, 207: blues music, 80, 107, 117n11, 122, 159, 197; hip hop, 62; jazz fusion, 6; slave songs, 18, 25, 46–47; spirituals, 35–38, 40, 185, 198
black nationalism/sovereignty, 64–76, 104, 163
black networked consciousness, 5–7, 5n8, 8, 14–15, 17–20, 25, 27, 29, 34, 37–40, 44–47, 49, 52, 54–55, 57–58, 61–64, 66–68, 71, 75, 79–81, 85, 88–90, 93–96, 99, 103–4, 112–17, 119–24, 128, 132, 136, 139–46, 144–46, 151–52, 154, 157, 157n5, 163–65, 170–71, 175–76, 181, 185, 192, 196
Black No More (Schuyler), 108, 108n5, 112, 129, 157, 211

black-on-black violence, 136, 143–44
black-o-sphere, 20, 49, 67, 186–96
Black Panther (Coogler), 1, 200
Black Panther Party for Self-Defense, 57, 71
Black Power Movement, 65, 160–61, 163–65, 169, 179n34, 184
black separatism, 51, 64, 69–71, 76, 112
Black Skin, White Masks (Fanon), 3, 149, 172, 183, 203
Black Thunder: Gabriel's Revolt: Virginia 1800 (Bontemps), 55n6, 157, 157n6, 199
Black to the Future (Dery), 2, 9, 29, 31–32, 39–40, 44, 102–4, 112, 122, 131, 201
"Black to the Future" (Mosley), 196, 209
blackness, positive images of, 63, 72–75
Blake, or the Huts of America (Delany), 3, 15–16, 34, 47, 53, 56, 63–69, 73, 75, 202
Bland, Sandra, 163
Bloch, Ernst, 4–5, 198
Blood of Emmitt Till, The (Tyson), 13n13, 213
blue-eyed devils, 165, 165n20
Blues, Ideology, and Afro-American Literature: A Vernacular Theory (Baker), 117n11, 121, 197
Boas, Franz, 108
Bodies in Dissent: Spectacular Performances of Race and Freedom (Brooks), 84, 89–90, 199
Bond, Hannah, 94. See also Crafts, Hannah
Bondsman's Narrative, The (Crafts), 94n14, 200
Bontemps, Arna, 55n6, 157, 157n6, 199
Bould, Mark, xi, 3, 3n5, 67, 70, 75, 161, 187–88, 199, 207
Bradbury, Ray, 156, 199
Bring the Jubilee (Moore), 156, 156n1, 208
Brooks, Daphne, 84, 89–90, 199. See also Afro-alienation
Brooks, Gwendolyn, 164, 164–65n19, 199
Brown Girl in the Ring (Hopkinson), 31, 205
Brown, Henry "Box," 18, 79, 88–90, 89n10, 94, 201, 210, 211–12
Brown, John, 78n3, 156n3

Brown, Michael, 14, 14n20, 127, 163
Brown, William Henry, 63, 63n16
Brown, William Wells, 18, 79, 94–95, 103, 199
Buffalo Soldiers, 169–70, 169n22, 174, 180, 182, 208
Burroughs, Edgar Rice, 110n7, 199
Bush, George H. W., 131, 131n2
Buckell, Tobias, 110n7, 199
Butler, Octavia E., 1, 1–3n1, 14n26, 20, 31, 31n5, 75, 75n27, 77, 77n2, 112, 124, 186, 199–201

Canada, 65–66, 90, 95, 97–99
Canavan, Gerry, x, 9, 200
cane/cane fields. See sugar cane/sugar cane fields
capital punishment, 13, 31, 133, 141, 143–44
capitalism, 2, 11, 34–35, 137, 162n15
Captain Blackman (Williams), 15, 17, 19–20, 66, 153–85, 212, 214
Caribbean, the, 53, 65, 75
Carrington, André M., xi, 77n1, 171, 171n23, 171n24, 200
Cartwright, Samuel A., 98, 200
Cash, Earl A., 154, 171, 174, 181–82, 200
Castile, Philando, 14, 14n24
Cerami, Charles A., 44, 200
Chang, Justin, 48, 200
Chesnutt, Charles W., 34–35, 200, 207
Child, Lydia Maria, 103, 200
Christianity, 33, 40–41, 45, 59, 62, 93, 145–46, 165, 190: Protestant, 40n9, 57, 64, 71, 145–46, 170, 190
"City, The" (Wu-Tang Clan), 62n14, 214
Civil Rights Act of 1964, 160
Civil Rights Act of 1968, 160
civil rights era/civil rights movement, 12–13, 13n12, 16, 57, 85, 158, 160, 163–64
Civil War. See American Civil War
Clansman: An Historical Romance of the Ku Klux Klan, The (Dixon), 156, 202
Clay's Ark (Butler), 124, 199
clones, 79, 196
Clotel; or the President's Daughter (Brown), 103, 199

code breaking, 29, 35–47
codes/cyphers, 37–38
Collected Essays of Ralph Ellison, The (Ellison), 127, 129, 133, 136–37, 151, 203
Collins, Addie Mae, 13
Colonial America, 11, 16, 18, 25–47, 49, 51, 81, 174
Colonial New England. See Colonial America
colonialism, 11, 36, 39–44, 50–52, 66, 72, 187–92, 187n1: and afrofuturism, 18, 25, 44, 187–92
Colonialism and the Emergence of Science Fiction (Rieder), 187n1, 210
color line, 107, 115, 120, 134, 139, 170, 173n26, 183
colorism, 8, 108n5, 164n16
"Comet, The" (Du Bois), 124, 202
Condition, Elevation, Emigration and Destiny of the Colored People of the United States, The (Delany), 115, 201
Confederacy, The/Confederates, 49, 155, 156n1, 176–78, 176n30, 178n33
Confessions of Nat Turner, The (Styron), 61, 212
Confessions of Nat Turner: The Leader of the Late Insurrection in Southampton, VA (Gray), 62, 62n15, 204
Conjure Woman, The (Chesnutt), 35, 200, 207
conjuring/conjurers, 25, 30, 31–35, 47, 56, 62, 66–67, 75n27, 197, 208
Conjuring Moments in African American Literature: Women, Spirit Work, and Other Such Hoodoo (Martin), 31, 208
connected black consciousness. See black networked consciousness
Conrad, Joseph, 72, 72n26, 187–89, 200
Coogler, Ryan, 1, 200
cotton/cotton fields, 9, 64, 85, 87, 100, 103
counterculture movement, 164, 171–72
counterfactual accounts, 55, 75n27, 156n3, 188
countermemory, 4, 35–36. See also memory
counternarratives, 84–94, 196
Crafts, Hannah, 94, 94n14, 200

cultural appropriation, 30, 44, 50, 188, 191, 196
cyberspace, 6, 159
"Cyborg Manifesto: Science, Technology, and Socialist-Feminism in the Late Twentieth Century, A" (Haraway), 96, 205
cyborg/monster/alien identity, 128–30, 132–34, 136–37, 139, 147–52
cyborgs, 19, 79, 96, 102, 110n7, 158–59, 196, 205

Dangerous Visions (Ellison), 164n18, 202
Dark Matter: A Century of Speculative Fiction from the African Diaspora (Thomas), 109, 201–2, 209, 212
Dark Princess, The (Du Bois), 108, 108n5, 168, 202
David Walker's Appeal, (Walker), 18, 49, 51, 57–61, 126, 213
Davis, Jefferson, 49
Davis, Thadious M., 69n22, 201
Death Bound-Subject: Richard Wright's Archaeology of Death, The (JanMohamed), 130n1, 143, 206
death penalty, the. See capital punishment
Declaration of Independence, The, 49, 60, 172
Defined by a Hollow: Essays on Science Fiction, Utopia, and Political Epistemology (Suvin), 5n6, 212
dehumanization of blacks/black bodies, 6, 44, 49, 79, 84, 91–92, 114, 128–29, 149, 156, 159, 172
Delany, Martin R., 3, 15–16, 18, 34, 47, 51, 53, 56, 63–69, 64n18, 75–76, 115, 157, 196, 201–2, 204–5, 211
Delany, Samuel R., 3n3, 20–21, 29, 39–40, 77, 77n2, 109–10, 109n6, 186, 196, 201, 212
Denmark Vesey: The Buried Story of America's Largest Slave Rebellion and the Man Who Led It (Robertson), 211
Dery, Mark, 2–3, 2n2, 3n3, 9, 29–31, 39–40, 44, 102–4, 109, 112, 122, 131, 201
Deslondes, Charles, 56–57
Diallo, Amadou, 13, 13n15
Dick, Philip K., 167, 202

Different Drummer, A (Kelley), 160, 160n8, 207
Dixon, Thomas, 156, 202
Do Androids Dream of Electric Sheep? (Dick), 167, 202
Dolezal, Rachel, 44n13
double consciousness, 7
Douglass, Frederick, 8, 11–12, 18, 25–28, 33, 36–38, 46, 57–58, 63, 78–79, 83–85, 94–96, 111–12, 184, 202
"Down at the Cross: Letter from a Region of My Mind" (Baldwin), 16n27
dozens, the, 107, 113, 117, 119
Drama of King Shotaway, The (Brown), 63, 63n16
Dred Scott Supreme Court Decision, 28
Du Bois, W. E. B., 7, 38, 71, 173n26, 108, 108n4, 108n5, 115, 123, 168, 168n21, 173n26, 202, 206
Dubey, Madhu, 118, 202
Due, Tananarive, 31, 31n5, 102, 102n16, 202
Dunbar, Paul Laurence, 40, 40n11, 202
dystopia/dystopian fiction, 26, 70, 102, 111, 127–52, 209

Easley, Nivi-Kofi A., 162, 162n15, 202
economic exploitation of blacks, 11, 51n3, 60, 72, 102, 135, 137, 159. *See also* American chattel slavery
education of blacks, 28, 59, 84, 140–41, 151, 190. *See also* literacy
1811 German Coast Uprising, 50, 56–57, 56n10
Ellison, Harlan, 164, 164n18, 202
Ellison, Ralph, 3, 3n5, 10–11, 16, 78, 108, 112, 119, 119n14, 127–29, 133, 136, 151, 158–60, 203, 215
emancipated blacks, 58, 60–61, 64, 175. *See also* free people of color
Enlightenment, The/Enlightenment ideas, 32–33, 41–42, 53–54, 78
Equiano, Olaudah, 18, 25, 32, 39–44, 47, 79, 81, 203
escaped slaves. *See* fugitive slaves
Eshun, Kodwo, 3–4, 6–7, 56, 119, 137, 149, 187, 203
ESP. *See* psionic powers

Essays, Moral, Political, and Literary (Hume), 42, 206
estrangement. *See* alienation
Everfair (Shawl), 75, 75n27, 211
Evers, Medgar, 13, 13n11, 163
extrasensory powers/extrasensory perception. *See* psionic powers

Fair, Ronald L., 160–61, 161n10, 203
Fanon, Frantz, 3, 149, 172, 183, 203
fantastic, the, 30, 61, 63–69, 72–73, 103, 108, 111
Farnham's Freehold (Heinlein), 156–57, 210
Faulkner, William, 10, 203
feminists/feminism, 64, 93, 107: second wave, 164
Fifteenth Amendment to the Constitution, 160, 180–81
Fifth Season, The (Jemisin), 1, 1–2n1, 102, 102n16, 197, 206
Figures in Black: Words, Signs, and the "Racial" Self (Gates), 64, 203
Fire in the Flint, The, (White), 157, 157n4, 214
Fire Next Time, The, (Baldwin), 16, 16n27, 198
Fire on the Mountain (Bisson), 77, 78n3, 156, 156n3, 198
Flight to Canada (Reed), 141, 210
folk romance, 107–8, 110, 118
folklore/folk traditions, 32–35, 38, 67, 79, 94, 107–26, 147, 162n14, 192n3: African, 101
"For My People" (Walker), 80, 80n5, 213
"For Saundra" (Giovanni), 164, 164–65n19, 204
"Forethought, The" (Du Bois), 173n26, 202
Forrest, Nathan Bedford, 174, 177, 177n31, 214
Fourteenth Amendment to the Constitution, 180–81
Franklin, Benjamin, 42, 44, 81
free people of color, 44, 54, 79, 82, 84–88, 174, 194–95, 210. *See also* emancipated blacks
freedom technologies, 17–18, 25–47, 79, 145: definition, 26
Freejacks, 174, 174n27, 176, 210

Fugitive Slave Act of 1850, 28, 93, 93n13, 101
fugitive slaves, 36–39, 51–73, 78–104, 194–96
"Further Considerations of Afrofuturism" (Eshun), 3–4, 36, 56, 119, 137, 149, 187, 203
future, black-determined, 59, 61, 67–73, 75, 79–80, 104, 143, 153–85

Gabriel's Conspiracy, 54–56, 55n6, 55n7, 55n8, 55n9, 63, 76, 157n6, 211: counterfactual account of, 55. *See also* Prosser, Gabriel
Gaines, Ernest J., 118n12, 203
Garies and Their Friends, The (Webb), 54, 213
Garner, Eric, 14, 14n19
Gates, Henry Louis, Jr., 35, 40, 42, 49, 64, 114, 117n11, 199–208, 212–14
gender, 93, 100, 103, 119–21, 125–26, 136, 172: antebellum/Victorian gender norms, 91, 91n12, 213; black masculinity, 172
genetics, 73–75, 75n27
genocide, 61, 156, 161, 170, 173, 194
genre fiction, 1–3, 20, 46, 74, 101–2, 110–11, 110n7, 130, 154, 163n16, 164–65, 171n23, 179n34, 186–87, 193, 255
German Coast Uprising, 18
Get Out (Peele), 1, 210
Gilroy, Paul, 7, 133, 204
Giovanni, Nikki, 164, 164–65n19, 204
God-breathing machines. *See* machines, black bodies as
Good House, The (Due), 31, 31n5, 202
"Goophered Grapevine, The" (Chesnutt), 34–35, 200
gothic, the, 130n1, 138
graphic novels, 61–62
Gray, Freddie, 61, 62n13
Gray, Thomas R., 62, 204
Great Getting' Up Morning: A Biography of Denmark Vesey (Killens), 55n6, 207
Great War, The. *See* World War I
Greenlee, Sam, 161, 161n12, 204
Griggs, Sutton E., 3, 18, 51, 63–64, 64n19, 69–76, 201, 204

Habeus Viscus: Racializing Assemblages, Biopolitics, and Black Feminist Theories of the Human (Weheliye), 94, 213
Haggard, H. Rider, 71–72, 72n24, 187, 204
Haitian Revolution, 18, 50, 53–55, 66–67, 76, 206, 209
Hammon, Jupiter, 43, 204
Hansberry, Lorraine, 134n4, 204
Haraway, Donna, 96, 205
"Harlem" (Hughes), 164–65n19, 205
Harlem Hellfighters, The, 174, 174n28, 180, 209
Harlem Renaissance, 113, 157, 207, 209
Harris, Trudier, 9, 102, 113, 205
Hayles, Katherine N., 140, 205
Heart of Darkness (Conrad), 72, 72n26, 187–89, 200
Heinlein, Robert A., 156–57, 205
historical erasure, 28–29, 48–57, 75–76, 196
history textbooks. *See* American history textbooks
Holiday, Billie, 194, 194n7, 208
hope/hope impulse, 4–8, 14–20, 25, 37–49, 62–63, 71, 75, 78–104, 108, 112, 135, 137, 142, 152–54, 164–65, 185–86, 195–96
Hopkins, Pauline, 3, 18, 51, 63–64, 64n20, 71–76, 187, 199, 201, 204–6
Hopkinson, Nalo, xi, 31, 31n5, 54, 75, 75n27, 113, 186, 205
horror fiction, 73, 131
Horton, Willie, 131–32n2, 132
"How 'Bigger' Was Born" (Wright), 128, 135, 137, 214
Hughes, Langston, 40, 40n11, 164, 164–65n19, 205–6
Hume, David, 41–42, 206
Hurston, Zora Neale, 6, 15, 17, 19, 107–26, 107n1, 108n2, 108n3, 118n13, 186, 198–200, 202–3, 205–7, 211, 214
Hynek, Joseph A., 86, 86n8, 206
hyperreal violence loop, 11–15, 19, 110n7, 110n8
hyperreality, 11–15, 83

"I Have a Dream" (King), 51n3, 207

I, Tituba, Black Witch of Salem (Condé), 31n4, 200
"I, Too" (Hughes), 40, 40n11, 205
"If We Must Die" (McKay), 164, 164–65n19, 208
Immortal Life of Henrietta Lacks, The (Skloot), 30n3, 211
imperialism, 53, 66, 72, 108n5, 168n21, 188
Imperium in Imperio (Griggs), 3, 18, 51, 63–64, 64n19, 69–76, 201, 204
In the United States of Africa (Waberi), 188, 188n2, 213
Incidents in the Life of a Slave Girl (Jacobs), 11, 18, 63, 78–79, 88, 90–94, 96, 194, 204, 206, 210, 212
indigenous futurism, 8, 78n4, 202
integrationists, 64
Interesting Narrative of the Life of Olaudah Equiano, The (Equiano), 18, 25, 32, 39–44, 47, 79, 81, 203
interstitial spaces, 90, 134, 207
Intuitionist, The (Whitehead), 192n3, 214
invisibility of blacks, 10–11, 93, 158–59
Invisible Man (Ellison), 3, 3n5, 10–11, 16, 78, 108, 112, 119, 128, 134, 158–60, 173, 203, 215
Irish, the, 80, 80n5, 194, 213
Islam, 16, 75n2, 165
Island of Dr. Moreau, The (Wells), 149, 149n7, 213
"I've Been to the Mountain Top" (King), 125, 207

Jackson, Denis, *See* Moreau, Julian
Jacobs, Harriett, 11, 18, 63, 78–79, 88, 90–94, 96, 194, 204, 206, 210, 212
James, C. L. R., 53, 206
Jameson, Fredric, 4, 4n6, 112, 206
JanMohamed, Abdul R., 130n1, 206
Jefferson, Thomas, 30, 40, 42–46, 51, 56, 59, 59n11, 67, 78–79, 153–54, 159, 198, 206
Jemisin, N. K., 1, 1–2n1, 102, 102n16, 197, 206
Jewel-Hinged Jaw, The (Delany), 110, 201
Jewels of Aptor, The (Delany), 109n6, 201
Jim Crow era/Jim Crow laws, 28, 63, 74, 112, 124, 127–52, 174, 180–83

John A. Williams: The Evolution of a Black Writer (Cash), 154, 171, 174, 181–82, 200
John Henry Days (Whitehead), 192n3, 214
Johnson, James Weldon, 97n15, 207
Johnson, Micah Xavier, 161n12
Jones, LeRoi. *See* Baraka, Amiri
Jungle, The (Sinclair), 151, 151n8, 211

Kant, Immanuel, 41–42, 207
Kearney, Douglas, 40, 40n11, 207
Kelley, William Melvin, 160, 160n8, 207
Kennedy, John F., 160
Kilgore, De Witt D., xi, 36, 84, 104, 109, 113, 128, 207
Killens, John Oliver, 55n6, 161, 161n11, 207
Kindred (Butler), 77, 77n2, 199
King Leopold II, 72, 72n25
King, Martin Luther, Jr., 13, 13n12, 51, 51n3, 125, 163, 207
King, Rodney, 13, 13n14
King Solomon's Mines (Haggard), 187, 204
Korean War, 166–68, 179n34, 181, 183, 212
Ku Klux Klan, 13, 63, 156, 157n3, 161, 177n31

labor-based technology, 6, 79, 128
Lacks, Henrietta, 30n3
Lagoon (Okorafor), 20, 20n29, 209
Larsen, Nella, 97n15, 207
Latinx futurism, 7–8, 78n4, 203
Laveau, Marie, 31, 31n4, 210
Lavender, Isiah III, x, 17, 72n26, 128, 170, 207–8
Leopard's Spots: A Romance of the White Man's Burden, 1865–1900, The (Dixon), 156, 202
"Letter to Thomas Jefferson" (Banneker), 51, 198
Life and Times of Frederick Douglass (Douglass), 95–96, 202
Lincoln, Abraham, 113
Lincoln Brigade. *See* Abraham Lincoln Brigade
linguistic coding, 18, 35
Lion's Blood (Barnes), 75n27, 77, 77n2, 198

literacy, 18, 25–27, 29, 35–47, 51, 57, 60, 84, 91, 195: anti-literacy laws, 52; white fears about black literacy, 57, 60
literacy technologies, 25–27, 29, 64, 133, 145
Long, Gavin Eugene, 161n12
loophole of retreat, 90–91, 194, 204, 212
lost-race tales, 71–72
Louisiana, 6, 14n23, 31, 50–51, 56–57, 56n10, 68, 85, 87–88, 98, 127, 174–76, 175n30, 181n12, 198, 210, 213: Avoyelles Parish, 85; Bayou Boeuf, 85
L'Ouverture, Toussaint, 50, 53–54, 66–67, 206
Loving v. Virginia, 103
lynching, 13, 56–57, 63–64, 64n17, 70, 70n23, 87, 124, 140, 148, 157n4, 160, 163, 177, 177n32, 194–95, 213

machines, black bodies as, 40, 40n11, 127–52, 159, 207: God-breathing, 79, 96; muscle machines, 114; natural machines, 78–79, 87, 96, 102, 128, 132, 159, 196
magic, 25, 30–35, 31n5, 47, 56, 62, 66–67, 75n27, 101–2, 102n16, 197, 208, 212, 215
Make America Great Again, 14
Mama Day (Naylor), 31, 31n5, 118n12, 205, 209
Man Who Cried I Am, The (Williams), 161, 214
Manifest Manners: Narratives on Postindian Survivance (Vizenor), 40, 213
"Many Thousands Gone" (Baldwin), 130, 152, 198
Many Thousands Gone (Fair), 160–61, 161n10, 203
maroons, 52, 52n4, 56, 66
Mars, 110n7, 156, 199
Martian Chronicles, The (Bradbury), 156, 199
Martin, Kameelah L., ix, 31, 34, 62, 208
Martin, Trayvon, 14, 14n18, 82, 126, 163
Marxism, 4, 151
McDole, Jeremy, 14, 14n22
McKay, Claude, 164, 164–65n19, 208
McNair, Denise, 13

medical experimentation on black bodies, 30, 30n3, 97, 193, 193n4, 211, 213
Melville, Herman, 165–66, 208
memory, communal/cultural/racial, 7, 76, 113–26, 165–83. See also countermemory
Metamorphoses of Science Fiction: : On the Poetics and History of a Literary Genre (Suvin), 129, 212
Middle Passage, the, 29, 43–44, 46, 79, 81, 115, 126, 212
Midnight Robber (Hopkinson), 54, 113, 205
Militants, The (Easley), 162, 162n15, 202
Miller, Warren, 160, 160n9, 208
minstrel songs/tradition, 184–85
miscegenation, 70–71, 73–74, 76, 103, 156, 172
"missing link," 148–49
Missouri Compromise, 28
mixed race people, 70, 72, 75n27, 97–98, 118–26, 155–56, 165, 184. See also mulattos
Moby-Dick; or, the Whale (Melville), 165–66, 208
monsters/monstrousness, 19, 84, 101, 128–34, 144, 147–49, 151–52
Moorcock, Michael, 164, 164n17
Moore, Ward, 156, 156n1, 208
More Brilliant than the Sun: Adventures in Sonic Fiction (Eshun), 6, 203
"More Perfect Union, A" (Obama), 10, 51n3, 209
Moreau, Julian, 161, 208
Morrison, Toni, 31, 31n5, 112, 118n12, 162–63, 171, 171n25, 209
Moses, Wilson J., 5, 209
Mosley, Walter, 196, 209
MOVE, 13
mulattos, 70, 72, 97–98, 156, 184 tragic mulatto/a trope, 126. See also mixed race peoples
Mules and Men (Hurston), 108, 118n13, 206
murder, 9, 12, 13n11, 14, 19, 163, 164n19, 60, 83, 124, 129, 133, 137, 139, 141, 144–45, 148–50, 161–63, 167, 176, 176n30, 177, 179, 181

My Bondage and My Freedom (Douglass), 33, 36, 46, 79, 83–85, 94, 202
My Soul to Keep (Due), 102, 202
myths/mythology, 38, 62, 94, 114, 193

Narrative of Henry Box Brown, Who Escaped from Slavery, Enclosed in a Box 3 Feet Long and 2 Wide, Written from a Statement Made By Himself, with Remarks upon the Remedy for Slavery (Brown and Stearns), 79, 88–90, 212
Narrative of the Life and Adventures of Henry Bibb (Bibb), 18, 33–34, 79, 97–99, 101–2, 198
Narrative of the Life and Adventures of Venture Smith, a Native of Africa: But Resident above Sixty Years in the United States of America, Related by Himself, A (Smith), 18, 79, 81–83, 81n7, 190, 212
Narrative of the Life of Fredrick Douglass (Douglass), 8, 11–12, 26–27, 36–38, 46, 57–58, 83, 202
Narrative of William W. Brown, A Fugitive Slave (Brown), 94–95, 199
Nat Turner (Baker), 61–62, 197
Nat Turner's Rebellion, 18, 48, 50, 56, 61, 66
Nat Turner's Slave Rebellion, Including the 1831 "Confessions" (Aptheker), 62, 197
Nation of Islam, 16, 165
Native Americans, 168–70, 174, 194n6
native science, 29, 62, 79, 118, 189
Native Son (Wright), 15–17, 19, 27, 127–52, 130n1, 133n3, 157, 164, 185–86, 198, 205, 208, 210–12, 214: 1940 edition, 130, 134, 214
naturalism, 133, 140, 143, 151
Naylor, Gloria, 31, 31n5, 118n12, 205, 209
"Necessity of Tomorrow(s), The" (Delany), 131, 201
"Negro Nation within a Nation, A" (Du Bois), 115, 202
Nelson, Alondra, 3, 5n8, 113, 115, 121, 128, 209
networked black consciousness. *See* black networked consciousness

New Jim Crow: Mass Incarceration in the Age of Colorblindness, The (Alexander), 25n1, 82, 146n6, 197
New York, 13n15, 13n16, 14n19, 20n29, 82, 84–85, 87, 90n11, 91, 93, 96, 161, 162n13, 174, 174n28, 177, 201: Bronx, 13n16; Glens Falls, 85, 87; Harlem, 159–60, 160n9, 162n13, 174, 174n28
New York City, 13n15, 14n19, 20n29, 85, 87, 96, 161, 162n13; Staten Island, 14n19
New York Fifteenth National Guard. *See* Harlem Hellfighters, the
1984 (Orwell), 137–38, 210
Northup, Solomon, 18, 78–79, 84–88, 209
Notes on the State of Virginia (Jefferson), 42, 51, 59n11, 78–79, 154, 206

Obama, Barack, 10, 15, 51, 51n3, 85, 209
"Observations on the Feeding of the Beautiful and the Sublime" (Kant), 42, 207
occult, the/occultism, 31, 33–34, 73, 75, 75n27, 204
occult practice, 33–34; contempt for, 33–34
Octavia E. Butler (Canavan), x, 9, 200
octoroons, 98, 184
"Ode to Ethiopia" (Dunbar), 40, 40n11, 202
Of One Blood, or the Hidden Self (Hopkins), 3, 63, 71–76, 187, 201, 205–6
O. J. Simpson murder trial, 149–50
Okorafor, Nnedi, 1, 2n1, 20, 20n28, 20n29, 75, 75n27, 207, 209–10. *See also* @Nnedi Okorafor
"On Being Brought from Africa to America" (Wheatley), 40, 214
one-drop rule, 72–74, 97–99, 156
Operation Burning Candle (Jackson), 162, 162n13, 206
Orwell, George, 137–38, 210

pan-Africanism, 73, 75, 113, 204
panopticon, 83–84
Parable of the Talents (Butler), 14n26, 199
parallel worlds/parallel universes, 19, 112, 115–16, 118–19
passing. *See* racial passing

Passing (Larsen), 97n15, 207
patriarchy, 103, 118–26, 189
Peele, Jordan, 1, 210
Philadelphia Fire (Wideman), 13n17, 214
Plains Wars, 169, 174, 183
planetary romance, 19, 110, 110n7, 110n8, 124
Playing in the Dark: Whiteness and the Literary Imagination (Morrison), 112, 209
playing white, 142–43, 147
Plessy v. Ferguson, 103
pocket universes, 77, 79, 88–94, 160, 186, 194
Poems on Various Subjects, Religious and Moral (Wheatley), 42, 214
poetry/poets, 16, 40–43, 40n10, 40n11, 63, 160, 164–65, 164–65n19, 198–99, 204–5, 208, 214
police brutality, 9, 11, 13–14, 14n18, 14n19, 14n20, 14n21, 14n22, 14n23, 14, 14n24, 61, 62n13, 82, 127, 159, 161, 163
porches as cultural spaces, 113, 116, 118–19, 122–23, 200, 205, 207
postapocalyptic future, 75n27, 157, 192n3
postbellum literature, 63–76
postrace era/postracial America, fantasy of, 13–14, 16, 50, 74, 85, 163
Power of the Porch: The Storyteller's Craft in Zora Neale Hurston, Gloria Naylor, and Randall Kenan, The (Harris), 113, 205
Price of the Ticket, The (Baldwin), 103, 198
Princess of Mars, A (Burroughs), 110n7, 199
Principle of Hope, The (Bloch), 4, 198
prison/industrial complex, 25, 57, 146
Prosser, Gabriel, 18, 50, 54–56, 55n7, 63, 67, 76, 157n6, 211
proto-science fiction, 72, 156–57
pseudoscience. *See* race: pseudoscientific theories about
psionic powers, 19, 112, 118–20
psychological warfare, 168–69
Public Enemy, 62, 62n15, 210
pulp magazines, 130–31, 150

quadroons, 98–99, 103, 184. *See also* mulattos

"Quadroons, The" (Child), 103, 200
Quest of the Silver Fleece, The (Du Bois), 108n4, 202
quilts. *See* slave quilts

Race: as an oppression technology, 109, 128–85; invention of, 82; pseudoscientific theories about, 9, 11, 43, 58, 64, 70, 74–75, 78, 97–98, 102–3
race criticism/theory, 4, 58, 78, 170, 198
Race in American Science Fiction (Lavender), 17, 170, 208
Race, Reform, and Rebellion: The Second Reconstruction and Beyond in Black America, 1945–2006 (Manning), 160n7, 208
Race, Rhetoric, and Technology: Searching for Higher Ground (Banks), 38, 198
race riots, 13n14, 13n16, 62n13, 63–64, 64n17, 159–60, 180, 180n36, 205
race war stories, 155–57
racial consciousness, 19, 61, 113–26, 140, 151, 172
racial passing, 71–74, 97–98, 97n15, 103, 108n5, 184, 205
racial purity, 70, 156, 159, 210
racial warfare, 1, 18, 55n8, 58, 59n11, 61, 63–64, 64n17, 66–67, 70–76, 135–85
racially motivated violence, 8–14, 19, 48, 60, 65–68, 71, 78, 82, 153, 156, 163–64, 164n16, 164–65n19, 175–78
"Racism and Science Fiction" (Delany), 20–21, 201
racism as a justification of slavery, 132
racist stereotypes of blacks: criminals/rapists, 12–14, 13n13–16, 14n18–25, 19, 27, 115, 127–52, 131n2, 140–41, 140–41n5, 155–57, 159, 169, 180, 185, 188; subhuman, 133–34, 141. *See also* science-fictional blackness
Raisin in the Sun, A (Hansberry), 134n4, 204
rape, 9, 91, 97, 99, 121, 143–45, 148, 167, 178–80; accusations of, 48n1, 140–41n5, 142–42n2, 180; of white women, 64n17; white fears of the rape of white women by blacks, 156, 179
Rasmussen, Daniel, 56n10, 57, 210
realism, 73, 75, 111, 193, 201, 255

rebellion. *See* slave insurrection
Red Record: Tabulated Statistics and Alleged Causes of Lynching in the United States, The (Wells-Barnett), 64n17, 124, 203, 213
Red Summer, 180, 180n37, 208
Reed, Ishmael, 141, 210
repatriation of slaves to Africa, 60, 63
Requiem for a Nun (Faulkner), 10, 203
resistance, 7, 15, 18, 29, 34, 41, 44–104, 196: passive, 16
revenge, 19, 48, 53, 60, 66, 161–62, 172, 177–79
revolt. *See* slave insurrection
revolution, 64–73, 153–85, 208: bloodless, 185
"Revolving Doors" (Bush campaign ad), 131
Rice, Tamir, 14, 14n21
Richard Wright: The Life and Times (Rowley), 131, 211
Rieder, John, xi, 170, 187n1, 190, 210
riots. *See* race riots
Robertson, Caroline, 13
Robertson, David, 55, 211
robots, 79, 147. *See also* cyborgs and machines, black bodies as
romance fiction, 110n8. *See also* folk romance, and planetary romance
Roof, Dylann, 55n8
Roosevelt, Theodore, 180
Roots, the, 62, 62n14, 211
Rose, Mark, 110n8, 211
Rowley, Hazel, 131, 211
Running a Thousand Miles for Freedom; Or, the Escape of William and Ellen Craft (Craft), 18, 79, 98–101, 200
Rusert, Britt, 66n12, 68–69, 211

Sag Harbor (Whitehead), 192n3, 214
Salem witch trials, 31, 31n6, 211
Salt Roads, The (Hopkinson), 75n27, 205
Samatar, Sofia, 190, 211
Sanders, Michael, 10, 203
Schalk, Sami, 77n1, 211
Schuyler, George S., 108, 108n5, 112, 123, 129, 157, 157n5, 211

science, 1, 29–31, 43–47, 66, 68, 72–73, 102: early American debates about, 4; as a mode of knowledge production, 30. *See also* race: pseudoscientific theories about
science fiction, 2–4, 3n3, 14–16, 20, 29, 43–44, 46, 54, 56, 63, 67, 75, 77, 83–104, 107–30, 155–56, 203: African American, 17, 75, 103–4, 155; contemporary, 75; cyberpunk, 186; Golden Age, 164; hard-boiled, 20n30; New Wave, 163–65, 164n17, 164n18, 186–87; social science fiction, 114–15; steampunk, 75n27. *See also* planetary romance and scientific romance
Science Fiction and the Mass Cultural Genre System (Rieder), 170, 210
science-fictional blackness, 9–15, 18–19, 26, 29, 52, 59–60, 63, 67, 78–79, 82, 103, 120, 124, 128, 132, 137, 148–50, 155, 158–59, 171, 193
science-fictional slavery, 81–84
scientific romance, 131. *See also* science fiction
Scott, Colin, 30, 211
Scottsboro Boys, the, 140–41, 140–41n3
segregation, 8, 15, 17, 25, 76, 103, 112, 115, 117, 119, 125–26, 129, 134–40, 159, 180
separatism. *See* black separatism
Seven Days society, 162–63
sexism, 91, 103, 118–26, 164n16, 179, 179n34
shape shifters/shape shifting, 20, 31n5, 96–97, 101–3, 111: failed shape shifting, 103
Shawl, Nisi, xi, 75, 75n27, 207, 211
She (Haggard), 72, 72n24, 187, 204
Siege of Harlem, The (Miller), 160, 160n9, 208
Signifying Monkey: A Theory of Afro-American Literary Criticism, The (Gates), 117n11, 203
Signs and Cities: Black Literary Postmodernism (Dubey), 118, 202
Simpson, O. J. *See* O. J. Simpson murder trial
Simulacra and Simulation (Baudrillard), 11–12, 198
Sinclair, Upton, 151, 151n8, 211

'Sippi (Killens), 161, 161n11, 207
Sixteenth St. Baptist Church bombing, 13
Skloot, Rebecca, 30n3, 211
slave insurrections, 7, 17–18, 29, 41, 46–76, 77n2, 112, 157, 157n6, 204–5, 209, 211: white fears of, 57–61
slave narratives, 9, 11–12, 18, 26, 43, 51, 77–104, 110n8, 188, 203
slave quilts, 18, 37n7, 38–39, 38n8, 47, 199, 202, 211
slave rebellions. *See* slave insurrections
slavery. *See* American chattel slavery
Small Acts: Thoughts on the Politics of Black Cultures (Gilroy), 133, 204
Smith, Venture, 18, 79, 81–83, 81n7, 190, 204, 212
social justice, 3, 44, 48–76, 125, 153–75
Sohn, Stephen Hong, 169, 212
"Somebody's Gotta Do It" (the Roots), 62n14, 211
Song of Solomon (Morrison), 31, 31n5, 162–63, 171n25, 209
Sons of Darkness, Sons of Light: A Novel of Some Probability (Williams), 161, 214
sorcery. *See* conjurers/conjuring and magic
Souls of Black Folk, The (Du Bois), 38, 202
Southern literature, 107–26. *See also* antebellum literature
*Southscapes: Geographies of Race, Region, and Lite*rature (Davis), 69, 69n22, 201
space-time continuum, 3, 36, 39, 58, 67, 69, 80
space-time travel, 15, 17, 75n27, 84, 111, 154, 157, 165, 172, 174, 196
Spanish-American War, 174, 180
Speculative Blackness: The Future of Race in Science Fiction (Carrington), 77n1, 171, 171n23, 171n24, 200
speculative fiction, 2n2, 31, 75, 102, 131, 157, 161, 165, 169, 171n23, 187, 192–93: Korean American, 169. *See also* science fiction
spiritual technologies, 25, 29–47, 62, 140
spirituality, 25–47
Spook Who Sat by the Door, The (Greenlee), 161, 161n12, 204
Stagger Lee (Dee), 162, 162n14, 201

stand-your-ground law, 14n18
Stearns, Charles, 88, 212
stereotypes. *See* racial stereotypes
Sterling, Alton, 14, 14n23, 127
Stonewall riots, 164
Stono Rebellion, 18, 50, 52, 76, 209, 213
storytelling, 19, 34–35, 37, 75, 111–25
Stowe, Harriett Beecher, 103, 210, 212
"Strange Fruit" (Holiday), 194, 194n7, 208
Styron, William, 61, 212
sugar cane/sugar cane fields, 9, 85, 87, 114
Sula (Morrison), 171n25
Sundquist, Eric J., 65, 212
supernatural, the. *See* fantastic, the
supernatural beliefs, 30, 33, 62, 189, 204
Suvin, Darko, 4, 5n6, 129, 212
syphilis, 193, 193n4, 207

Tate, Greg, 3n3, 9, 44, 122, 131
Tal, Kali, 163, 163n16, 179, 179n34, 212
Tales of Nevèrÿon (Delany), 77, 77n2, 201
technoculture, 2n2, 3, 7, 17, 30–32, 102, 109, 159
technologies of resistance. *See* resistance technologies
technology, 2–3, 32–33, 61, 68, 72, 102
"Technology and Ethos" (Baraka), 140, 198
technospiritual, 7, 103
telepathy. *See* psionic powers
Tell My Horse: Voodoo and Life in Haiti and Jamaica (Hurston), 108, 118n13, 206
temporal dislocation, 2, 148
temporality, 4, 45, 47, 119, 155, 178, 195
terrorism, domestic/terrorists, 13, 63, 156, 157n3, 161, 177n31
Their Eyes Were Watching God (Hurston), 6, 15, 17, 19, 107–26, 107n1, 110n7, 110n8, 186, 198–200, 202–3, 205–7, 214
Things Fall Apart (Achebe), 20, 186–92, 197, 211
Thirteenth Amendment to the Constitution, 180–81
Thomas, Sheree R., x, 10, 64, 109, 212

INDEX

Thomas, Timothy, 13, 13n16
Three-Fifths Compromise of, 1787, 49
369th Infantry Regiment. *See* Harlem Hellfighters, the
Till, Emmett, 13, 13n13, 163, 141, 213
time. *See* space-time continuum and space-time travel
Tituba, 31, 31n4, 210
"To His Excellency George Washington" (Wheatley), 42
To Wake the Nations: Race in the Making of American Literature (Sundquist), 65, 212
Traitor: A Story of the Fall of the Invisible Empire, The (Dixon), 156, 202
transhistorical feedback loop, 6–8, 14–15, 17–19, 27, 29, 37–47, 49, 52–53, 57, 62–64, 67, 74–75, 78–80, 102, 104, 125–26, 132, 135, 140, 150, 153–55, 165, 167–68, 172, 175–77, 181, 192, 196
trauma, collective, 2, 36, 56, 77, 84
Trials of Phillis Wheatley, The (Gates), 40, 204
trickster mythology, 34–35, 101–2, 205
trickster technologies, 18, 77, 79, 94–103
Trump, Donald J., 14, 82
Turner, Nat, 1 8, 41, 47–48, 48n1, 56, 61, 63, 66–68, 80, 197, 200, 204, 212
Tuskegee experiment, 193, 193n4, 207
Twelve Years a Slave (Northup), 18, 78–79, 84–88, 209
Twenty-fourth Infantry Regiment of the United States Army, 166, 169, 174, 180, 180n36

UFO Experience: A Scientific Inquiry, The (Hynek), 86, 86n8, 206
Uncle Tom's Cabin (Stowe), 103, 212
Underground Airlines (Winters), 77–78, 78n3, 214
Underground Railroad, The, 37–39, 98, 101, 193–96, 202, 214
Underground Railroad, The (Whitehead), 20, 98, 187, 193–96, 214
Union Army, 174, 176–78 176n30. *See also* United States Army
Unite the Right rally, Charlottesville, Virginia, 82

United States Army, 154, 166–67, 169, 181–83
utopia/utopian fiction, 4–5, 72–75, 103, 110, 112–13, 171n23, 171n24, 196: utopian studies, 4–5. *See also* afrotopia

vernacular technology, 19, 117–19, 118n12, 147
Vesey, Denmark, 18, 50, 54–57, 63, 67, 211
Vietnam War, 19, 154–55, 162, 162n13, 166–67, 171, 178, 181, 183, 204, 207
virtual realities, 30–31
Vizenor, Gerald, 40, 213
"Voodoo of Hell's Half-Acre, The" (Wright), 131
Voting Rights Act of 1965, 160

Waberi, Abdourahman A., 188, 188n2, 206, 213
Walker, David, 18, 41, 49, 57–61, 63, 126, 210, 213
Walker, Margaret, 80, 80n5, 213
War of 1812, 174–75
War of the Worlds (Wells), 192, 213
"Warning" (Hughes), 164–65n19, 206
Warren, Kenneth W., 16, 213
Washington, Booker T., 71, 158
Washington, George, 42, 67, 81, 113
"Way in the Middle of the Air" (Bradbury), 156, 199
Webb, Frank J., 54, 213
webbed black awareness. *See* black networked consciousness
Weheliye, Alexander G., 94, 213
Wells, H. G., 149, 149n7, 192, 213
Wells-Barnett, Ida B., 64n17, 124, 213
Wesley, Cynthia, 13
Western civilization, 102, 132, 188, 191: beliefs about science, technology, and progress, 1, 15, 30, 73, 112, 118
westerns, 130
"What Did I Do to Be So Black and Blue?" (Armstrong), 10
What Was African American Literature? (Warren), 16, 213
Wheatley, Phillis, 18, 25, 39–43, 20n10, 47, 63, 76, 112, 204, 214

white nationalism, 82
white racial violence, 14n18, 14n19, 14n20, 142n21, 14n22, 63–76, 64n17, 14n23, 82–83, 175–78
White Skin, Black Masks (Fanon), 3, 149, 172, 183, 203
white slavery, 77n2, 99, 157–58
white supremacy/white supremacists, 2, 9–12, 16, 40–47, 49, 54, 56, 64, 67, 74, 103, 109, 115, 118, 135, 140, 142, 144, 149, 152, 156, 161, 163n16, 168, 170, 172, 186
White, Walter, 157, 157n4, 214
Whitehead, Colson, 20, 98, 187, 192n3, 193–96, 214
whiteness, hegemonic, 63–76, 142
Who Fears Death (Okorafor), 2n1, 75, 75n27, 209–10
Wideman, John E[dgar], 13n17, 214
Wild Seed (Butler), 31, 31n5, 75n27, 112, 199

Williams, John A., 15, 17, 19–20, 66, 153–85, 200, 209, 212, 214
Winters, Ben H., 77–78, 78n3, 214
Womack, Ytasha, 36, 102, 214
World War I, 171, 171n25, 174, 179n34, 180, 184
World War II, 2, 158, 174, 179n34, 181–84, 182n38, 184, 188
Wright, Richard, 15–17, 19, 27–28, 46, 125, 127–52, 130n1, 131, 133n3, 135, 137, 158, 164, 185–86, 198–99, 203, 205–6, 208, 211, 214
Wu-Tang Clan, 62, 62n14, 214

X, Malcolm, 51, 51n3, 163, 165n20, 214

Yaszek, Lisa, 3, 3n5, 44, 68, 108, 149, 159, 191, 215

Zimmerman, George, 14n18, 82
Zone One (Whitehead), 192n3, 214
Zulu Heart (Barnes), 75n27, 198

NEW SUNS: RACE, GENDER, AND SEXUALITY IN THE SPECULATIVE
Susana M. Morris and Kinitra D. Brooks, Series Editors

Scholarly examinations of speculative fiction have been a burgeoning academic field for more than twenty-five years, but there has been a distinct lack of attention to how attending to nonhegemonic positionalities transforms our understanding of the speculative. New Suns: Race, Gender, and Sexuality in the Speculative addresses this oversight and promotes scholarship at the intersections of race, gender, sexuality, and the speculative, engaging interdisciplinary fields of research across literary, film, and cultural studies that examine multiple pasts, presents, and futures. Of particular interest are studies that offer new avenues into thinking about popular genre fictions and fan communities, including but not limited to the study of Afrofuturism, comics, ethnogothicism, ethnosurrealism, fantasy, film, futurity studies, gaming, horror, literature, science fiction, and visual studies. New Suns particularly encourages submissions that are written in a clear, accessible style that will be read both by scholars in the field as well as by nonspecialists.

Afrofuturism Rising: The Literary Prehistory of a Movement
 ISIAH LAVENDER III

The Paradox of Blackness in African American Vampire Fiction
 JERRY RAFIKI JENKINS

CPSIA information can be obtained
at www.ICGtesting.com
Printed in the USA
LVHW092238041019
633251LV00001B/3/P